D1613101

MODERN SLAVERY AND HUMAN TRAFFICKING

The Victim Journey

Edited by
Carole Murphy and Runa Lazzarino

With a foreword by Patricia Hynes

First published in Great Britain in 2023 by

Policy Press, an imprint of
Bristol University Press
University of Bristol
1–9 Old Park Hill
Bristol
BS2 8BB
UK
t: +44 (0)117 374 6645
e: bup-info@bristol.ac.uk

Details of international sales and distribution partners are available at
policy.bristoluniversitypress.co.uk

British Library Cataloguing in Publication Data
A catalogue record for this book is available from the British Library

ISBN 978-1-4473-6363-7 hardcover
ISBN 978-1-4473-6365-1 ePub
ISBN 978-1-4473-6366-8 ePdf

The right of Carole Murphy and Runa Lazzarino to be identified as editors of this work has been asserted by them in accordance with the Copyright, Designs and Patents Act 1988.

Cover design: Andrew Corbett
Front cover image: The cover art work was produced by survivors of modern slavery at Bakhita House, a safe house for women, with guidance from art teacher John Bateson-Hill
Bristol University Press and Policy Press use environmentally responsible print partners.
Printed and bound in Great Britain by CPI Group (UK) Ltd, Croydon, CR0 4YY

FSC
www.fsc.org
MIX
Paper | Supporting
responsible forestry
FSC® C013604

We would like to dedicate this volume to all the victims and survivors of modern slavery and human trafficking in the world, with the hope that this book will shine a light on their journeys and raise awareness of the obstacles they face, their personal agency and resilience when dealing with challenges, and the healing process experienced in supportive care. This volume is also offered to all those compassionate frontline practitioners and dedicated researchers who devote their lives to better understand and confront the unacceptable issue of human-to-human exploitation.

To Viola and Nicolò, infinitely wishing them all the possible light on their short, precious journeys. Runa

To Caitlin and Max, for accompanying me on my research and writing journey. Carole

Contents

List of figures and table

Figures

Table

List of abbreviations

ASEAN	Association of Southeast Asian Nations
ASO	Assessment of Survivor Outcomes
ATMG	Anti-Trafficking Monitoring Group
BASNET	Black and Minority Ethnic Anti-Slavery Network
CBH	Caritas Bakhita House
CE	criminal exploitation
CECM	Complex Experience Care Model
CJS	criminal justice system
CPC	Child Protection Compact Partnership
CPS	Crown Prosecution Service
CQC	Care Quality Commission
CRT	critical race theory
CSE	child sexual exploitation
CSEM	child sexual exploitation materials
GRETA	Group of Experts on Action against Trafficking in Human Beings
HTOR	Human Trafficking for the purpose of Organ Removal
IJM	International Justice Missions
ILO	International Labour Organization
M&E	monitoring and evaluation
MS PEC	Modern Slavery and Human Rights Policy and Evidence Centre
MS-COS	Modern Slavery Core Outcome Set
MSHT	modern slavery and human trafficking
NGO	non-governmental organisation
NRM	National Referral Mechanism
ODA	Official Development Assistance
OECD	Organisation for Economic Co-operation and Development
OSEC	online sexual exploitation of children
PTSD	post-traumatic stress disorder
SDGs	Sustainable Development Goals
THOA	Transplantation of Human Organs Act
THOTO	Transplantation of Human Organs and Tissues Ordinance
TIP	Trafficking in Persons
UDHR	Universal Declaration of Human Rights
UNGP	United Nations Guiding Principles
UNODC	United Nations Office on Drugs and Crime
WPGA	WePROTECT Global Alliance

Notes on contributors

Karen Anstiss is Manager of Caritas Bakhita House, a safe house for women survivors of modern slavery. In 1983, Karen joined the Metropolitan Police, and her career spanned 31 years. In 1985, Karen trained to deal with victims of sexual abuse. She was on the Metropolitan Police Sexual Offences Steering Group which was instrumental in the creation of Sapphire, a unit which investigated serious sexual violence. In 2009, Karen worked on the Metropolitan Police Trafficking Team, working closely with different faith groups in supporting victims of trafficking. After retirement in 2014 Karen became part of the project team which developed and then opened Caritas Bakhita House in June 2015.

Debbie Ariyo is Founder and Chief Executive of AFRUCA – Safeguarding Children which supports children and young people who have experienced trafficking, modern slavery and exploitation. She is an expert in forced migration with experience of delivering diaspora led initiatives to address human trafficking. She is Founder and Chair of the UK Black and Minority Ethnic Anti-Slavery Network which works to improve equality, diversity and inclusion in the UK anti-slavery space. Debbie is an Advisory Board member of the UK Modern Slavery Policy Evidence Centre and the *Journal of Modern Slavery*.

Craig H. Barlow is a human trafficking and modern slavery expert. As Consultant to the Organization for Security and Cooperation in Europe and the Office for Democratic Institutions and Human Rights, he has contributed to the forthcoming international *National Referral Mechanism Handbook*. With 25 years of statutory safeguarding experience, he has trained social workers, police officers and health professionals in the field of child and vulnerable adult safeguarding and is a leading practitioner in the field of human trafficking. Craig developed the Systemic Investigation, Protection and Prosecution Strategy for assessing cases of modern slavery and trafficking (2017).

Anta Brachou recently obtained her PhD at the University of Hull researching human trafficking from Albania. Her project focuses on the 4Ps Paradigm to look at Prevention, Prosecution, Protection and Partnerships. After graduating from University of Westminster (BA Criminal Justice) and UCL (MSc Crime Science), Anta briefly worked in Albania as an associate at a legal consultancy firm and, in 2015, she returned to London to work in the voluntary sector with women affected by the criminal justice system and victims of trafficking. She currently works as Research Officer at the Bakhita Centre for Research on Slavery, Exploitation and Abuse.

Sarah Burch is Director of Research and Research Students in the Faculty of Health, Education, Medicine and Social Care at Anglia Ruskin University, Cambridge, UK. She is an experienced academic and research manager and has also worked in a range of public sector organisations, principally with older and disabled people. These experiences underpinned her commitment to social policy and research that focuses on wellbeing and need across the life course, while supporting vulnerable and disenfranchised groups within societies.

Mike Dottridge has worked in the field of human rights for four decades. He was employed by two organisations between 1977 and 2002 (Amnesty International and Anti-Slavery International). Since 2002 he has worked independently, undertaking evaluations for international organisations and non-governmental organisations. From 1995 onwards he has focused on the rights of adults and children who experience severe economic or sexual exploitation. He is the author of numerous articles and books on slavery, servitude, forced labour, child labour and human trafficking. He was a trustee of the United Nations Fund on Contemporary Forms of Slavery from 2011 until 2016.

Imogen Fell is Head of Programme Management for International Justice Mission's Centre to end online sexual exploitation of children. Imogen's academic interests include online and offline forms of child sexual exploitation and non-governmental organisation responses to child protection in Southeast Asia. During her PhD, Imogen conducted fieldwork in the Philippines and worked as a visiting researcher at the Social Development Research Centre, De La Salle University, Philippines. At the Social Development Research Centre, she was involved in UNICEF Philippines's research on online sexual abuse and exploitation of children.

Anne-Marie Greenslade is Lecturer in Law at Leeds Beckett University, teaching Perspectives on Law and Society, Public Law, International Human Rights Law and Anti-Terrorism Law. She successfully completed her PhD on evaluating frontline services for modern slavery survivors in October 2021. Her previous experience supporting refugees in Kosovo fuelled Anne-Marie's interest in human rights, and she later worked as an independent advocate for rape survivors, which drove her decision to become a legal scholar with the aim of contributing to policy change for victims of traumatic crime.

Jon Hackett is Associate Professor, Film and Communications, and Head of Communications, Media and Marketing at St Mary's University, Twickenham. With Dr Mark Duffett of the University of Chester he is the author of the recent *Scary Monsters: Monstrosity, Masculinity and Popular Music* (Bloomsbury, 2021). He teaches a postgraduate module on Mediating Trafficking, Migration and Diaspora at St Mary's and is researching political cinema, including representations of trafficking on screen.

Rune Henriksen is an expert on conflict, terrorism and organised crime. He is the Deputy Director of RHIPTO Norwegian Center for Global Analyses, where his research has focused on the links between organised crime and non-state armed groups, including violent extremist groups, to understand how the financing from illegal activity facilitates political goals. He holds a PhD from the London School of Economics. His recent publications include *Human Trafficking: An Organised Crime* (Hurst, 2019).

Kathryn Hodges is a registered social worker with over 20 years' experience in social care practice and higher education. Dr Hodges is Co-Founder of PraxisCollab and Honorary Visiting Fellow at the Bakhita Centre for Research on Slavery, Exploitation and Abuse. Much of her work explores the decisions and choices individuals make when seeking help and support, the complexity of help seeking, and the relational aspects of care. With Lara Bundock (The Snowdrop Project), she co-authored the *National Training Standards for the Identification, Care and Support of Victims / Survivors of Modern Slavery and Human Trafficking* (Skills for Care).

Sasha Jesperson is a consultant with extensive experience in technical delivery, strategic planning, research and analysis, and monitoring and evaluation to address organised crime, human trafficking, modern slavery and migration in complex and conflict environments. She has worked with a range of governments, donors and institutions to strengthen policymaking and programming and to build the evidence base on organised crime and conflict. She holds a PhD from the London School of Economics. Recent books include *Human Trafficking: An Organised Crime* (Hurst, 2019) and an edited volume *Militarised Responses to Transnational Organised Crime* (Palgrave, 2018).

J. Julia: Depending on the context, she uses the terms survivor and expert by experience interchangeably. Expert by experience when it comes to contributing her expertise to the abolition of modern slavery and survivor when it comes to remembering how it was, how it is today, and where she is now. She recently graduated with a first-class degree in Criminology and Sociology. She is deeply committed to social justice. While working in the criminal justice system or charitable organisations such as youth justice services, she would like to apply what she has learned about social problems and inequality and their detrimental effects on society.

Runa Lazzarino is a sociocultural anthropologist, specialised in health and migration. Runa started investigating recovery/reintegration processes and care/assistance discourses and practices for exploited migrants and human trafficking survivors in 2008. Runa's research interests revolve around transcultural and global (mental) health/care, exploited migrants (victims of human trafficking, conflict, and abuse), social and cultural norms and determinants of health, participatory and creative interventions and evaluations. Runa obtained her PhD in human trafficking in 2015, and is now based at Oxford and Middlesex University.

Carole Murphy is Associate Professor of Criminology and Sociology at St Mary's University. She played a key role in establishing the Bakhita Centre for Research on Slavery, Exploitation and Abuse and is currently Director of the Centre. Her main research interests are in human trafficking, modern slavery, exploitation and abuse, and examining intersections with social problems, inequalities, addiction and health/mental health issues.

Neena Samota is Programme Lead in Criminology and Sociology at St Mary's University. As an applied, critical criminologist, she has over 20 years of research, evaluation and policy development experience in criminal justice with a specialised interest in race, gender and age. Her chapter 'Race, ethnicities, and the criminal justice system' features in *The Oxford Textbook of Criminology* (Case et al, Oxford University Press, 2021). Her research interests include crime, criminal justice, inequalities, migration, human rights and the politics of multiculturalism. Neena has advocacy and governance experience in the charitable sector and is a trustee of StopWatch and Voice4Change England.

Karen Sanders is Professor of Politics and Communication and Research Lead at St Mary's University's Institute of Business, Law and Society. She is co-editor of the *Routledge Companion to Journalism Ethics* (Routledge, 2021). She has published widely in interdisciplinary journals including the *European Journal of Communication* and the *International Journal of Press and Politics*, authoring key texts such as *Ethics and Journalism* (SAGE, 2003) and *Communicating Politics in the 21st Century* (Palgrave Macmillan, 2009). Visiting professor at the University of Navarra, Karen is a founding member of the Journalism Studies Department at Sheffield University and spent ten years at Spain's CEU San Pablo University.

Trevor Stammers was Reader in Bioethics at St Mary's University in London, UK, where he was also Co-Director of the Centre for Bioethics and Emerging Technologies. Trevor was also on the teaching faculty for the Masters programme in Bioethics and Medical Law established in 2002, which now has hundreds of graduates worldwide. He is the author of over 60 papers and has been published in a number of books, most recently from Bloomsbury, Cambridge University Press and Oxford University Press. Dr Stammers' research interests include both genomic editing and the ethics of organ acquisition for transplantation.

Colleen Theron is a tri-qualified solicitor and founder of Ardea International, a specialist company that provides sustainability, business and human rights and modern slavery expertise to companies. Colleen is a fellow of IEMA, a research fellow of the Bakhita Centre for Research on Slavery and Abuse (St Mary's Twickenham) and a lecturer at Birkbeck University on human rights and business. She has over 30 years of legal and commercial experience of working with business, organisations and non-governmental organisations across sectors and provides training and online resources on human rights, modern slavery and sustainability issues.

Thi-Diem-Tu Tran is a lecturer for the BA Criminology and Sociology at St Mary's University Twickenham, London, where she teaches Modernity and Global Societies as well as Social Theories. Dr Tran's research focuses on migration, media representation of migrants, and human trafficking. Diem-Tu holds a MA in Migration and Diaspora Studies from the University of London, SOAS. She has broad professional experience in the area of assisted voluntary return of asylum seekers and support of unaccompanied minor refugees. Since 2017, she has been acting as a researcher for St Mary's Bakhita Centre for Research on Slavery, Exploitation and Abuse.

Ruth Van Dyke is Visiting Fellow in the Bakhita Centre for Research on Slavery, Exploitation and Abuse at St Mary's University, and teaches on the MA in Human Trafficking, Migration and Organised Crime. Ruth has been involved in evaluating anti-slavery interventions, for example Justice & Care's Victim Navigator programme. She wrote *What Looks Promising for Tackling Modern Slavery: A Review of Practice-based Research* (St Mary's, 2020). Ruth has published work on policing responses to modern slavery, and the development of the Modern Slavery Act. She has been a long-standing member of the Modern Slavery and Exploitation Group.

Emily Vaughn is a lived experience consultant who has worked with many organisations including the Human Trafficking Foundation and Hope for

Justice. She is a Sunday times best-selling author with her memoir 'Enslaved' and is usually found challenging the Home Office on their failures.

Anna Westin is a lecturer, writer, Pilates instructor, Somatic trainee and musician. In her role as Director of the JAM Network UK, she uses creative expression and movement in her work with survivors of trafficking. She lectures at St Mellitus College, East Midlands and is a visiting fellow and lecturer at St Mary's University, Twickenham. Anna recently published her second book, entitled *Embodied Trauma and Healing: Critical Conversations on the Concept of Health and Rupture* (Routledge).

Acknowledgements

We would like to thank the survivors who participated in many studies for the purposes of research, reflected in and contributing to the richness of this book. We would also like to thank the voluntary sector organisations who facilitated access to data and participants, reviewers, the contributors and the editors at Policy Press for all their support and advice. We are grateful to Arianna Schiavo, Dr Anta Brachou and Dr Anne-Marie Greenslade for their help in the management of this book project. We also extend thanks to our families who supported us through the journey of putting this book together.

Foreword

Patricia Hynes
Professor of Social Justice
Helena Kennedy Centre for International Justice
Sheffield Hallam University

Journeys begin with an idea of movement. The idea of a journey to escape indebtedness, ensure family is taken care of and/or imagine a better way of living is a courageous and honourable endeavour. Journeys often begin with such rational decision-making but can be based on limited or unreliable information about costs, lengths of journeys, legal requirements or situations en-route and at destinations. Once journeys begin, they can become progressively more precarious with structures of border control, migration management plus other harms inherent in global systems designed to deter mobility. The original motivations for movement can also be demolished by others who seek to gain for their own benefit and exploit individual circumstances, changing people's lives. That journeys involve such painful and potentially violent processes leads us on to think about resilience, coping and the extraordinary capacity of people to survive.

We know stigma can be both a driver and outcome of human trafficking. As our own research tells us, individual circumstances too often involve stigmatising norms around divorce, pregnancy out of marriage, domestic violence, the perception of shameful employment or being seen to be in debt which can drive people to make decisions to survive and maybe envision the ability to grow and thrive, even against all odds. Paying attention to the cyclical nature of such journeys is important, as an additional element – return, sometimes referred to as reintegration, repatriation or, less euphemistically as deportation – challenges those advocating a rights-based or user-centred approach to human trafficking.

Journeys are life-changing and transformative experiences. However, in human trafficking studies, they are also under-researched. This book details the beginning, middle, and the end of human trafficking from a range of perspectives. A key strength is that it is written in collaboration with practitioners. Additionally, two survivors – or experts by experience – of trafficking have contributed to the introduction of this book with an acknowledgement that survivors may not wish to dwell in spaces of victimhood for too long and slowly move away from such negative experiences in their lives over time.

To make preparations and plan for a journey feels like an exciting prospect. But there is nothing exciting about being arrested and jailed for crimes committed under coercion or coercive control, nothing thrilling about crossing deserts and being detained in Libyan detention centres or being held in the dark in basements for months on end, nothing compelling about the day-to-day lived realities of human trafficking, and nothing friendly about organs harvested from living human beings and/or those rendered immobile by imprisonment as atonement for real of supposed crimes with their kidneys.

One might expect a book about journeys to focus in on solely ethnographic accounts. This book defies this, beginning with an exploration of organised crime recruitment strategies, showing how human trafficking is ever-evolving, with agile and dynamic actors continually developing new tactics to avoid detection and with law enforcement strategies from other areas such as drug trafficking used to also counter human trafficking. It then details various forms of human trafficking, including for the purposes of organ removal, that relies on shifting legislation, practices, patterns and markets. Children exploited online in the Philippines brings to the fore how demand, combined with resource inequities and power imbalances between the so-called Global North and South, can be at the heart of exploitation.

Who would want to be called or continue living with the label of 'victim of trafficking'? Being a 'victim' and representations of those who are trafficked through film, the media and the judicial system highlights how complex representations of the experience of 'enslavement' are. 'Race', the volume goes on showing, is an often forgotten factor in conceptualising and analysing human trafficking in the UK. The legacies and impacts of colonialism and imperialism are now finally beginning to reach debates about 'modern slavery', allowing for a deeper historical consciousness to inform and enrich our thinking.

Practices, resilience and constrained choices around aftercare – that construct people affected by trafficking as vulnerable and traumatised within a system that is not informed by user-knowledge – are detailed. Given the heterogeneity of experiences considered, we need to be hungry to learning what works for whom and when and in what contexts, otherwise trauma can threaten survivors with its permanent story. It is therefore essential that books, such as this one, address the needs of individuals, understand value-based services and value monitoring and evaluation process to ensure avoidance of further harms.

It has been a delight to provide a Foreword for this book which is sure to be a valuable contribution at this critical point of time where there is a war and risk of exploitation in Ukraine, the threat of people being sent to Rwanda for asylum processing, and children and young people being treated with disbelief and hostility by those tasked to protect them. In particular, I hope this book will also be a useful tool for practitioners working to ensure the dignity and safety of people are upheld and their fundamental human rights are protected.

Preface

The concept for this book comes from the many conversations I have had with practitioners and policymakers about the reflection, recovery and (re)integration of survivors in the UK context, and consultations with survivors about their lived experience of recovery support and opportunities for (re)integration. Having conversations with survivors has been a critical element in the development of this book from an idea to a final text. Two of these survivors are known to me through their personal agency in choosing to engage with me in conversations about education, survivor agency and survivor voice. Both survivors have been inspirational in terms of their willingness to share their stories of the recovery and integration available in the UK, offering an insight into the similarities and differences in their experiences as domestic and international survivors accessing support.

After ten years of working with victims and survivors of exploitation and abuse, I was keen to establish a research centre that would address key challenges facing society, including human trafficking and modern slavery. I set up the Bakhita Centre for Research on Slavery, Exploitation and Abuse (formerly the Centre for the Study of Modern Slavery) at St Mary's University, Twickenham in 2015 to respond to growing awareness of human trafficking and modern slavery in the UK and internationally; to recognise the impact on victims and survivors with complex and intersecting needs; and to ensure timely and focused evidence-based responses. Centre staff, honorary fellows and affiliates have worked together to build a body of research evidence that is practice focused and applied, and which is represented in many chapters in this book. Going forward, survivors (experts by experience) will be key partners in the work of the Centre.

Carole Murphy

Introduction: Victim journeys, survivors' voice

Runa Lazzarino, J. Julia, Emily Vaughn and Carole Murphy

This volume started taking shape during the year of the fifth anniversary of the UK Modern Slavery Act 2015, which also coincided with the 20th anniversary of the Palermo Protocol (UNODC, 2000). The Act is the first piece of legislation making use of the term modern slavery, and arguably has contributed to establishing the UK as the leader in what seems to be an irreversible and criticised shift from the human trafficking to the modern slavery paradigm (Bunting and Quirk, 2017; Bravo, 2019; Lazzarino, 2019). Also prompted by this changing context, the editors of this volume felt it was time to take stock of what the landscape of tackling what is now increasingly referred to as the field of modern slavery and human trafficking (MSHT) looked like.

With this collaborative book project, the editors aimed to answer a broad range of questions in relation to MSHT. They wanted to gain a better picture of what new interventions were being trialled in policing and policy, including the impact that the UK Act was having in prosecuting traffickers and supporting victims, for example. Other aspects of interest were recruitment upstream in source contexts, and the role of business in tackling exploitation and trafficking along supply chains. The editors also wanted to explore which services were available to survivors, to what extent they were user-centred, and how their effectiveness was evaluated. At the discourse level, the volume wanted to target the role of ideologies, and national and international political agendas in the construction of the problem of MSHT. To this end, the editors decided to structure this work along the journey of victims/survivors of MSHT, into and within the UK, from recruitment through representation to (re)integration, in diverse fields of trafficking and exploitation, and from an array of disciplines and angles. By offering a plethora of contributions that cover different moments of the victim journey, and doing this from different perspectives, professional roles and positionings, the editors wanted to equip readers with tools to enable them to build up their own, better informed, views of the victim's journey.

The volume attempts to unpick many of the complexities of MSHT, in the UK and beyond. It brings together expertise from academics, practitioners, and consultants to offer novel insights and grounded suggestions for better public awareness, policies and practices in a diverse and fractured landscape.

With this volume, the editors have tried to reduce the knowledge-creators/ evidence-users gap, and to target, as a second-tier audience, practitioners, and policymakers. First and foremost, this book has tried to do so by having nine out of 13 chapters written either in collaboration with practitioners, or by researchers who are/have also been practitioners (or vice versa). The perspective of these contributors is inevitably informed by some form of hands-on experience and speaks back to that. The researcher-practitioner is better positioned to speak to both policymakers and victim/survivors. This is because they sit at the intersection between critically synthesising and generating new knowledge from data collection, on the one hand, and, on the other, are, or have been, embedded into the practicalities and everyday obstacles of systems in the encounter with service users/survivors. Furthermore, some of the chapters are fully based on interventions/ evaluations and practical, frontline experience, and they are rich in practical recommendations. In other chapters, the editors have asked all authors to add an ad hoc section on practical implications/recommendations for policies/ practices. However, we (Lazzarino and Murphy) would also like to remind readers that one of the benefits of the book is that it is not only a manual, but a collection where contributors come also from academic disciplines including sociology, philosophy, criminology and media studies, hence contributing to theorisation, dissemination, critical thinking and awareness raising.

The approach to MSHT underpinning this book is critical. The call for a decolonisation of the discourse of MSHT, that we make at the end of this introduction, speaks to the establishment of a less rhetorical and less instrumental MSHT system. MSHT – as it is used in this volume – embeds and embraces several criticisms within the neo-abolitionist 'old v new slaveries' rhetoric, as well as criticism of the ongoing expansion of a modern/ contemporary slavery framework. Accordingly, the terminological choice of combining modern slavery and human trafficking is far from suggesting that the two terms are simply interchangeable. Human trafficking and modern slavery belong to two distinct historical and political genealogies (O'Connell Davidson, 2017; Allain, 2018). The link between old and new slaveries, and their respective abolitionist movements, is far from being straightforward (Patterson, 2012).[1] More recently, as mentioned, modern slavery seems to be supplanting the human trafficking framework, which dominated the humanitarian, legal and media landscapes alike in the 15 years following the Palermo Protocol. Together with the inclusion of a reference to modern slavery in the UN Sustainable Development Goal 8.7, the UK Modern Slavery Act 2015, now followed by the 2018 Australian Act, epitomises the current trend towards 'the new moralistic policy frame' of modern slavery (Chuang, 2014; Broad and Turnbull, 2018). The concept has turned into a widespread discursive reality, further stretching the definition contained in the last international convention on slavery of 1956 (United Nations, 1956;

see also Chapter 8 in this volume). However, modern slavery is not a robust concept (Gadd and Broad, 2018). As an umbrella term for practices such as trafficking, debt bondage, forced labour, forced sex work, forced marriage and other practices involving exploitation, modern slavery risks being a catch-all term with little analytical and practical purchase (Miers, 2003).[2] The modern slavery framework, as we argue in this introduction, produces a binary conceptualisation of freedom versus unfreedom, victim versus perpetrator, good versus bad (O'Connell Davidson, 2015; see Chapter 9 in this volume), which ignites the establishment of an emergency, self-justifying anti-MSHT system. In this type of system, little is heard of the experiences and context of victims/survivors and their perpetrators. This book begins to counteract this position, starting with this introduction.

A further challenge of this project has been to weave in and bring to the fore victims/survivors' voice in trying to respond to the necessity for greater and better collaborative knowledge production and service design in critical MSHT studies. In this respect, the co-authorship of this preamble with an international (J. Julia, hereafter JJ) and a domestic (Emily Vaughn, hereafter EV) survivor serves a few interrelated ends. Firstly, it constitutes a tangible effort to participatory knowledge production, which is guided by the ethical principle of no-harm and rests on the awareness of power disparities and the effort to reduce them. Secondly, this introductory collaborative experiment tends towards overcoming survivors' voice as tokenism. The survivor is not *given* free voice, because this is considered a politically correct act per se. The survivor is here involved as *author* and expert, who in part decides what to speak or not (Spivak, 1988) – as survivor – and in part is asked to follow editorial guidelines serving the rationale of the collection – as author. A third purpose of having a co-created storytelling at the onset of this collection is of standing as a more classic introduction, and of gluing the chapters together.[3]

Reflecting the overall organisation of the collection, a simple plot structure has been agreed for this collaborative introduction, articulated along a tripartition of beginning, middle and end of the victim journey. While this is an easy way to tell stories, the structure must not be taken too strictly, and each part has broader ramifications and connections, as the chapters will show. The involvement of two survivor co-authors, and the presence of their story and critical elaboration of it, function as an enclosing voice to all the chapters where victim/survivors' voice is instead collected, revisited, engaged with, yet offered by someone else (that is, researchers and practitioners). In other words, the first-person storytelling woven into the opening of this collection aims to point to the current dearth of survivors' participation in both knowledge- and practice-production in MSHT studies and systems. Accordingly, we will first travel through our collaborative victim journey, which will serve to present the sections and chapters of the volume. And we will close with a quick overview of the state-of-the-art of survivors' participation in MSHT studies, accompanied by some self-reflective considerations on how to contribute to de-Westernise/decolonise the discourse of MSHT.

Victim journeys

Beginning: one day (1)

> At the age of 23 years I was married and life looked promising. Although we did not have much, we had enough to keep us going. (JJ)

The commencement of a journey entails a change in status quo, a disruption. Sometimes social actors want to depart from such a change perceived as negative, or the journey coincides with the disruption itself. The departure can be geographical, and entailing migrating, or can be experiential, marking an abandonment of previous ways of living. Some victims' stories run along a journey in and out of abuse and exploitation, without entailing an international migration, and sometimes since early childhood, as in the case of EV, the domestic survivor co-author of this introduction.

> My trafficking experiences were historic, starting from the age of 11 which was drug trafficking and then at 14 which was sex trafficking up until the age of 20. (EV)

The story of JJ, the international survivor co-author, is representative of an experience which is also geospatial.

> Life took a very negative turn and what looked like a home turned into a battlefield. My children and I were subjected to endless physical and emotional pains until I realised that if I did not leave, I was going to end up dead. I left and went back to the village so I could recollect myself. I became very desperate ready to do anything to make ends meet so I could feed my children. (JJ)

The story of the victim/survivor journey, for some yet-to-be victims, starts with the creation of life conditions that are experienced as unbearable – a disruption or a disillusion, as mentioned. The sense of needing to change those conditions seems urgent. In the case of migration journeys, other unplanned and unimagined decisions and changes can precede that of migrating abroad. The perspective of the self-realisation pathways as wife and mother, for example, may be suddenly shattered. In an analogous way, others take decisions around the life of a child, and what should be a playful and joyful childhood turns into a nightmare to be forgotten. Several factors, such as domestic violence and addiction – but also more subtle disappointments and dissatisfactions – can unexpectedly alter those life dreams and future expectations of becoming and being a 'normal' person in society, regardless of the kind of normality we are conceiving. Largely, in the same way that those dreams are socially forged, so are the factors making them collapse. This is the case of JJ.

> My culture does not embrace women who have failed marriages. So my stay in the village was like adding salt to my injury due to the stigma attached to single mothers, divorcees or failed marriages. More often women are blamed when their marriages fail, society looks down on such women and drives them to either going back to their abusive husbands or engage in things that lends them to trouble or things they would have never engaged in if it were not for the poverty and marriage troubles. When I went back to the village, I became the laughing stock, and I would walk with my head down. This made me very vulnerable and more depressed not to mention my family looking at me as an embarrassment. (JJ)

Social and gender norms contribute to establishing the horizon of what is acceptable and desirable for social actors; norms mark the boundary between what is normal and what is not. Often, discriminating social norms combine with structural forces of unequal partitions of wealth and health. This combination has tragic effects, which become exceptionally atrocious in minors' exploitation. In the case of child victims of MSHT, we cannot talk of unexpected opportunities and decisions to change which are taken by the future victims themselves. Child victims' embryonic life dreams and plans are crashed completely by someone else's actions. The victim journey *happens* to them – maybe due to a decision taken by their parents, who in turn had little margin of choice.

In JJ's journey, discriminating gender norms, rooted in heteronormative ideologies which favour specific types of marriage, family and women's roles, turn divorce into a failure. For this, stigma and self-stigma stain the sense of self of the woman. Furthermore, JJ's husband's gambling addiction and violent behaviour are to be framed within a series of broader factors, such as destitution, social inequalities, social suffering and the legacy of colonialism. Taken together, these factors constitute socio-structural determinants of intergenerational and community poor health, violence and inequality. Similar factors of structural violence affect EV, her family and her exploiters. Fundamentally, this is the terrain where MSHT recruitment occurs, and this terrain is shared by both victims and traffickers, as Henriksen and Jesperson suggest in Chapter 1. The authors concentrate on the fast-evolving recruitment tactics of organised crime groups in MSHT as an international business linked with outward migration drivers. The common terrain of everyday and structural violence shared by victims and their traffickers is epitomised by the 'criminal pyramid scheme'. In this phenomenon, communities and families are located in the middle of the pyramid and have the role of encouraging potential victims to migrate. Potential and actual victims make up the largest layer of the pyramid: they are expected to profit and send their earnings home. By exploring the complex realities that influence the drivers of migration that result in exploitation, Chapter 1 challenges the dominant assumptions around victimhood and recruitment.

> One day I met a man who promised to get me a job abroad and all my problems will come to an end. I was desperate because I could barely make ends meet. I took the offer and spoke to my family who in return came together and helped me out as this would have meant their faces were saved from shame as well as financial support. The journey was arranged by the man and my part was just to hand over the money and follow instructions. As I began my journey to the UK, I had hope and dreams. Dreams to turn my life around, to give the best education to my children and certainly to be the best mother in the world. (JJ)

The recruitment moment can be approached in terms of an encounter between the personal dimension and the wider picture of MSHT international business, shaped by market forces and structural inequalities. When the encounter corresponds, a simple occurrence becomes an opportunity, and a chat becomes a promise of life change. The following three chapters in this collection continue painting the broader context for that 'one day' and the moment when the life of a yet-to-be victim forever changes. In Chapter 2, Stammers offers the extreme example of organ removal, which is one form of MSHT, too often neglected. Organ trafficking is a very good example to demonstrate both the global nature of MSHT and its underpinning supply-demand market dynamics. International policies against the international organ trade, or the censure on forced organ harvesting, are often curtailed, or circumvented, by domestic demand and competing agendas. Stammers adopts a legal lens to explore the scale of the problem post-COVID-19, its nature and practice in India, China, Nepal and Pakistan, along with the difficulties of implementing effective action against it. Fell and Jesperson (Chapter 3) explore a similarly horrific form of MSHT, which is the online sexual exploitation of children (OSEC). OSEC is a widespread and rampant issue, particularly for minors in the Global South. The case study country of the chapter is the Philippines, and the authors challenge the expectation on local governments to confront international demand. The latter poses in fact complex problems to local states who struggle to access adequate resources to ensure that risks to children can be minimised. International forces and power disparities emerge clearly, along with the necessity to act upstream, at the very centre of Global North countries' agendas and policies.

The geopolitical Global North–South disparity of Chapter 3 becomes sharply socioeconomic in EV's story, where the Global North–South divide is a finer line of social inequalities within one of the world's richest countries.

> In early 2019 I decided to talk to an old friend who reminded me of some of the rapes she had reported from 2000–4 which added to my flashbacks, and it was then that things started to make more sense and I was piecing together what had happened. … I started to request my police files and everything any professionals had on me which helped me build a picture of my past. I Googled it one day and it came up with the words modern slavery, so I called the modern slavery helpline number as I wasn't sure what happened to me was that so was shocked when they said it was trafficking. (EV)

Global North countries, like the UK, have the responsibility to implement measures, both in source countries in the Global South and within their own national boundaries. Cooperation within the international community is necessary, since MSHT sees the crossing of national borders, when it is not a domestic crime. If international child trafficking for sexual exploitation occurs, national systems of both source and destination countries, together with the international system, are rotten at several junctions. The inevitable international interconnections and Global North responsibilities within MSHT could hardly be more palpable when examining supply chains, the topic of Chapter 4. Theron's chapter closes Part I of the volume, 'Recruitment: business and tools', which concentrates on macro aspects of MSHT – connected with structural, upstream and pull factors at the root of MSHT (that is recruitment, supply chain and business, demand) – and formal, legislative tools and policies to combat them, internationally and nationally. Theron addresses how business practices have an impact on 'creating' victims of MSHT through their own operations and supply chains. Making reference to United Nations Guiding Principles and the UK legislation, Theron provides examples of how companies purposefully, or inadvertently, exploit people in their business and supply chains. In its second half, Chapter 4 jumps forward to post-trafficking assistance, exploring how businesses can actively help survivors in their recovery, by providing job opportunities. In this way, the chapter casts a bridge between Part I and III of the volume, while also paving the way across that bridge, which revolves around the experience of being a victim – the focus of Part II.

Middle: one day (2)

Potential, yet-to-be victims enter exploitation, and, *one day*, they realise that they are, or they have been, victims. This acknowledgement can be imagined as a second important turning point along MSHT victims' journey: a sudden, or a more slowly evolving, realisation that the hopes and expectations attached to the life course/migration endeavour are not actualising. This awareness – when it does happen – can be fuelled by the severe restrictions in different areas of one's individual freedom and severe abuses in different realms of the individual life, identity and body. The awareness must be followed by the acceptance of being a victim, which in itself involves a margin of decision.

> One day this man told me there is nothing for free and he has been housing me and feeding me and it was my time to pay the debt. He forced himself on me and from then everything turned from worse to worst. He started to bring men in the house to sleep with me and then he would be paid, this progressed to a point that he could take me to other's houses and hotels and wait outside as men did the unthinkable to me. During my captivity there were days I thought I will not see tomorrow following threats, hunger and mental breakdown, not forgetting the unthinkable filthy acts committed by those who purchased sex from me through my 'boss'. (JJ)

JJ and EV's experience of exploitation resonates with that of millions of other children, women and men. Sexual abuse is one of the most atrocious forms of human-to-human violence, and when it is profit-oriented, it forces reflection around human nature and ethics, from the individual to the macro-political level.

Part II of this volume revolves around being a victim. The aim is not to explore unimaginable, and sometimes unspeakable, experiences of abuse, which can be so atrocious as to sit repressed for years in the mind. EV gives us a poignant picture of her struggle to make sense of her mental illness symptoms – a journey along her troubled mind to rustle up her trafficking-related atrocious suffering. However, the approach in the second part of the book is neither psychological nor phenomenological.

> One day I was picking my young daughter up at school and noticed a male police officer there which caused me to have a panic attack in the school and freak out. I wasn't sure why at the time, but it was from there that I started to have regular panic attack episodes, severe anxiety and started to get fearful and lost my confidence. I started to withdraw and isolate myself and suffer with severe anxiety, this was

in 2017. I went to my doctors and was prescribed medication and I went to herbalists and tried homeopathic therapies, but nothing was working. In 2018 I started to feel worse and on high alert, I hadn't taken any of the prescription I was prescribed because I didn't want to feel out of control or become addicted so I threw them all away. In 2018 I started to have flashbacks and a bit of social anxiety and was scared to be around people, it was then I started to piece together some of my past. I started to remember bits and certain things that had happened and I started to look through some of my belongings that I had kept from the past which is when more memories started coming to light. I hadn't heard of modern slavery until 2019. (EV)

The experiences of 'enslavement', and what it means to be a victim, are in Part II critically addressed from the point of view of the film industry (Chapter 5), the media (Chapter 6), race and migration (Chapter 7) and the judicial system (Chapter 8). All of these are ways to conceptualise victims, exploited by perpetrators and by wider victimising discourses, where stories, like those of EV and JJ, are often politicised, or depoliticised, and turned into MSHT stereotypes. Stereotyping can be a way of mitigating shocking truths, making them psychologically manageable, but also more distant and abstract, almost fictional. In the case of MSHT, victims' story stereotyping has a depoliticising effect. The gaze is diverted from political and economic structural responsibilities of governments and businesses towards simplified stories of good versus bad, victims versus perpetrators, voluntary versus forced (Doezema, 2002; Anderson, 2008; O'Connell Davidson, 2015). Surveying MSHT films, Hackett's contribution (Chapter 5) is precisely rooted in the assumption that representations of MSHT on screen play a role in constituting victim and survivor narratives as well as awareness of MSHT within the public domain. However, they do so serving various interests, commercial or otherwise. The way victims/survivors are talked about in the film industry is informed by ideologies fuelling stereotypes and popular fears, which often serve ambivalent political ends and impact services, advocacy, and activism.

Ambiguity and reductionism are also key words in Tran and Sanders' chapter (Chapter 6), where authors analyse social media representations of MSHT within the larger framework of migration to the UK. British social media platform Facebook is shown to mostly represent a specific perspective of the host society, not giving a nuanced picture of undocumented migration as a complex socioeconomic phenomenon. Supported by anti-migration policies and legislation (such as the Nationality and Borders Bill in the UK), MSHT appear not to be explicitly associated with undocumented migration, opening up ambiguous discursive representations and negative attitudes regarding 'unwanted' undocumented migrants, who are criminalised, stigmatised and seen as invaders and liars.

Many are the times that I am defending my case. How more painful can it be than been subjected to months, to years of uncertainty, years of trying to belong, or even to trying to get your identity back. By identity I mean once you are identified as a victim/survivor/suspect of human trafficking you are labelled. You are either referred to as survivor or victim. It is not easy to be okay while you feel like an open book, a prisoner, or a suspect. It is not easy to run away from these labels because even if you are free from your trafficker you are never free from segregation and stigma. (JJ)

Ambiguous attitudes can easily turn into suspicion and even hostility, and often it is a mix of these that permeates anti-trafficking systems. Becoming a victim is not an easy label per se, yet it becomes even more cumbersome when, with that attached identity, come also other experiences, identity positionings and labels. One of those is the identity of suspect and potential criminal, within a system of civic stratification that establishes who is to be believed and who is not (Leerkes et al, 2018). Officially embracing the identity as victim entails a deprivation and the threat of loss of one's own identity and sense of self. It also entails enduring being a second-class resident, dwelling in the uncertainty of whether, next time, one will be believed, or reviewed again, or one will be got rid of by deportation (JJ).

I was torn between entering the NRM [National Referral Mechanism] and doing the DtN [Duty to Notify] form instead.[4] I was worried if I did the NRM would social services become involved as I had a child and would they assume she was at risk even though it was historic. (EV)

At the age of 12, I was sexually assaulted by someone I know. I am a victim of domestic violence, gambling, trafficking and a mother who left her children, hoping to make a better life. But does the process put all these into consideration? The answer is no. The answer is you are a suspect awaiting to prove themselves as victim so that you can become an equal human being. (JJ)

Both Chapters 7 and 8 critically engage with criminal justice systems and approaches. In Chapter 7, MSHT are conceived as discursive, fresh sites that craft victims, suspects and offenders. Samota and Ariyo show how, often invisibly, racialisation and racism are useful concepts to interrogate these overlapping categories. The authors also demonstrate how these are concepts used to justify enforcement policies that continue to adversely affect non-White/non-Global North populations. The chapter discusses the evidence on policing of immigration and crime in the UK, and elsewhere in Europe, that invokes race in ways that classify certain communities as suspect. This is particularly alarming because often the same communities experience harsh and dangerous conditions when fleeing persecution, and other forms of violence, from domestic to structural.

A critical vein runs also through Barlow's contribution (Chapter 8) around the UK judicial system in light of the Modern Slavery Act 2015. With reference to cases that have been before the civil and criminal courts since 2015, it is argued that the implementation of the Act is currently falling short of its ambition.

> I was supposed to have been referred into the NRM in January of 2019; that was a referral sent from the modern slavery helpline to the police. The police never told me that a referral had been made until the April, I was told they needed to find out what the NRM was, and they needed to get guidance on how to complete the form from the Home Office. I was also told that modern slavery offences never existed before 2015 and that what happened to me was just bad luck. I was told the investigation would be closed due to other cases of the same nature being returned for investigation and closed. (EV)

Echoing EV, Barlow argues that the criminal and civil justice systems suffer from a lack of knowledge and understanding of the complexity and organisation of these MSHT-related crimes and maintain flawed assumptions about both victims and perpetrators. Focusing on the UK response to criminal exploitation, the author argues that the systems tend to embody sceptical attitudes towards MSHT cases, while also being slow in conducting appropriate investigations. This has a deleterious impact upon victims, who can even be criminalised, re-victimised, and are too often re-traumatised and further humiliated. A glaring example of this is during the police interviews, where survivors are invisible, and all that matters is to 'accomplish the authorities' mission, that is to catch the perpetrator and close the case', as JJ argues.

End: one day (3)

> One day I managed to run away. I was rescued and after some time I was taken for treatment and that is when I was taken in safe house owned by charity organisation. Later the police, Migrant Help and the Home Office took over my case. I lost everything, my dignity was stripped away, I lost my identity and most of all I have turned from a victim to a suspect. It has been three years since I arrived in the UK. Two years since my case was taken over by the Home Office. This

journey has not been easy because you lose your place as the victim and become a suspect. (JJ)

Coming out of exploitation, both in tangible terms – running away from your exploiters – and in psychological terms – lifting the cover off your memory and past experiences – is a further step along the victim journey. Usually, but not necessarily, and depending upon the circumstances of each survivor, following the end of the period of abuse and exploitation, care is sought. The MSHT system of assistance is however necessarily imbued with the same package of intersecting postcolonial ideologies around migration, race, gender and victimhood, that are explored in Part II of the volume. As EV and JJ clearly express in relation to the UK, survivors entering the system of assistance, on the one hand, carry a burdensome label – that of victim/survivor – which, on the other hand, they have to keep proving and fighting about in order to obtain adequate care and services. Chapter 9 by Lazzarino and Greenslade is built upon the fundamental ambiguity of MSHT systems of assistance. The authors explore several phases of post-MSHT care, from the moment of self-identification and the decision to enter the system, or not, and subsequent psychotherapeutic assistance, education and job placement. All throughout, the system – in the UK and in other Global South contexts – oscillates between a construction of survivors as traumatised and vulnerable victims, on one side; and, on the other side, practices and policies pivoting around a criminalising vein of suspect, stigma and disempowerment.

I felt out of the loop as to what was going on. I finally entered the NRM in June of 2019 and received my conclusive grounds in the August. I was referred to an organisation straight away but felt uncomfortable as it was very foreign based, very heavy on immigration and asylum and I felt this would not meet my needs. I asked if it would be possible to have an English-speaking support worker but was told that I could not. I felt upset, stuck and triggered. I didn't have any support or a case worker for nearly four months until via Twitter, they told me it was unlawful and I shouldn't be left on my own and managed to find me a support worker and legal representation over 200 miles away with a new provider who could only do phone support as she was not permitted to travel. I was told I would have to manage everything myself but would have phone support when I needed it. Having no support worker to help with things and having no consistency was tough, I struggled doing legal aid forms myself, I struggled with talking to lawyers myself as I could never remember what we had discussed, I couldn't apply for PIP [Personal Independence Payment][5] when my PTSD [post-traumatic stress disorder] was at its worst and I needed time off as I didn't know how to fill in the forms. I never had the foundation to build on a relationship with my support worker which made trust issues really hard. I felt alone. I had no risk assessments done so I could have been back in exploitation but no one would have known. Mentally, physically and emotionally I was on my own and I had to be quite independent in knowing and learning what was going on around me. (EV)

The concept of 'subjection' (Butler, 1997) used in Chapter 9 helps bind survivors' recovery and reintegration processes in terms of a constant fluctuation between being-defined and self-defining, being-made and self-making. In other words, this means self-rebuilding via subjugation to the paradoxical and insensitive systems of trafficking aftercare. The system is inadequate to the point of failing to assist both migrants and its own citizens, as EV tells us.

The inadequacy of the MSHT system of assistance can be attributed to the same postcolonial gaze running through the whole MSHT discourse. Under this gaze, human-to-human exploitation is perceived as happening to others, to immigrants, and to the non-Western Other (Newton, 1997; Kapur, 2002; Kempadoo, 2012). Consequently, a biased system is unprepared, leaving survivors fundamentally alone, not seen and recognised in their very complex set of cultural and individual needs. Such a system can further impede on survivors' ability to process what has happened to them and reconstruct their sense of self.

Charity organisations are working tirelessly to help women like me. But as I dealt with a few of them I felt like their hands are tied and there is only so much they can do. Policies and legislations that are laid down for them restrain them. Many women are not just victims of trafficking but are victims of domestic violence, FGM [female genital mutilation], poverty, religious cults and many other things, but does the process stops to think how one ended up in that position? Secondly there are blanket policies that are used on all victims. These policies do not put into consideration individual circumstances. The majority of frontline employees either do not know how to handle people like me seeking asylum or under NRM, or it is the stigma. Going through the process leaves you unconfident, drained and uncertain. (JJ)

As underlined here, abuses and exploitation linked to MSHT are to be read against the backdrop of broader configurations of structural inequality, violence and discriminating gender norms. The identity as victim/survivor interacts with that of vulnerable migrant and citizen, woman, daughter, student, representative of a different cultural and ethnic background, and beneficiary of assistance. All these positionings and experiences constitute both avenues for self-realisation and intersecting lines of oppression (Smith, 2000; Crenshaw, 2017), echoing the ambivalence in power-imbalanced relationships (Bhabha, 1984). Hodges, Brachou and Burch bring attention, in Chapter 10, to the intersecting lived experiences of women victims of sexual exploitation, to depict the intertwining and intricate identities and situations that make up their journeys. Drawing on the findings of two evaluation studies of support provisions, the chapter addresses the gendered discourse framing the different ways victims/survivors support needs are defined and met by policymakers, commissioners and support services. The three contributors also show how the nature and quality of help can make female survivors' lives more precarious and vulnerable.

> I have dreams just like any other person, I am a law-abiding citizen, I never wanted this kind of life, I just found myself misled and exploited due to my desire to end my suffering. But the constant suspicion and stigma attached to this journey shrinks my dreams every day ... every day I have constant fear and uncertainty and I don't know If I will ever see my children again. I want to work with youth justice or women after I finish my studies because I still believe there is still good in people even though I have suffered in the hands of the same human beings. (JJ)

Hodges, Brachou and Burch however set out actions needed to provide services to women that are adequately helpful and supportive, such as the application of cultural mediation. A positive vein is present also in the following two chapters of Part III of this volume around 'Caring: practices and resilience'. In this section, attention is turned towards the voices of survivors, as service users, and practitioners, as service providers. Both experiences and practices of assistance are articulated in light of key concepts – such as gender, trauma, resilience and creativity. Better tools to understand which care works better are also discussed.

> I am now studying without having to explain myself or to feel ashamed of myself in front of my classmates, because no one knows my story and I can use my name and I don't have the Home Office card attached to my every move, at least at university, I use my student card just like any other student. Although in private I have days that I would have flashbacks and I would have mental breakdown, I would say that I have been given this chance to do something with my life, give me a reason to dust myself and look forward for tomorrow. (JJ)

In Chapter 11, Murphy and Anstiss cast light onto caring for survivors of MSHT in a residential safe house setting in the UK and show how this type of values-based intervention may contribute to the development of psychological capital (Luthans et al, 2007). Not too dissimilar from the concept of self-making underpinning Chapter 9, psychological capital is characterised by self-efficacy, optimism, hope and resilience. The authors explore the development of psychological capital resources in a group of survivors participating in a safe house-based support programme in the UK. The programme's specific values, the authors highlight, contribute to ongoing empowerment of survivors during reintegration into the community.

In Chapter 12, Westin makes the case for therapeutic approaches offered by imaginative arts-based activity and movement to be integrated into programmes of assistance to recovery. These alternative approaches to tending to the traumatic experience of trafficking offer ways of reconnecting with the lived body, through the embodied medium of the arts, and can enable the survivor to live a reconstructed experience of the self. This is because imagination enables a living of future-oriented experience, even as the traumatic experience is still cognitively fragmented and silenced.

> After I went to the safe house, things were much better, I felt safe and cared for, but I was far from being free. There were days I would have mental breakdowns or panic attacks, and even though I was free, I felt like I had just begun another journey of constant surveillance and constant opening up things that I would rather take to my grave. But this was a part of proofing myself and I guess part of healing. But all this has left me without any self-confidence and even though I always try to put up a smile I have a dying self inside. (JJ)

On the one hand, there is the need to decolonise care from Western-centred concepts and practices (as biomedicine-informed and language-based therapies, for example); but simultaneously, it is also urgent and necessary to push the monitoring and evaluation (M&E) of services for survivors of MSHT up the agendas of researchers, practitioners and policymakers, as an aid to improving services. This is the important task of the concluding chapter of the whole volume, by Van Dyke and Dottridge (Chapter 13). Based on their long-term hands-on experience, the authors explore the purposes of M&E and look at what is to be monitored and evaluated in a wide range of services, such as basic needs, life skills and employment. They also show the role of indicators and methods of verification related to service outputs/outcomes and impact. The authors review various monitoring models that have been tried in other countries and challenges, such as ethical issues, time constraints, and data availability and collection.

A key point that Van Dyke and Dottridge make in relation to M&E and its ethics is the extent to which survivors have been involved in service design, delivery and evaluation.

Survivors' voice

A state-of-the-art of survivors' involvement in MSHT studies and systems is lacking. Mapping it is the next step in the editors' agenda (Lazzarino and Murphy, in preparation). What is known, at this stage, is that overall, there is a dearth of survivor-informed research and practice (Steiner et al, 2018; Lazzarino et al, 2022), as identified at the onset of this introduction. The embryonic presence of survivors in MSHT studies and systems is because extensive research of this kind is costly (both in terms of time and budget); additionally, it is because access to survivors is difficult and requires a long-term process of building the necessary partnerships and non-governmental organisations' commitment to participation. Another reason concerns the ethical considerations that must be a priority in survivors' inclusion, and which must be carefully evaluated to avoid instrumentalisation and re-traumatisation; and finally, because, despite the terminology being around for half a century, radically participatory, co-produced knowledge in academia and services in the public and third sector is a 'new Zeitgeist' (Alford, 2014; Palmer et al, 2019). Evidently, it is also the case that not all survivors are willing to become advocates or activists, or to be embedded into MSHT studies and systems in any capacity and roles in the different fields of prosecution, policies, prevention or protection. Several survivors resolve to leave behind that identity and expertise, and cultivate different aspirations, vocations and roles.

Looking at what is changing instead, survivors' expert voice in knowledge creation and dissemination is making its way in several realms. Tools are being developed to support the creation of survivor-informed organisations, national referral mechanisms, and to monitor and evaluate survivors' involvement (Sanar Wellness Institute and NHTTAC, 2018; Survivors Voices, 2021; OSCE, 2022). There are examples of survivors' involvement in multimodal research, with current cases spanning from documentary ethnofiction (Mai, 2016) to ethical storytelling techniques (Haji et al, 2022) and photovoice (Lockyer and Koenig, 2020). Legal debates around definitions of slavery (Nicholson et al, 2018), ways to envision post-trafficking citizenship (Laurie et al, 2015), mental health recovery (Wright et al, 2020) and design of ad hoc education modules for healthcare providers (Sheets, 2021) have seen the participation and the authorship of survivors. Survivor-authored and informed literature has been analysed to hear survivor perspectives on the inclusion of leaders with experience in the anti-trafficking system (Lockyer, 2020).

The presence of survivor expertise in the anti-MSHT system, such as the Human Trafficking Foundation in the UK, is becoming increasingly visible, with growing cases of leadership, advocacy and activism. Organisations founded and constituted entirely by survivors (for example, Shakti Samuha in Nepal and Survivor Alliance in the US and UK) are examples of this. There are cases where survivors have been actively involved as experts and peer-supporters within organisations' design and delivery of service (such as Liberty Shared from Hong Kong, River of Life in the Philippines, Sanjog, and Integrated Rural Community Development Society in India; and King's Daughter's Organization in Namibia) (Lazzarino et al, 2022). These international examples, along with the increasing participation of survivors as experts, beyond the tokenistic storytelling, in conferences, awareness raising and partnership events (for example, the first conference of the Commonwealth Parliamentary Association UK [CPA UK] and the UK Modern Slavery and Human Rights Policy and Evidence Centre [MS PEC]) are promising, but insufficient still. Furthermore, much peer-support and grassroots work, as well as survivor involvement in the anti-trafficking system and in research, may remain anonymous and invisible. More research is needed to understand to what extent, how, and with which motivations, outcomes and experiences victims/survivors become active in MSHT studies and systems.

Notes

[1] Briefly put, human trafficking is in continuity with the anti-prostitution abolitionist movement of the late 19th century, which sought to fight, in particular, women's mobility (Doezema, 2010; Kempadoo, 2012; see Chapter 5 in this volume too). The United Nations Office on Drugs and Crime Palermo Protocol (United Nations, 2000) reflects such historical preoccupation with sex work, together with states' revitalised concern with undocumented migration and international terrorism around the beginning of the 21st century (Anderson, 2008; Aradau, 2008; see Chapter 6, this volume). Modern slavery has no legal basis within international provisions (Allain, 2017). The term conjures up imagery of predominantly male transatlantic chattel slavery and it is associated with the history of its legal abolition (Bravo, 2011). This history saw a progressive definitional expansion of what could be considered as slavery, at least from a political and rhetorical, but not legal, standpoint, reflecting new political and economic exigencies (Miers, 2003). Explanatory efforts and critical analyses of the MSHT, as terms and approaches, and of the relationship between the two are ongoing (Weitzer, 2015; Stoyanova, 2017; Patterson and Zhuo, 2018).

[2] In the British provision, 'slavery, servitude and forced or compulsory labour' and 'human trafficking' remain separated within the same Act and referred to as per the international definitions.

[3] The collaborative process of co-authorship with J. Julia (JJ) and Emily Vaughn (EV) worked in this way. As a first step, Runa Lazzarino (RL) drafted a first version of this introductory text, where there appeared the idea of involving two survivor co-authors who could narrate and critically reflect on their own journey as victims/survivors. As a second step, Carole Murphy (CM) mentioned this idea with a few survivor students and

participants, and JJ and EV were the ones who accepted to contribute, as an international and a domestic survivor respectively. CM gave them a few cues to follow, if they wished so, to write their stories, which they could however tell as freely as they felt like. After receiving JJ and EV's texts, RL read them and weaved them in what became a new draft of the introduction, trying to balance their voice with the voice and aims of the volume's editors, as well as with the voices of the contributors of the volumes' chapters. This new text was sent back to CM who provided further input and feedback, and then again to JJ and EV, for their comments, feedback and editing. RL embedded all the co-authors' feedback and drafted the version of introduction that we are here offering to readers.

[4] NRM stands for National Referral Mechanism, and it is described by the UK government as a 'framework for identifying and referring potential victims of modern slavery and ensuring they receive the appropriate support'. The NRM was introduced in 2009 and provides support with a minimum 45-day reflection period for the victim if certain conditions are met. In order for a potential victim to access the NRM this must be initially referred by an authorised agency, known as a First Responder. The DtN is the Duty to Notify introduced in 2015, also referred to as MS1, and is a way to inform the authorities of a suspected/potential adult case of modern slavery who wants to remain anonymous and does not want specialist support (https://www.gov.uk/government/publications/human-trafficking-victims-referral-and-assessment-forms/guidance-on-the-national-referral-mechanism-for-potential-adult-victims-of-modern-slavery-england-and-wales, accessed 14 January 2022).

[5] PIP stands for Personal Independence Payment and it is a UK government benefit and financial support for a long-term physical or mental health condition or disability (https://www.gov.uk/pip).

References

Alford, J. (2014) The multiple facets of co-production: Building on the work of Elinor Ostrom. *Public Management Review*, 16(3): 299–316.

Allain, J. (2017) Contemporary slavery and its definition in law. In A. Bunting and J. Quirk (eds) *Contemporary Slavery: Popular Rhetoric and Political Practice*. Vancouver: UBC Press, pp 36–66.

Allain, J. (2018) Genealogies of human trafficking and slavery. In R. Piotrowicz, C. Rijken and B.H. Uhl (eds) *Routledge Handbook of Human Trafficking*. New York: Routledge, pp 3–12.

Anderson, B. (2008) 'Illegal migrant': Victim or villain? *ESRC Centre on Migration, Policy and Society – Working Paper no 64*.

Aradau, C. (2008) *Rethinking Trafficking in Women: Politics Out of Security*. Basingstoke and New York: Palgrave Macmillan.

Bhabha, H. (1984) Of mimicry and man: The ambivalence of colonial discourse. *October*, 28: 125–33.

Bravo, K.E. (2011) The role of the transatlantic slave trade in contemporary anti–human trafficking discourse. *Seattle Journal for Social Justice*, 9(2): 555–97.

Bravo, K.E. (2019) *Contemporary State Anti-'Slavery' Efforts: Dishonest and Ineffective*. SSRN Scholarly Paper. Rochester: Social Science Research Network.

Broad, R. and Turnbull, N. (2018) From human trafficking to modern slavery: The development of anti-trafficking policy in the UK. *European Journal on Criminal Policy and Research*, 25: 119–33.

Bunting, A. and Quirk, J. (2017) Contemporary slavery as more than rhetorical strategy? The politics and ideology of a new political cause. In A. Bunting and J. Quirk (eds) *Contemporary Slavery: Popular Rhetoric and Political Practice*. Vancouver: UBC Press, pp 5–35.

Butler, J. (1997) *The Psychic Life of Power: Theories in Subjection*. Stanford: Stanford University Press.

Chuang, J. (2014) Exploitation creep and the unmaking of human trafficking law. *The American Journal of International Law*, 108(4): 609–49.

Crenshaw, K. (2017) *On Intersectionality: Essential Writings*. New York: The New Press.

Doezema, J. (2002) Who gets to choose? Coercion, consent, and the UN Trafficking Protocol. *Gender & Development*, 10(1): 20–7.

Doezema, J. (2010) *Sex Slaves and Discourse Masters: The Construction of Trafficking*. London: Zed Books.

Gadd, D. and Broad, R. (2018) Troubling recognitions in British responses to modern slavery. *The British Journal of Criminology*, 58(6): 1440–61.

Haji, A.A., Baya, R., Brady, E., McCabe, H., Manji, Y. and Otiende, S. (2022) Participatory photography, ethical storytelling, and modern slavery survivor voices: Adapting to COVID-19. In M.C. S. Gonçalves, R. Gutwald, T. Kleibl, R. Lutz, N. Noyoo and J. Twikirize (eds) *The Coronavirus Crisis and Challenges to Social Development: Global Perspectives*. Cham: Springer International Publishing, pp 371–80.

Kapur, R. (2002) *The Tragedy of Victimization Rhetoric: Resurrecting the Native Subject in International/Postcolonial Feminist Legal Politics*. Rochester: Social Science Research Network.

Kempadoo, K. (2012) Abolitionism, criminal justice, and transnational feminism: Twenty-first-century perspectives on human trafficking. In K. Kempadoo, J. Sanghera and B. Pattanaik (eds) *Trafficking and Prostitution Reconsidered: New Perspectives on Migration, Sex Work, and Human Rights*, 2nd edn. Boulder, CO: Paradigm Publishers.

Laurie, N., Richardson, D., Poudel, M. and Townsend, J. (2015) Co-producing a post-trafficking agenda: Collaborating on transforming citizenship in Nepal. *Development in Practice*, 25(4): 465–77.

Lazzarino, R. (2019) Fixing the disjuncture, inverting the drift: Decolonizing human trafficking and modern slavery. *Journal of Modern Slavery*, 5(1): 1–31.

Lazzarino, R. and Murphy, C. (in preparation) Survivor voice in modern slavery and human trafficking studies, practice and policies: A review.

Lazzarino, R., Wright, N. and Jordan, M. (2022) Mental healthcare for survivors of modern slavery and human trafficking: A single point-in-time, internet-based scoping study of third sector provision. *Journal of Human Trafficking*, https://doi.org/10.1080/23322705.2021.2024043.

Leerkes, A., Engbersen, G., Snel, E. and de Boom, J. (2018) Civic stratification and crime: A comparison of asylum migrants with different legal statuses. *Crime, Law and Social Change*, 69(1): 41–66.

Lockyer, S. (2020) Beyond inclusion: Survivor-leader voice in anti-human trafficking organizations. *Journal of Human Trafficking*, 8(2): 135–56.

Lockyer, S. and Koenig, C.J. (2020) At the intersection of method and empowerment: Reflections from a pilot photovoice study with survivors of human trafficking. *Journal of Human Trafficking*, https://doi.org/10.1080/23322705.2020.1809300.

Luthans, F., Avolio, B.J., Avey, J.B. and Norman, S.M. (2007) Positive psychological capital: Measurement and relationship with performance and satisfaction. *Personnel Psychology*, 60(3): 541–72.

Mai, N. (2016) *Travel Documentary Ethnofiction*. Available from: https://raifilm.org.uk/films/travel/ (accessed 2 January 2021).

Miers, S. (2003) Slavery: A question of definition. *Slavery & Abolition*, 24(2): 1–16.

Newton, K.M. (1997) Homi K. Bhabha: 'The other question: The stereotype and colonial discourse'. In K.M. Newton (ed) *Twentieth-Century Literary Theory: A Reader*. London: Macmillan, pp 293–301.

Nicholson, A., Dang, M. and Trodd, Z. (2018) A full freedom: Contemporary survivors' definitions of slavery. *Human Rights Law Review*, 18(4): 689–704.

O'Connell Davidson, J. (2015) *Modern Slavery: The Margins of Freedom*. London and New York: Palgrave Macmillan.

O'Connell Davidson, J. (2017) Editorial: The presence of the past: Lessons of history for anti-trafficking work. *Anti-Trafficking Review*, 9: 1–12.

OSCE (Organization for Security and Co-operation in Europe) (2022) *National Referral Mechanisms: Joining Efforts to Protect the Rights of Trafficked Persons*. Warsaw: OSCE Office for Democratic Institutions and Human Rights.

Palmer, V.J., Weavell, W., Callander, R., Piper, D., Richard, L., Maher, L., Boyd, H., Herrman, H., Furler, J., Gunn, G., Iedema, R. and Robert, G. (2019) The participatory zeitgeist: An explanatory theoretical model of change in an era of coproduction and codesign in healthcare improvement. *Medical Humanities*, 45(3): 247–57.

Patterson, O. (2012) Trafficking, gender and slavery: Past and present. In J. Allain (ed) *The Legal Understanding of Slavery: From the Historical to the Contemporary*. Oxford: Oxford University Press, pp 324–6.

Patterson, O. and Zhuo, X. (2018) Modern trafficking, slavery, and other forms of servitude. *Annual Review of Sociology*, 44(1): 407–39.

Sanar Wellness Institute and NHTTAC (2018) *Toolkit for Building Survivor-Informed Organizations*. US Department of Health and Human Services, Administration for Children and Families, Office on Trafficking in Persons.

Sheets, K. (2021) Human trafficking education module for healthcare providers: Reviewed and informed by survivors of sex trafficking. *Doctor of Nursing Practice Projects*. Available from: https://scholarworks.seattleu.edu/dnp-projects/18/

Smith, B. (ed) (2000) *Home Girls: A Black Feminist Anthology*. New Brunswick: Rutgers University Press.

Spivak, G.C. (1988) Can the subaltern speak? In C. Nelson and L. Grossberg (eds) *Marxism and the Interpretation of Culture*. London: Macmillan, pp 271–313.

Steiner, J.J., Kynn, J., Stylianou, A.M. and Postmus, J.L. (2018) Providing services to trafficking survivors: Understanding practices across the globe. *Journal of Evidence-Informed Social Work*, 15(2): 151–69.

Stoyanova, V. (2017) *Human Trafficking and Slavery Reconsidered: Conceptual Limits and States' Positive Obligations in European Law*. New York: Cambridge University Press.

Survivors Voices (2021) *Survivor Involvement Ladder 2021*. Available from: https://survivorsvoices.org/involvement-ladder/ (accessed 8 January 2020).

United Nations (1956) *Supplementary Convention on the Abolition of Slavery, the Slave Trade and Institutions and Practices Similar to Slavery*. New York: United Nations.

United Nations (2000) *Protocol to Prevent, Suppress and Punish Trafficking in Persons*. New York: United Nations.

UNODC (United Nations Office on Drugs and Crime) (2000) *Protocol to Prevent, Protect and Punish Trafficking in Persons Especially Women and Children, Supplementing The United Nations Convention Against Transnational Organised Crime*. New York: United Nations.

Weitzer, R. (2015) Human trafficking and contemporary slavery. *Annual Review of Sociology*, 41(1): 223–42.

Wright, N., Hadziosmanovic, E., Dang, M., Bales, K., Brookes, C., Jordan, M. and Slade, M. (2020) Mental health recovery for survivors of modern slavery: Grounded theory study protocol. *BMJ Open*, 10(11): e038583.

PART I

Recruiting: business and tools

This part includes contributions exploring macro aspects of modern slavery and human trafficking (MSHT) – connected with structural, upstream and pull factors at the root of MSHT (that is, recruitment, supply chain and business, demand) – and formal, legislative tools and policies to combat them, internationally and nationally.

1

Criminal pyramid scheme: organised crime recruitment strategies

Sasha Jesperson and Rune Henriksen

Introduction

While the experiences of victims of modern slavery and human trafficking (MSHT) are becoming better understood, a greater threat emerges from the involvement of organised crime. The profit motives and violence associated with organised crime makes MSHT more dangerous for victims and difficult to detect and address. As law enforcement has sought to respond to the role of organised crime in MSHT, the tactics being used to facilitate MSHT have evolved. In many countries, particularly where there is demand for outward migration, a worrying trend has emerged where communities, families and victims themselves become complicit in their own recruitment, becoming invested in their own exploitation and subsequently reluctant to seek assistance. This chapter traces the creation of a 'criminal pyramid scheme', with criminals at the top driving the recruitment and exploitation of victims, communities and families in the middle, encouraging potential victims to migrate, and victims themselves making up the largest layer, expecting to profit and send their earnings home by exposing themselves to exploitation.

Human trafficking as an organised crime

Following the adoption of the UN Convention on Transnational Organised Crime, the head of what was then the UN Drug Control and Crime Prevention Programme (now United Nations Office on Drugs and Crime [UNODC]) argued that human trafficking was the fastest growing form of organised crime. Pino Arlacchi pointed to 'reports that drug traffickers are switching to human cargo to obtain greater profit with less risk' (UN News, 2001). That was in 2001, and one of the protocols to the UN Convention focused specifically on human trafficking – seeking to prevent and punish traffickers and protect victims of trafficking. UNODC was subsequently tasked with assisting state parties in drafting legislation, developing strategies and providing resources to implement the protocol.

Although the protocol came into force as international law in 2003, the UK Anti-Trafficking Monitoring Group released a report in 2012 pointing out that 'little is known about the profile of people who essentially fuel this criminal industry, what level they occupy within the criminal chain, their characteristics and personal circumstances, their reasons for becoming involved in trafficking activities, their perceptions of their activities and their opinion of those they traffic' (Anti-Trafficking Monitoring Group, 2012).

UNODC itself highlighted how the landscape of organised crime, and particularly the actors involved, has changed.

> The overall common ground in this respect is that there not only exists an enormous diversity in the landscape of organised criminal involvement in both phenomena but that overall, there is an enormous diversity as to the different actors active in these markets. The actors involved may be organised criminal groups, individual traffickers or smugglers, or even friends and family of migrants or trafficking victims. (UNODC, 2010, p 7)

Despite the lack of understanding on what form organised crime takes in relation to human trafficking, it is increasingly being recognised as an organised crime problem. This is primarily because it is such a lucrative industry. In 2014, the International Labour Organization estimated that the profits made from forced labour amounted to US$150.2 billion per year (ILO, 2014). This breaks down to $99 billion from commercial sexual exploitation, $34 billion in construction, manufacturing, mining and utilities, and $9 billion in agriculture, including forestry and fishing (HRF, 2017). Not all of this profit is harnessed by criminal groups, however, as it also includes savings within the industry by using cheaper forms of labour. The figure also includes $8 billion that is saved annually by private households that employ domestic workers in exploitative conditions. Craig et al also argue that 'it is difficult to conclude other than that we all do [profit], however unknowingly, in the goods we buy which come from unknown destinations' (Craig et al, 2018, p 19). Despite this dispersal of profits, trafficking remains a lucrative activity for criminal groups. A UNODC estimate from 2012 claims that traffickers make US$32 billion annually and this has likely increased since then (UNODC, 2012).

A major motivator for organised criminal groups to engage in human trafficking is the low threshold costs, the low risk of getting caught, and the fact that this business model can be conducted anywhere in the world (Jesperson et al, 2019). In addition, criminal groups can capitalise on the desire of many individuals to migrate. O'Connell Davidson (2017, p 159) cites research on debt-financed migration and debt bondage, where migrants know the risks, but nonetheless consider the potential benefits worthwhile.

They 'invariably want to move, and generally have excellent reasons for wishing to do so'.

In some cases, however, the role of criminal groups is redundant. In the UK at least, forced or exploitative labour occurs at a greater rate than sexual exploitation, and this is primarily a result of increasing deregulation of the UK economy, opening the door to low wages, long hours, insecure contracts, poor working conditions and limited organising by trades unions (Craig et al, 2018). These factors mean organised crime networks are not necessary to circumvent labour regulations – employers or agencies can exploit workers directly. These circumstances have created a role for 'middlemen' who exploit individuals from their own country of origin, finding them jobs, but charging them for travel and accommodation. When their language skills are not adequate, they may be duped into opening a bank account that they don't control. The Gangmasters Labour Abuse Authority explained that:

> [S]ometimes ... workers are being exploited, but they are being exploited by somebody who works for the same company that they do. ... In that situation you find that it's either, for example, Lithuanian workers exploited by a Lithuanian who works for the same company, or, for example, a Slovak Roma exploited by a Czech Roma who are in the same company. (Cited in Allain et al, 2013, p 36)

The ease with which anyone can become involved in the exploitation or trafficking of people reduces the need for organised crime networks. However, crossing borders still requires more technical expertise, and the profit motive creates a desire from criminal groups to get involved.

This chapter engages primarily with human trafficking, defined in the Palermo Protocol to the UN Convention on Transnational Organised Crime as a crime against the individual, where they are coerced into exploitation. However, there is significant overlap with people smuggling (see Chapter 6, this volume). Although defined as a crime against the state, as migrants generally seek out the services of a smuggler to assist in crossing borders, the vulnerability of these migrants, and their reliance on smugglers, makes them vulnerable to exploitation, which can shift their categorisation from people smuggling to human trafficking, as has often been the case for migrants passing through Sudan, which is discussed in this chapter.

Learning from countering other crimes

Much of what is known or thought about organised criminal involvement in human trafficking comes from research on other forms of criminality. Human trafficking is viewed as one aspect of a rapid growth in all forms of organised crime. Drug trafficking has received the most attention, both in research and responses. Accordingly, it is from drug trafficking that the response to human trafficking has drawn most of its lessons. Although there are increasing discussions of building the toolbox to address organised crime, particularly from development agencies, the main strategies to address organised crime continue to rely on law enforcement techniques, particularly arrest and seizure.

For drug trafficking, this approach involves crop eradication and decapitation or 'kingpin' strategies, where the head of an organised crime group is targeted by law enforcement, in source countries, arresting traffickers and seizing commodities in transit, and arresting users and distributors in destination countries, while also attempting to disrupt networks along the transit route. For human trafficking, this translates to arresting traffickers in source countries and disrupting criminal networks, which may include tracking financial flows and asset seizure. In transit countries, law enforcement also attempt to arrest traffickers and disrupt the networks, while in destination countries the focus is also on arresting facilitators of exploitation, and potentially arresting users, depending on the type of exploitation and the legislation in place. Even in response to drugs however, law enforcement approaches have not been effective. Successful law enforcement strategies rarely stop organised crime, they merely push it elsewhere.

There is still some value in applying the strategies to tackle drug trafficking to human trafficking. Phil Williams contends that:

> [O]ne of the most pernicious and demeaning aspects of trafficking in women and children is that it reduces people to the status of commodities. Understanding this, however, is also an important insight since it suggests that what we are seeing is the operation of a commodity market that is subject to the same kinds of laws, impulses and trends as any other illicit market, whether drugs, nuclear materials, illicit arms, fauna and flora or art and antiquities. (Williams, 2007, p 127)

A Centre for Social Justice report also identified several cases that involved similar structures to drug trafficking networks – 'power pyramids', with 'divisions of foot soldiers who will play their role in whichever division they are employed to operate within to recruit, transit or run the daily management of controlling victims' (CSJ, 2015, p 40). Shelley also points out how traffickers interact with other criminal networks: 'they obtain false documents for their victims from criminal specialists, hire thugs from outside their network to intimidate women and traffic labourers, and move their proceeds through established money-laundering channels' (Shelley, 2010, p 83).

But there are challenges with addressing human trafficking through law enforcement strategies. Because human trafficking involves a human commodity, strategies to respond place victims at risk. Some of the investigative techniques applied to drug trafficking, such as controlled deliveries, where police track the delivery of a shipment and then move in for arrests, or covert tactics and surveillance, put individuals at risk of exploitation. For these tactics to be effective, the crime has to have taken place, giving law enforcement the evidence they need to prosecute a case. This creates a tension between the need to safeguard victims, the development of criminal intelligence and the collection of evidence. As a result, there is a heavy reliance on testimony, which is particularly difficult because of the trauma experienced by victims, but also because of potential threats against family members from other control mechanisms, such as *juju* in the Nigerian context, a curse where victims believe their family members will be harmed if they report their case.

The methods of criminal groups also differ between human trafficking and other illicit activity such as drug trafficking. While there are some overlaps in the need for false documentation, corruptible border officials, the use of violence and conduits to launder money, other areas differ significantly. Recruitment of victims is very different from harvesting drugs. There is a need for large numbers of victims, and there is a tendency for traffickers to target their own communities to capitalise on the trust that exists (Jesperson et al, 2019). In addition, other strategies are used, such as advertising for false jobs, or marriages. Transport and entry rely on bribes to border officials or the receipt of visas through clandestine means, but human cargo needs to be fed, housed and delivered in a reasonable condition (Jesperson et al, 2019). Finally, compared to inanimate commodities, the victim needs to be controlled upon arrival – they need to be housed and prevented from escaping, usually through coercive control, including violence, the confiscation of documents, psychological intimidation and threats to family (Jesperson et al, 2019). These factors require a more nuanced understanding of how organised crime is involved in human trafficking, in order to identify more strategic entry points for intervention.

The growth of the criminal pyramid scheme

Organised crime has become renowned for its agile and dynamic nature – its ability to remain two steps ahead of law enforcement. This adaptability was cited by Marc Goodman in the *Harvard Business Review*, in a think piece that discussed what business can learn from organised crime. Goodman was referring to the use of technology by the attackers of the Taj Mahal Palace hotel in Mumbai in 2008 – which resulted in 'one of the best orchestrated, most technologically advanced terrorist strikes in history' (Goodman, 2011, np). One of the lessons learned was to outsource to specialists, highlighting how the hierarchical structures of mafia type organisations have long been abandoned for more agile networks that bring in individuals with specific expertise. This has been increasingly important with the rise of credit card fraud and other online criminal activity. The 2017 Serious and Organised Crime Threat Assessment, released by Europol, recognised this as an emerging feature of criminal markets, where organised crime groups openly advertised ad hoc opportunities, and particularly with online crime, the true identity of these individuals may never be known. This is just one example of how organised crime has evolved to avoid detection and disruption.

But a shift in route hasn't been the only way organised crime has evolved. The primary focus has been removing risk to evade arrest even if some of the product is lost in the process. For example, many high value commodities, such as drugs and arms, have traditionally relied on high volume transfers. Drug trafficking originally relied on multi-tonne shipments, which are easier to detect and when seized create a larger blow on the drug trafficking organisation.

Increasingly, organised crime networks are shifting to low volume, high frequency activity. As Edwards and Jeffray (2015, p 69) point out in their report on the illicit trade in tobacco, alcohol and pharmaceuticals in the UK, 'organised crime groups have begun to realise that law enforcement agencies find it much more difficult to respond to illicit trade when goods are broken down and transported in smaller consignments'. These strategies have made the illicit trade in tobacco, alcohol and pharmaceuticals particularly lucrative because there is a 'lower risk of detection, and sanctions for offences are typically less severe' (Edwards and Jeffray, 2015, p 69). As a result, it has become a key strategy for minimising the risk associated with criminality.

An important feature, though, for the illicit trade in tobacco, alcohol and pharmaceuticals is the difficulty in distinguishing it from legitimate commodities. In many instances, organised crime networks are merely engaging in tax evasion but with genuine products. This does not mean it does not do serious damage – between 1994 and 2002, the Montenegrin economy was kept afloat through cigarette smuggling (Sisti, 2008). Once passed on to the end market, these goods cannot be separated from those imported officially.

When high value commodities are too lucrative for organised crime networks to ignore, the networks that facilitate trafficking seek to distance themselves from the actual transaction. For decades now, the higher levels of drug trafficking organisations have been far removed from the actual production and distribution of drugs, making them difficult to target in law enforcement operations. For example, the use of drug mules was adopted to move drugs because if they are arrested, there is no direct link between them and the organised crime network that employed them, and only a small amount of product is seized. When West Africa was at its peak for cocaine trafficking, flights would have scores of mules on the same plane because law enforcement couldn't arrest them all. In one operation, every passenger on a flight from Nigeria was searched, and after more than 100 were found to be carrying cocaine, there was no more capacity to keep searching.[1]

Other methods have also been adopted. Rather than using light aircraft and yachts to move cocaine across the Atlantic, the tactic of rip-on/rip-off was used. This involves a smaller quantity of drugs being placed inside a container just before it is sealed, and removed as soon as it arrives, before customs search the full container. Such a strategy relies on bribing the appropriate people, but it results in high frequency, low volume shipments that displaces the risk to lower levels of the criminal network.

For people smuggling, criminal networks have developed strategies to remove their presence altogether. As the 'migrant crisis' was getting underway in 2014 and 2015, two ships were intercepted en route from Turkey to Italy. The *Blue Sky M*, with nearly 1,000 passengers on board, was intercepted on 31 December 2014 in Greek waters, and the *Ezadeen*, with over 350 passengers on board, was brought into an Italian port on 2 January 2015 (BBC News, 2014; *The Independent*, 2015). Both of these vessels had been left without crew and were sailing on autopilot. On the *Blue Sky M*, one of the passengers, Rani Sark, was reportedly promised a payment of US$10,000 to control the ship. People who are prepared to risk their lives to escape conflict are then left to face the consequences, while those facilitating the trade remain unidentified and continue to be able to fill boats with more willing passengers.

In line with the entrepreneurialism frequently attributed to criminal groups, this phenomenon took advantage of European policies to ensure the safety of passengers after the boats were abandoned, which promotes ongoing business. The Italian government stepped up their patrols of the Mediterranean in October 2013 after two boats carrying migrants from Libya sank off the island of Lampedusa (BBC News, 2013). Frontex, the EU's border agency, also launched a surveillance mission in the Mediterranean in October 2014 to control the area, monitor the border and carry out search and rescue (EC, 2014). These operations ensured that passengers were not left to drown. But they also resulted in the prosecution of many people smugglers, requiring a new strategy from criminal groups. By leaving the boats without crew, criminal groups evade law enforcement and can continue their activities.

People smugglers use many existing skills of criminal groups. The boats have all been flying flags of countries with inadequate regulations for shipping companies, or that lack the capacity to monitor vessels, such as Sierra Leone, Moldova and Tonga. This allows criminal groups to use boats that are discarded by shipping companies and sold off cheaply for scrap metal. It also makes it difficult to track the owners of the ships. These tactics are used in other forms of illicit activity such as drug trafficking and illegal fishing. As a form of illicit entrepreneurship, this approach fits with a new trend of criminal groups avoiding violence so as not to draw attention to their activities. The criminal facilitators also provide good conditions for passengers, with reports of mattresses and other comforts on board, thereby maintaining a positive reputation and ensuring future business. Criminal groups have also managed to distance themselves from the activity, making it difficult to disrupt.

Controlling a human commodity

Criminal networks involved in human trafficking, however, do not have the same capacity to distance themselves from their commodity. The challenge for networks that facilitate human trafficking is their 'commodity' can escape and tell authorities about their ordeal. This requires strategies to control the commodity. The movement of human trafficking victims does employ similar strategies to drug trafficking, using foot soldiers to recruit, transit or control victims (CSJ, 2015). But because human trafficking victims are 'enduring if re-placeable "commodities" that are consumed repeatedly rather than just once', the potential for continued profit has resulted in more innovative control mechanisms (Williams, 2007, p 133). This may include physical, psychological and emotional abuse, sexual assault, confiscation of identification and money, isolation, renaming victims, leveraging the vulnerability of victims, promising to meet the needs of victims, with the aim of creating a fear to leave (Polaris, nd). There is not just one strategy employed; traffickers identify what is likely to work with a particular victim and exploit it.

Because of the need for control, human trafficking is renowned for being violent. Glenny identified that Bulgarian organised crime networks that became involved in sexual exploitation regularly used rape and violence to coerce their victims into submission (Glenny, 2008). But it is not just physical violence that is used. Hopper and Hidalgo highlight how psychological abuse and coercion is easier to conceal and is widespread: 'coercive systems utilize high levels of control, exposure to chronic stress and threat, isolation, provocation of fear, and the creation of a sense of helplessness in victims' (Hopper and Hidalgo, 2006, p 191). Given the vulnerability of many victims when they are in a country other than their own, these tactics are extremely effective. Much more is understood about the control of victims of sexual exploitation, but Bales et al report that psychological abuse is also applied to victims of labour exploitation: 'cut off from contact with the outside world, they can lose their sense of personal efficacy and control, attributes that mental health professionals have long considered essential to good mental and physical health' (Bales et al, 2005, p 3).

A growing body of research has emerged on control methods linked to sexual exploitation. This can include the confiscation of travel documents, the use of violence, the threat to harm family members and a financial dependency upon the human trafficker (Hughes, 2000). This research has been expanded by Hughes, who explored the form of isolation and threats, also including shame, humiliation and culturally specific forms of control, through an analysis of sex trafficking from Ukraine (Kelly, 2002). Based on empirical research on the sex trade in the Netherlands, Ioannou and Oostinga have developed a typology – victim as object, involving direct possession and subjugation of victims; victim as vehicle, involving emotional and psychological control through threats; and victim as person, involving control through manipulation (Ioannou and Oostinga, 2015).

What has been found across all forms of violence, whether physical or psychological, is that victims become 'increasingly dependent on the perpetrator, not only for survival and basic bodily needs, but also for information and even for emotional sustenance' (Herman, 1992, p 81). This has been linked to trauma-coerced attachment or trauma bonds, terms developed to explain the unidirectional bond that emerges between hostages and their hostage takers, as a result of the trauma that has been experienced (see, for example, Sanchez et al, 2019; Doychak and Raghavan, 2020). The result is that victims are reluctant to testify against their traffickers, meaning law enforcement need to rely on other methods to build a case (see, for example, Kitroeff, 2012). The knock-on effect is that authorities see victims as unreliable. The Centre for Social Justice uncovered cases where law enforcement had been working for over a year before victims decide to withdraw from providing oral evidence (CSJ, 2015).

For traffickers, this is the ideal situation, as it has been difficult to build cases without victim testimony. As discussed earlier, many of the evidence collection techniques applied to other forms of organised crime are dangerous to victims of human trafficking. However, it is a resource-intensive activity controlling victims. In some examples, trafficking networks have employed people specifically to manage the control of victims. In the same vein as the strategies discussed to remove risk and increase profit, human traffickers have also sought out other control mechanisms that are more cost-effective.

Moving to less direct forms of control

One factor that crosses all forms of criminality is that criminal groups adapt their activity to the market dynamics that are present. Accordingly, how each type of criminality adapts will differ and needs careful analysis. In relation to human trafficking, a criminal pyramid scheme has emerged, where all layers are complicit in denying and hiding the criminality.

When seen as an organised crime problem, 'criminals are presented as the main beneficiaries of human trafficking' (Sharapov, 2015, p 94). But the situation is more complex than this binary distinction suggests. Offenders are generally established as the polar opposite of victims, but in many cases this distinction is inappropriate as many traffickers were previously trafficked and have worked their way up to become the exploiters (De Shalit et al, 2014; Szörényi and Eate, 2014; Moore and Goldberg, 2015). This is evident in Nigeria, where the goal of many girls travelling to Europe is to become a madam.[2]

For the Nigerian trafficking industry, a series of control measures have been in place that reduce the need for violence. This is not to say that violence is completely removed from the transaction – in Libya, as conditions deteriorated, violence and extortion became commonplace. However, to control women and girls, *juju* rituals have been used extensively. During the ritual, the girls' hair or fingernails are taken and they swear an oath to a deity. This process binds the girl to the contract to repay her debt for transportation. Girls are genuinely scared of the ritual and believe they will be plagued by nightmares or go crazy if they do not fulfil their obligation.

The use of *juju* manipulates culturally specific conventions to control girls in order to minimise the need for direct oversight. The girls instead self-discipline as they are indirectly controlled by their fear of *juju*. This is particularly useful when they are working on the street and direct control is not possible. Non-governmental organisations providing assistance to Nigerian girls state that *juju* prevents the girls from sharing their experiences. In one case, a young woman took months to reveal her story, sharing a little bit at a time to test what would happen.[3]

Other mechanisms are also used in case the power of *juju* is not enough. In some cases, a contract is signed by a lawyer and the girl's family, adding another layer of pressure to adhere to the agreement. When girls do breach the contract, there are often reprisals against the family. For example, one girl went to the police in Ceuta, Spain, and her family's home in Nigeria was burnt down.[4]

These control mechanisms are imposed by the recruiters, but they have been coming under increased pressure. Counsellors have been working with trafficked women to overcome the belief in *juju*. The Oba, or monarch of Benin City in Edo State, also placed a curse on perpetrators of human trafficking and traditional priests who conduct *juju* rituals with girls about to be trafficked in an attempt to undermine the power of the rituals (Ebegbulem, 2018).

Accordingly, a different strategy emerged in parallel. Within Nigeria, there is a powerful narrative of success linked to 'making it' in Europe. As long as girls return with money, no questions are asked about the work they were doing. These returning girls are then powerful and can even 'buy a husband'.[5]

Figure 1.1: A criminal pyramid scheme

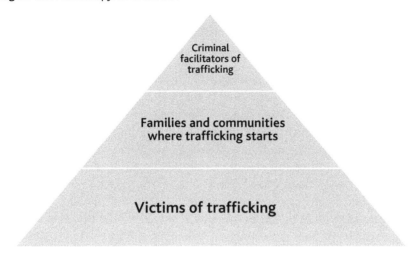

Previously, madams would visit Benin City with their expensive clothes to appeal to girls and young women and offer them work in Europe. As awareness around the nature of the work increased, it is mostly acknowledged that they are madams that worked their way up. This creates an aspiration among girls travelling to Europe to become madams – they all think they will be one of the lucky ones, even though they have to make it through 3–5 years of exploitation first to pay off their debt.[6] These aspirations however prevent girls from speaking about the criminal facilitators of trafficking, as their ultimate goal is to move up in the business. Accordingly, victims themselves become the bottom, and largest later in the criminal pyramid scheme.

The pressure from families and the broader community creates a middle layer of pressure to maintain silence around the criminal actors involved in trafficking. The economy of Edo State in Nigeria, where many girls are recruited from, has depended on the income from trafficking. As a result, civil society organisations that seek to prevent trafficking have come under attack. Families that invest in the girls want to see a return on their investment. If the girls call home to complain about the conditions, a common response is along the lines of 'so-and-so's daughter made enough to buy them a house'.[7]

The Nigeria example highlights the emergence of a criminal pyramid scheme (see Figure 1.1) – the criminal facilitators, including recruiters, transporters and madams, make the most money and have an interest in maintaining discretion – this is the top of the pyramid. The middle layer includes families and communities that are eager to profit from the exploitation of young women and girls. Accordingly, they are not going to speak out about the trafficking industry. At the bottom of the pyramid are the trafficked girls themselves. Some of the girls have been silenced by *juju* or a contract demanding that they repay their debts. But increasingly, these girls are driven by aspirations to become madams themselves, which helps maintain their silence.

While the presence of a criminal pyramid scheme is the most obvious in the Nigerian case, it is identifiable in any case where the distinction between human trafficking and people smuggling is not clear-cut, in any case where the 'victim' has something to gain. For instance, in Sudan there have been examples of direct involvement by police or authorities in the transportation of migrants. However, there have been numerous examples where authorities are paid off by smugglers to allow passage or look the other way. There have been cases of police taking migrants out of camps and handing them over to smugglers. In one case, several refugees were removed from Wad Sharifa camp in mid-2017. Police guards were tied up, which made it appear to be a kidnapping, but the refugees were found in the desert waiting for smugglers.[8] In this example, the migrants become complicit with the smugglers, even though there is a risk that the relationship may become exploitative and shift into the category of human trafficking.

When the relationship becomes exploitative along the journey, migrants have no avenue for recourse, or do not know what avenues exist, so they are unable to report exploitation and therefore contribute to the impunity of their exploiters. One entrepreneurial resident of Kassala state spent her days by the *hafir*[9] with a large stick. When migrants approached to drink from the *hafir* she charged them five Sudanese pounds, threatening to call the police if they did not pay. Not wanting to be picked up by police, the migrants paid or refrained from drinking, but they did not seek to have the water broker arrested or removed. As such, she was able to continue collecting revenue from migrants passing by.[10]

This is perhaps a minor example compared to silence regarding large-scale trafficking networks, but it is indicative of a larger trend – unless the exploitation exceeds the perceived potential benefit of the migrant, they will remain silent. Part of the role of brokers and smugglers is the selling of a dream – they need the perception of benefit to be significant enough to excuse horrific practices. This is evident in the number of Eritrean women who make use of long-term contraceptive implants, because they know of the likelihood of rape or sexual assault along their journey, but the perceived benefit of arriving in Europe has made this worth the risk.

Albania and Vietnam offer two different cases, as the main trend in relation to human trafficking is the movement of minors with the aim of working in the destination country. While this can be seen as people smuggling, because the migrants are under 18, it is legally deemed as human trafficking as the potential for consent is considered absent. Because of the desire for families to send their children to work abroad, there are parallels to the family and community pressure placed on Nigerian girls.

In Albania, minors usually come from middle-class families that may have to sell their house to send their child to Europe or the UK, and there is an expectation that this will be repaid when the child is successful in gaining employment. The process is similar for Vietnam, but it is more likely that the family will enter into debt bondage, with an implicit threat of violence. To earn enough to repay these debts and contribute to family income, these minors often end up in exploitative industries – from cannabis farms to nail bars to drug distribution – because of the earning potential. The Centre for Social Justice found that 'traffickers often do not need to resort to physical violence which would make the exploitation more visible. Trafficked children do not consider themselves to be in an exploitative situation, but rather perceive their exploitation as loyalty to their family' (CSJ, 2015). Accordingly, in these cases, neither the family nor the child will reveal the criminal facilitators that brought them to their destination.

Conclusion

While some criminal groups use violence to maintain control, and can be more obvious with their wealth, there has been a shift among many organised crime groups towards more discrete methods to avoid attracting unwanted attention from law enforcement. This was the driving force behind the reduction of violence and the increasing business-like nature of organised crime groups. Each form of criminality has also developed tactics to strengthen the profit-making potential of their activities and minimise risk.

Traditionally, human trafficking has been violent and coercive, which relied on complicity from border officials in order to facilitate passage to destination countries. However, by giving communities, families and even victims a stake in the business – an aspiration that they will benefit, even if distant – they are more likely to be complicit and protect the criminal groups that facilitate their movement. This approach builds on the methods of psychological control that have been used by traffickers in the past and minimises the need for more physical forms of control, leading to the emergence of criminal pyramid schemes where all parties have an interest in protecting the business.

Individuals are exploited when they have limited choices, and others will be ready to take advantage of that lack of choice, exploiting these individuals to make a profit. Often, those who choose to leave the situation that they are in do so determinedly. While it is dangerous to ignore the risks to which they are exposed, by labelling them all as victims who have naively trusted ruthless criminals is not adequate as it takes away their agency in the process. However, this creates challenges for attempts to tackle the criminal actors that facilitate human trafficking. What is needed is a more nuanced understanding of the dynamics of human trafficking from different countries. By unpacking the different stages of the victim journey, this volume begins to fill this gap, but these details need to be combined with detailed country knowledge to develop a tailored response.

Notes

[1] Interview, Lagos, Nigeria, August 2014.
[2] Interviews with civil society organisations, Nigeria, September 2017.
[3] Interview, UK, July 2017.
[4] Interview, Lagos, September 2017.
[5] Interview, Lagos, September 2017.
[6] Interview, Lagos, September 2017.
[7] Interview, Benin City, September 2017.
[8] Interview, Kassala, November 2017.
[9] Water source.
[10] Interview, Kassala, November 2017.

References

Allain, J., Crane, A., LeBaron, G. and Behbahani, L. (2013) *Report: Forced Labour's Business Models and Supply Chains*. London: Joseph Rowntree Foundation.

Anti-Trafficking Monitoring Group (2012) *All Change: Preventing Trafficking in the UK*. London: Anti-Slavery International.

Bales, K., Fletcher, L. and Stover, E. (2005) *Hidden Slaves: Forced Labour in the United States*. Berkeley: University of California Press.

BBC News (2013) Italy steps up migrant boat patrols after tragedies. *BBC News* [online] 14 October. Available from: http://www.bbc.co.uk/news/world-europe-24515906 (accessed 12 June 2021).

BBC News (2014) Blue Sky M: Hundreds rescued from abandoned cargo ship. *BBC News* [online] 31 December. Available from: http://www.bbc.co.uk/news/world-asia-30646778 (accessed 12 June 2021).

Centre for Social Justice (CSJ) (2015) *A Modern Response to Modern Slavery*. London: CSJ.

Craig, G., Balch, A., Lewis, H. and Waite, L. (2018) Editorial introduction. In G. Craig, A. Balch, H. Lewis and L. Waite (eds) *The Modern Slavery Agenda: Policy, Politics and Practice in the UK*. Bristol: Policy Press, pp 1–28.

De Shalit, A., Heynen, R. and van der Meulen, E. (2014) Human trafficking and media myths: Federal funding, communication strategies, and Canadian antitrafficking programs. *Canadian Journal of Communication*, 39(3): 385–412.

Doychak, K. and Raghavan, C. (2020) 'No voice or vote': Trauma-coerced attachment in victims of sex trafficking. *Journal of Human Trafficking*, 6(3): 339–57.

Ebegbulem, S. (2018) 'Our gods will destroy you': Oba of Benin curse human traffickers. *Vanguard News* [online] 10 March. Available from: https://www.vanguardngr.com/2018/03/gods-will-destroy-oba-benin-curse-human-traffickers/ (accessed 12 June 2021).

EC (European Commission) (2014) Frontex joint operation 'Triton': Concerted efforts to manage migration in the Central Mediterranean. *EC* [online] 7 October. Available from: http://europa.eu/rapid/press-release_MEMO-14-566_en.htm (accessed 12 June 2021).

Edwards, C. and Jeffray, C. (2015) *On Tap: Organised Crime and the Illicit Trade in Tobacco, Alcohol and Pharmaceuticals in the UK*. London: RUSI.

Glenny, M. (2008) *McMafia: Crime Without Frontiers*. London: Bodley Head.

Goodman, M. (2011) What business can learn from organized crime. *Harvard Business Review*, November. Available from: https://hbr.org/2011/11/what-business-can-learn-from-organized-crime (accessed 12 July 2022).

Herman, J. (1992) *Trauma and Recovery: The Aftermath of Violence – From Domestic Abuse to Political Terror*. New York: Basic Books.

Hopper, E. and Hidalgo, J. (2006) Invisible chains: Psychological coercion of human trafficking victims. *Intercultural Human Rights Law Review*, 1(18): 185–209.

HRF (Human Rights First) (2017) *Human Trafficking by the Numbers*. Available from: https://www.humanrightsfirst.org/resource/human-trafficking-numbers (accessed 12 June 2021).

Hughes, H. (2000) The 'Natasha' trade: The transnational shadow market of trafficking in women. *Journal of International Affairs*, 53(2): 1–18.

The Independent (2015) Abandoned migrant 'ghost ship' arrives in Italy carrying hundreds of Syrian refugees. *The Independent* [online] 3 January. Available from: http://www.independent.co.uk/news/world/abandoned-ghost-ship-carrying-hundreds-of-syrian-refugees-arrives-safely-in-italy-9955399.html (accessed 12 June 2021).

International Labour Organization (ILO) (2014) *Profits and Poverty: The Economics of Forced Labour*. Available from: http://www.ilo.org/wcmsp5/groups/public/---ed_norm/---declaration/documents/publication/wcms_243391.pdf (accessed 12 June 2021).

Ioannou, M. and Oostinga, M.S.D. (2015) An empirical framework of control methods of victims of human trafficking for sexual exploitation. *Global Crime*, 16(1): 34–49.

Jesperson, S., Henriksen, R., Barry, A.M. and Jones, M. (2019) *Human Trafficking: An Organised Crime?* London: Hurst.

Kelly, E. (2002) *Journeys of Jeopardy: A Review of Research on Trafficking in Woman and Children in Europe*. Geneva: International Organization of Migration.

Kitroeff, N. (2012) Stockholm Syndrome in the pimp–victim relationship. *New York Times* [online] 3 May. Available from: https://kristof.blogs.nyti mes.com/2012/05/03/stockholm-syndrome-in-the-pimp-victim-relations hip/ (accessed 12 June 2021).

Moore, A.S. and Goldberg, E.S. (2015) Victims, perpetrators, and the limits of human rights discourse in post-Palermo fiction about sex trafficking. *The International Journal of Human Rights*, 19(1): 16–31.

O'Connell Davidson, J. (2017) The right to locomotion? Trafficking, slavery and the state. In P. Kotiswaran (ed) *Revisiting the Law and Governance of Trafficking, Forced Labor and Modern Slavery*. Cambridge: Cambridge University Press, pp 157–78.

Polaris (nd) *Human Trafficking*. Polaris Project. Available from: https://pol arisproject.org/victims-traffickers (accessed 12 June 2021).

Sanchez, R.V., Speck, P.M. and Patrician, P.A. (2019) A concept analysis of trauma coercive bonding in the commercial sexual exploitation of children. *Journal of Pediatric Nursing*, 46: 48–54.

Sharapov, K. (2015) 'Traffickers and their victims': Anti-trafficking policy in the UK. *Critical Sociology*, 43(1): 91–111.

Shelley, L. (2010) *Human Trafficking: Global Perspectives*. Cambridge: Cambridge University Press.

Sisti, L. (2008) The Montenegro connection. *Organised Crime and Corruption Reporting Project*. Available from: https://www.reportingproject.net/unde rground/index.php?option=com_content&view=article&id=7&Itemid= 20 (accessed 12 June 2012).

Szörényi, A. and Eate, P. (2014) Saving virgins, saving the USA: Heteronormative masculinities and the securitisation of trafficking discourse in mainstream narrative film. *Social Semiotics*, 24(5): 608–22.

UN News (2001) Human trafficking fastest growing form of organized crime: UN anti-crime chief. *UN News*. Available from: https://news. un.org/en/story/2001/11/19272-human-trafficking-fastest-growing- form-organised-crime-un-anti-crime-chief (accessed 12 June 2021).

UNODC (UN Office on Drugs and Crime) (2010) *Organised Crime Involvement in Trafficking in Persons and Smuggling of Migrants*. Vienna: UNODC.

UNODC (2012) Human trafficking: Organized crime and the multibillion dollar sale of people. *UNODC*. Available from: http://www.unodc.org/ unodc/en/frontpage/2012/July/human-trafficking_-organised-crime- and-the-multibillion-dollar-sale-of-people.html (accessed 12 June 2021).

Williams, P. (2007) Trafficking in women: The role of transnational organised crime. In S. Cameron and E. Newman (eds) *Trafficking in humans: Social, cultural and political dimensions*. New York: United Nations University Press, pp 126–58.

2

Organ trafficking: a neglected aspect of modern slavery

Trevor Stammers

Introduction

Organ trafficking is a heinous violation of both human rights and medical ethics but nevertheless it remains, if not entirely forgotten, the often-overlooked element of trafficking in people. Though organ trafficking involves thousands of people globally, it gains far less attention in terms of research output and media coverage than any other element of people trafficking.

This chapter aims to raise the profile of organ trafficking among academics researching in human trafficking overall. It explains how the various elements of organ trafficking are defined and how they relate to and differ from transplant tourism and organ markets. Some of the most important international declarations on organ trafficking are outlined, alongside some selective national legislation. Shifting global patterns of organ trafficking are illustrated with an emphasis on Asia. Some of the difficulties in curbing such trafficking are then considered followed by some recommendations for increasing effective prevention, prosecution of perpetrators, and protection and support of victims.

Organ transplantation, human trafficking for the purpose of organ removal and organ trafficking

It is a medical truism that organ transplantation in the 21st century has become a victim of its own success. Since the first successful kidney transplant was carried out in 1954 (Merrill et al, 1956), organ transplantation has grown exponentially as a life-saving procedure across the globe. The World Health Organization's Global Observatory on Donation and Transplantation records the total number of solid organ transplants in 2019 at 153,863.

However, this is only a fraction of the ever-rising need for organs, a need greatly increased by the 2020–1 COVID-19 pandemic. No country in the world, even prior to the pandemic, has been able to meet the demand for organs from within its own borders, except for Iran (Ghods and Mahdavi,

2007). If people know they will die from organ failure, some will not hesitate to acquire an organ illegally if they cannot get one legitimately within their own healthcare system. Organ traffickers know this and are only too willing to profit from their victims' bodies being utilised to meet this demand. Regrettably, some healthcare professionals are also willing to either knowingly collude in organ trafficking for profit or at least turn a blind eye to it.

The victims of human traffickers are typically members of hidden populations for whom no reliable sampling frame exists. Characterising them has been likened to 'describing the unobserved' (Tyldum and Brunovskis, 2005: 1). If this is true overall, it is especially difficult in the case of those trafficked for organs. In a recent paper characterising 128 victims from the Association of Southeast Asian Nations countries, only one was trafficked for organs (Cho et al, 2018: 108). Donor victims of organ trafficking are usually young men (except in India where most are young women) and economically deprived (Lomero-Martínez et al, 2017). Even some of the latest specialist reports are remarkably short on detail concerning the vulnerabilities of organ-trafficked people. For example, a July 2021 Interpol Analytical Report on organ trafficking in North and West Africa simply notes that the victim-donors 'are usually unemployed youth and people in vulnerable situations (for example, victims of multiple ways of exploitation such as sexual or labour trafficking or asylum seekers)' (Interpol Analytical Report, 2021: 16). They only receive a fraction of the money they were promised and are unlikely to report the offences against them because of shame or fear of retaliation.

It has taken a long time for organ trafficking to be eventually recognised, defined with increasing clarity and incorporated into both national and international law and protocols, the most important of which are considered next, particularly in regard to definitions of types of organ trafficking and related activities.

The Palermo Protocol and the Declarations of Istanbul 2008 and 2018

The adoption by the 2000 UN General Assembly of its Protocol to Prevent, Suppress and Punish Trafficking in Persons, Especially Women and Children, now widely known as the 'Palermo Protocol', is probably the most significant milestone in combating human trafficking.

The Protocol in Article 2 defined 'trafficking in persons' as:

[T]he recruitment, transportation, transfer, harbouring or receipt of persons, by means of threat or use of force or other forms of coercion, of abduction, of fraud, of deception, of the abuse of power or of a position of vulnerability or of the giving or receiving of payments or benefits to achieve the consent of a person having control over another person, for the purpose of exploitation. Exploitation shall include, at a minimum, the exploitation of the prostitution of others or other forms of sexual exploitation, forced labour or services, slavery or practices similar to slavery, servitude or the removal, manipulation or implantation of organs. (United Nations, 2000)

What is now referred to as Human Trafficking for the purpose of Organ Removal (HTOR), came at the very end of this lengthy definition and its location was to prove symbolic of the neglect of this element of human trafficking in subsequent years. In 2008, the Transplantation Society and the International Society of Nephrology convened in Turkey a Summit specifically on organ trafficking. This resulted in the Declaration of Istanbul (International Summit on Transplant Tourism and Organ Trafficking, 2008), which strongly condemned not only organ trafficking but also what it termed 'transplant tourism' and 'transplant commercialism'. The Declaration received considerable criticism for putting these three in the same moral category (Radcliffe Richards, 2013: 83–7). Furthermore, it did not distinguish clearly between trafficking in organs and trafficking people for their organs.

When the Declaration of Istanbul was eventually updated in 2018, its definitions of both organ trafficking and HTOR became much more precise in response to criticism of the earlier version.

Organ trafficking consists of any of the following activities:

- removing organs from living or deceased donors without valid consent or authorisation or in exchange for financial gain or comparable advantage to the donor and/or a third person;
- any transportation, manipulation, transplantation or other use of such organs;
- offering any undue advantage to, or requesting the same by, a healthcare professional, public official, or employee of a private sector entity to facilitate or perform such removal or use;
- soliciting or recruiting donors or recipients, where carried out for financial gain or comparable advantage; or
- attempting to commit, or aiding or abetting the commission of, any of these acts.

HTOR is the recruitment, transportation, transfer, harbouring, or receipt of persons, by means of the threat or use of force or other forms of coercion, of abduction, of fraud, of deception, of the abuse of power or of a position of vulnerability, or of the giving or receiving of payments or benefits to achieve the consent of a person having control over another person, for the purpose of the removal of organs. (Transplantation Society and International Society of Nephrology, 2018)

The 2018 updated Declaration also made much clearer the distinction between travelling abroad for a transplant and transplant tourism, stating:

Travel for transplantation becomes transplant tourism, and thus unethical, if it involves trafficking in persons for the purpose of organ removal or trafficking in human organs, or if the resources (organs, professionals and transplant centres) devoted to providing transplants to non-resident patients undermine the country's ability to provide transplant services for its own population. (Transplantation Society and International Society of Nephrology, 2018)

With these influential definitions in mind, the different patterns of tackling organ trafficking are illustrated with a focus on India, Nepal, Pakistan and finally China, where it remains a particularly persistent crime. The type of offences vary greatly however from one country to another and illustrate the difficulties of both effective legislation against and policing of HTOR and organ trafficking.

Organ trafficking in India

The Transplantation of Human Organs Act (THOA) 1994 (Indian Society of Organ Transplantation, 1994) was implemented in India in early 1995. The Act was needed both to recognise the criteria of brain death as acceptable to permit organ donation and also to combat trafficking in human organs. Under THOA, permitted expenses included reimbursement of loss of earnings to the donor, but other payments were restricted. Donation was only permitted to close family members. Advertisements to obtain or sell an organ were also regulated and violations punishable.

One of the legal loopholes however was that non-related donations were allowed, where the donor could prove evidence of 'affection and attachment' to the recipient to a local authorisation committee, to demonstrate it was not a commercial transaction. This resulted in organ traders staging photos and forging documents to mislead such committees into thinking brokered vendors were friends of the recipient (Raza and Skordis-Worrall, 2012: 87). The effectiveness of THOA 1994 in reducing organ trafficking also appears to have been severely compromised by India's determination to maintain its importance as a centre for medical tourism (including provision of transplants to foreign nationals) while simultaneously trying to comply with increasing international pressure against organ trafficking. Even after the Declaration of Istanbul 2008 stated both organ trafficking and transplant tourism should be banned, India appeared reluctant to curb the latter.

'The Government of India opposes organ trafficking and has a nuanced position on medical tourism', cautiously suggest some Indian researchers, who continue:

> India is hub [sic] of 'Medical Tourism' since many of the hospitals in India are comparable in expertise with the western standards while the cost is much cheaper. India is promoting 'Medical Tourism' as a policy. Transplant of Human Organs Act, 1994, does not prohibit foreign nationals from getting the transplant done in India. (Agarwal et al, 2012: 112)

It was perhaps such apparent ambivalence that at least in part meant that illegal practice in transplants continued. In 2004, police apprehended a senior surgeon in Mumbai for his alleged role in facilitating trade in human kidneys (Mudur, 2004: 246). Dr Suresh Trivedi, a nephrologist at the Bombay Hospital and Medical Research Centre was arrested for allegedly passing requests for kidneys to agents who would find poor donors and fabricate documents showing they were distant relatives or friends of the patients. Each donor would receive 30,000–50,000 rupees, but a recipient would be charged up to 200,000 rupees for the kidney.

In January 2008, police uncovered an Indian organ trafficking ring of four doctors and 40 support staff who transplanted 400–500 kidneys into 'transplant tourists' (Gentleman, 2008). Sarkar (2014: 487) comments on this case that 'the severe shortage of organs for transplant in India reflects the international imbalance in supply and demand. Inevitably, there are people who see the potential for making a lot of money; hence there is a flourishing black market in organs in India'.

Goyal et al (2002: 1591) reported finding 'widespread evidence of the sale of kidneys by poor people in India despite a legal ban'. Within a month, these researchers were able to identify and interview over 300 people in Chennai who had sold a kidney, 96 per cent of them to pay off existing debts. Nearly all of their interviewees would not recommend selling a kidney.

With continuing widespread evidence of trafficked organs in India well after the passing of the THOA 1994, the Act was amended in both 2008 and 2011. Penalties under the Act were increased from a maximum of five years' to ten years' imprisonment. Though the gradual tightening of the law did not eliminate organ trafficking in India, it did curb it to some extent. However, it also resulted in an influx of transplant tourism to surrounding countries such as Pakistan and more recently Nepal.

Organ trafficking in Pakistan

The first successful kidney transplant in Pakistan was carried out in 1979 (Rizvi and Naqvi, 1996) but organ trafficking there has a more recent history. A report (Ilyas et al, 2009) from Pakistan's largest public transplantation centre, the Sindh Institute of Urology and Transplantation, showed that 75 per cent of renal transplantation in 1991 was from living, related donors. But by 2003, 80 per cent of transplants were from living, *unrelated* donors. One of the main reasons for this reversal involved India's introduction of the 1994 THOA, banning all commercial organ dealings there. Consequently, large numbers of international patients travelled to Pakistan, which had no organ trafficking legislation at the time.

Around two-thirds of the population of Pakistan live in rural areas with around a quarter of the population living below the national poverty line in 2005; life expectancy was 65 years, and half the population was illiterate (National Archives, 2005). Many, especially in Punjab, were 'bonded labourers' working for wealthy landowners and, given such pre-existing vulnerabilities, they were targeted to supply organs to transplant tourists from the Middle East, Europe and the US (Walsh, 2005; Evans, 2017).

The universal story of poor outcomes for 'vendors' is played out in Pakistan with up to 98 per cent of them reporting a deterioration in their health up to a year after organ removal (Naqvi et al, 2007). Mental health also deteriorated not only in those providing organs but also in their families, who suffered both stigmatisation in their communities and felt pressure to sell their organs also (Moazam et al, 2009). Organ-selling frequently led to the vendor being in a worse economic situation, being unable to work as well as they had done before the surgery (Budiani-Saberi and Delmonico, 2008). 'Instead of families moving up the socioeconomic ladder, they remained in the same social strata with the kidney trade only reinforcing and further increasing social and economic inequality within Pakistan's society' (Raza and Skordis-Worrall, 2012: 86).

Two-thirds of the 2,000 transplants carried out in Pakistan in 2006 were into foreign nationals (Efrat, 2013). With growing international pressure to curb the organ trade, Pakistan passed its 'Transplantation of Human Organs and Tissues Ordinance' (THOTO) in 2007 (Government of Pakistan, 2007). This legislation, *inter alia*, specifies that 'donation by Pakistani citizens shall not be permissible to citizens of other countries' with a penalty for violation of ten years' imprisonment and a substantial fine. Living donors also must be 18 years old or over, donation must be voluntary and to a close blood relative defined as spouse, parent, son, daughter or sibling. A Human Organ Transplant Authority was also mandated to be set up to monitor institutions carrying out transplantations nationally. THOTO eventually resulted in the Transplantation of Human Organs and Tissues Bill being passed in 2010 (Bile et al, 2010).

Following the passage of the initial Pakistan Ordinance and then, the 2010 Bill, illegal organ trafficking fell markedly. Documented patient numbers travelling for a kidney transplant in Pakistan from Kuwait alone, for example, fell from a high of 23 in 2002 to zero between 2008 and 2011 (Al-Mous cited in Ali, 2016) However, over time, networks of private hospitals in Pakistan have recommenced trafficking in vended organs and transplanting them into transplant tourists from other countries. A Jordanian recipient died in 2014 during an illegal transplant carried out in a private hospital near Lahore by Dr Fawad Mumtaz and Dr Altamash Kharal. Dr Kharal was reported as having forged the woman's death certificate in an attempt to cover up the two doctors' involvement in organ trafficking. They were eventually arrested (*Dawn*, 2017), reportedly while preparing to transplant kidneys into two Omani transplant tourists.

This incident precipitated a plea in 2017 from a team of Karachi doctors for the Pakistan government to focus on increasing awareness of deceased donation and promoting it as a means to reduce the pressure from organ shortages, which, in part, drives both organ trafficking and transplant tourism. Pakistan, with a population at that time of 200 million, had deceased donors numbering in single figures only (Fatima et al, 2017).

Organ trafficking in Nepal

Nepal is another of India's neighbours where organ trafficking has increased, in part due to the tightening of the law in India. According to the National Human Rights Commission, Office of the Special Rapporteur on Trafficking in Women and Children's (2011) report, at least 22 of the 77 districts on Nepal had an organ trade present in 2009. In one district, Kavrepanalchok, close to Kathmandu, 300 people had sold their kidneys. Another report in 2012 estimated the number of kidney sellers at ten times that (Centre for Legal Research and Resource Development, 2012) . Two-thirds of victims were male, most between 20 and 50 years of age, and were

> driven by extreme poverty and were lured by the promise that they would earn a large amount of money that they could use to pay off loans or to buy a house or a piece of land. Many were illiterate and deceived into believing that the organ removal would have no adverse effects on their health or that the kidney would regrow. (Gawronska, 2021: 2)

Traffickers in Nepal have had no hesitation in capitalising on the chaos and misery in the wake of natural disasters. *The Lancet* (Cousins, 2016 reported on how the April 2015 earthquake not only worsened the poor medical condition of those who had already been trafficked to India for their kidneys but also suggested that HTOR had increased in the Kavre region. The founder of the Nepal Institute for Development Studies in Kathmandu, Ganesh Gurung, commented: 'After the earthquake, people were so vulnerable. When you have no option and no money, you sell a kidney … a higher percentage than before have gone to sell their organs' (Cousins, 2016: 833).

The use of trafficked organs within Nepal has also increased since the establishment of a national domestic transplant system in 2017 (Shrestha, 2018). Gawronska (2021: 3) cites three reasons for believing the illicit organ trade in Nepal is likely to increase:

1. With some three million patients with diabetes in Nepal, the numbers requiring kidney transplantation are going to increase.
2. Anecdotal evidence continues of physicians in Nepal being approached by patients willing to purchase a kidney.
3. The growing transplant infrastructure in Nepal where over half the population lives either below or on the poverty line means inevitably it will be a target country for the wealthy to look for organs for transplantation.

Organ transplantation in Nepal is regulated by the Human Body Organ Transplantation (Regulation and Prohibition) Act, 2055 (1998) (Nepal Law Commission, 1998) and the subsequent regulations introduced in 2015 by the Human Body Organ Transplantation (Regulation and Prohibition) Legislation, 2073. Under paragraph 24, those carrying out illicit transplants 'shall be punished with imprisonment for a term not exceeding five years and a fine not exceeding five hundred thousand rupees'. However, 'if the person from whom an organ is extracted dies as a result of that wound or pain within three months, the person who commits such an offense shall be punished with life imprisonment, with confiscation of entire property'.

Human trafficking is separately regulated by the Human Trafficking and Transportation (Control) Act 2007. Section 4.1 specifically includes HTOR as one of the forms of human trafficking punishable under Section 15 of the Act by up to ten years in prison and a fine of 200,000 rupees.

This all sounds very watertight, but the UN Palermo Protocol 2008 defined human trafficking as the 'recruitment, transportation, transfer, harboring or receipt of persons'. The Nepali Human Trafficking Act however distinguishes the offence of human transportation from that of human trafficking. 'This distinction was inspired by the wish to emphasize the element of movement present in the offense of human transportation and to adjust the penalties' (Gawronska, 2021: 5). Though the definition of human trafficking in the Human Trafficking Act includes 'the removal of a human organ in breach of transplant regulations', it does not include any of the acts and illicit means specified by the Palermo Protocol. As Gawronska notes, not including acts of recruitment means that 'the Nepali definition may pose problems for prosecutors who wish to indict a recruiter of an organ donor for human trafficking' (2021: 11). One of her principal concluding recommendations (Gawronska, 2021: 12) is for Nepal to merge the separate offences of human transportation and trafficking into one as in the UN Protocol.

Organ trafficking in China

China represents particularly difficult issues since the country is associated with both transplant tourism and providing trafficked organs for its own citizens. It is the only country in the world known to systematically use organs from prisoners (Huang et al, 2008), many of whom are prisoners of conscience, mainly Falun Gong practitioners, but also Uyghur Muslims and Christians. There are also reports of organ harvesting from still living prisoners, who are killed by the removal of vital organs (Paul et al, 2017: 12–13). Despite substantial evidence of their occurrence, these practices were consistently denied up until 2005 (Sharif et al, 2014). Even subsequently, there can be little doubt widespread organ trafficking continued on a national scale (Trey et al, 2016). It is estimated that 90 per cent of transplants carried out in China in 2010 were removed from prisoners (Delmonico et al, 2014).

In 2014, in accordance with the Hangzhou Resolution agreed at the China Transplant Congress (Huang et al, 2014), the Chinese government announced it would no longer harvest organs from prisoners from 2015. The Chinese leadership stated that civilian organ donation cannot coexist alongside the transplantation of organs from executed or coerced prisoners (Huang et al, 2015). A group of Chinese psychiatrists hailed the new guidance as an 'important step in the right direction for medical ethics in China' (Xiang et al, 2016). They however received a stinging rebuttal:

> Contra Xiang et al, when people are being killed for their organs, a mere 'step in the right direction' is insufficient and unacceptable in medical ethics. A real step in the right direction would be providing uncensored and transparent access to China's transplant and organ donation numbers and permitting independent international inspections. (Rogers et al, 2016: 553)

There was no change in 2015 in China's transplant regulations or laws; prisoners of conscience were even excluded in the guidance and the practice of organ removal remained legal in all prisoners provided it was with their alleged 'consent'. Organisations such as the Transplantation Society, however, refuse to accept the validity of such consent, as imprisonment, by definition, implies the deprivation of liberty and vulnerability to coercion that renders voluntary consent unreliable. A 2017 review paper of the state of organ transplantation in China has a chilling set of conclusions:

> The unethical practice of organ procurement from executed prisoners in China is associated with a large scale of abuse and a cascade of severe human rights violations, including, we contend, organ explantation from still alive human beings, and, upstream, conditioning the supply of prisoners exploited per se or then solicited to 'freely' offer organs as atonement for real or supposed crimes. Those involved in organ harvesting from still alive prisoners must be prosecuted. The unethical practice of lethally procuring vital organs from the living must be prevented by a law prohibiting use of prisoner organs generally, supporting change in the practical legal, medical and popular culture surrounding transplantation in China. (Paul et al, 2017: 8–9)

Further evidence that little has changed in China since the supposed reforms is found in a recently published forensic analysis of data from the China Organ Transplant Response System and the Red Cross Society of China. This concluded that:

> [The] evidence points to what the authors believe can only be plausibly explained by systematic falsification and manipulation of official organ transplant datasets in China. Some apparently non-voluntary donors also appear to be misclassified as voluntary. This takes place alongside genuine voluntary organ transplant activity, which is often incentivized by large cash payments. (Robertson et al, 2019)

Further evidence of the ability of accessing organs at very short notice is provided by reports early on in the COVID-19 pandemic that a patient in respiratory failure due to COVID-19 infection had successfully been given a double lung transplant. The report states that '[t]he transplanted lungs were donated by a non-local patient after brain death and transported to Wuxi by high-speed railway in seven hours' (Keyue, 2020). This however prompts questions about how they were obtained so quickly when the waiting time for a single lung from a suitable donor often runs into years. Coincidentally, within days of the lung transplant in China, the judgement of the independent China Tribunal in the UK (2020) into forced organ harvesting was published. The present author attended one day of the hearings and heard harrowing first-hand accounts of systematic organ harvesting from prisoners of conscience. Paragraph 382 of the judgement, noting the short waiting times of typically two weeks for organs in China, states:

Such waiting times are not compatible with conventional transplant practice and cannot be explained by good fortune. Predetermining the availability of an organ for transplant is impossible in any system depending on voluntary organ donation. Such short-time availability could only occur if there was a bank of potential living donors who could be sacrificed to order. (China Tribunal 2020)

Improving prevention of organ trafficking and protection of victims

The patterns of organ trafficking in India, Pakistan, Nepal and China, though very different, all demonstrate clearly the difficulty of drafting and implementing effective legislation both to protect victims and prosecute traffickers. There are, however, particular elements of organ trafficking that, in theory at least, should make it easier to prevent and prosecute than human trafficking for sex work or forced labour. This section considers some of the factors specific to preventing organ trafficking and other relevant issues related to the prevention of human trafficking in general.

Education and prosecution of healthcare professionals

In spite of almost universal condemnation of organ trafficking in medical literature, there are healthcare professionals, specifically of course transplant surgeons, across the world who are prepared to engage in it and many more prepared to turn a blind eye to it. The present author has heard of cases in the UK where doctors have suspected that their patient has been transplanted with a trafficked organ but have preferred to not follow up on their suspicions. Many medical staff will be totally unaware of the existence of organ trafficking in their country, or of what to look for and ask about in order to detect it.

There are a few organisations specifically seeking to educate healthcare professionals about human trafficking (including organ trafficking) such as Relentless in the US and Vita Network in the UK; a few articles on clinical indicators of patients who may have had trafficked organs removed or transplanted are also now available (De Jong and Ambagtsheer, 2016).

Medical staff as a whole, and doctors especially, have the lives of other people in their hands daily and should be held accountable to a high standard of ethical conduct. If no medics were prepared to facilitate the transplantation of trafficked organs, the whole chain involved in such crimes would immediately be ended (Stammers, forthcoming). The punishments for direct involvement by doctors should be commensurately high. The legal loopholes which encourage lighter sentences for clinicians in Nepal, for example, need to be closed and international pressure increased on those states such as China, which expect surgeons to participate in transplanting trafficked organs.

Part of the education surrounding organ trafficking is about the nature of the crime and placing it on a continuum with transplant tourism and organ trading (Stammers, 2019: 237–53). One of the reasons identified for the failure of Nepal's legislation to curb organ trafficking was the desire to retain and indeed promote Nepal as a thriving centre for transplant tourism (Gawronska, 2021: 5).

Reducing the domestic need for organs

Both the Madrid Resolution on Organ Donation (2011: SS29–31) and the Declaration of Istanbul (Transplantation Society and International Society of Nephrology, 2018: Principle 1) point out that reduction in domestic organ needs would minimise illegal organ removals. Such reduction can be attempted by both instituting public health programmes to reduce the incidence of conditions causing organ failure, especially diabetes and alcohol liver damage, and by maximising the number of deceased and living donations. The COVID-19 pandemic, however, has badly hit the effectiveness of both of these.

An increase in obesity has been widely noted during the pandemic and obesity is a major factor in the development of diabetes – one of the most common causes of kidney failure, thereby building up a legacy of increasing need for kidneys for decades ahead. COVID-19 itself also causes both respiratory and renal failure leading to increased need for those lungs and kidneys. In terms of donation, COVID-19 reduced living donations in the UK to a third of pre-pandemic levels – a pattern repeated across the globe. The likely overall effect of the pandemic as global travel reopens is a large surge in organ trafficking (Greenbaum et al, 2020; United Nations Office on Drugs and Crime, 2021 Todres, 2021).

Improving successful prosecution of the entire trafficking chain

A large number of individuals are involved in an organ trafficking ring. Of the total of 24 people indemnified in the trafficking networks of four cases prosecuted in Nepal, only five were convicted (Gawronska, 2021: 13). The domestic law tends to focus on charged individuals rather than on breaking up entire trafficking networks. A tendency compounded by the next factor – a lack of both domestic and international law to tackle organised crime in general and organ trafficking in particular.

Improving drafting of domestic and international law to tackle organised crime

Mention was made earlier that China only drew up official guidance and made no change in the law to curb domestic organ trafficking from prisoners and to deter transplant tourism. In Nepal, the drafting of separate offences of human trafficking and of human transportation has also meant that those guilty of organ trafficking have either escaped prosecution or obtained lighter sentences. Even these laws are drafted for specific individual criminals and neither the South Asian Association for Regional Cooperation (SAARC) Convention on Preventing and Combating Trafficking in Women and Children for Prostitution, or the SAARC Convention on Mutual Assistance in Criminal Matters, 2008, has even a definition of organised crime.

Things are little better beyond Asia. A repeated pattern of domestic laws is that where there is opportunity to apply their force on their own citizens for involvement abroad (usually in being the recipients of trafficked organs) this is rarely taken. For example in the US, though the National Organ Transplant Act 1984 prohibits the sale of organs, it is difficult to trace any prosecutions of US citizens who have been transplanted with purchased organs abroad and returned to the US. In 2008, Gill from the University of California Los Angeles (UCLA), described a series of 33 patients who had a kidney transplant in this way. Delmonico, commenting on this series, wryly notes: 'The UCLA group makes no conclusion regarding the ethical propriety of this practice, disclaiming social circumstances that may have propelled these patients to travel for transplantation' (Delmonico, 2009: 249). There is certainly plenty of evidence that '[t]he difference between domestic enforcement regimes for sex trafficking against children and for labor trafficking of illegal immigrants, and the enforcement regime for international organ trafficking remains noteworthy' (Francis and Francis, 2010: 288). This remains a big obstacle to tackling a global organised crime.

In an attempt to improve the record on curbing HTOR and organ trafficking, there have been suggestions to separate it from organ trading, since the latter does not necessarily involve the trafficking of humans for organs or trafficked organs (Columb et al, 2017). Some leading experts in the field though have argued this move would not help and would probably make matters worse (Capron and Delmonico, 2015). A separation that might well help combat organ trafficking, however, is that of organ trafficking from the other two main areas of people trafficking – for sex work or for forced labour. Whereas efforts to curb sex trafficking and forced labour are complex and expensive, organ trafficking should be much easier in comparison. For example, essential participants in organ trafficking such as physicians and hospital administrators can and should engage in open political process to prevent this particular form of trafficking. The same does not apply so readily in sex trafficking (Efrat, 2013).

Conclusion

If those most adversely affected by organ trafficking are to receive the protection, help and long-term support they require and deserve, it is essential that they are recognised as victims under domestic law and that adequate funding is made available to provide and pay for the necessary services. Those who undermine the status of organ vendors as victims (Radcliffe Richards, 2012; Columb et al, 2016) by insisting that would not sell their organs if they did not foresee overall benefit, do these victims no favours by their attempts to defend organ sales.

Though the Nepali Human Trafficking Act establishes the rights of victims to medical treatment and support, its focus is solely on victims of sex trafficking sold into prostitution and it is therefore unclear whether a person from whom an organ has been illegally removed actually qualifies as a victim under the Act. Even if they do, victims are unaware they qualify for help and their funding for such help is totally inadequate (Gawronska, 2021: 14). Furthermore, the Act does not guarantee protection from the perpetrators and brokers involved as mandated by the UN Convention against Transnational Organized Crime (2000: Article 25). There is a still a long way to go before the many victims of organ trafficking in Nepal receive any adequate protection in law, let alone in practice. This story is repeated across the world and the plight of victims will only be intensified by the ongoing knock-on effects from COVID-19. There is much yet to be done.

References

Agarwal, S.K., Srivastava, R.K., Gupta, S. and Tripathi, S. (2012) Evolution of the Transplantation of Human Organ Act and law in India. *Transplantation*, 94(2): 110–13.

Ali, N.S. (2016) Of human organs, desperate poverty and greed. *Dawn*, 16 September.

Bile, K.M., Qureshi, J.A.R.H., Rizvi, S.A.H., Naqvi, S.A.A., Usmani, A.Q. and Lashori, K.A. (2010) Human organ and tissue transplantation in Pakistan: When a regulation makes a difference. *Eastern Mediterranean Health Journal*, 16: 159–66.

Budiani-Saberi, D.A. and Delmonico, F.L. (2008) Organ trafficking and transplant tourism: A commentary on the global realities. *American Journal of Transplantation*, 8(5): 925–9.

Capron, A.M. and Delmonico, F.L. (2015) Preventing trafficking in organs for transplantation: An important facet of the fight against human trafficking. *Journal of Human Trafficking*, 1(1): 56–64.

Centre for Legal Research and Resource Development (2012) *Human Organ Harvesting: Kidney Transplantation & Trafficking in and from Nepal*. Kathmandu: Centre for Legal Research and Resource Development.

China Tribunal, Final Judgment (2020) Available from: https://chinatribu nal.com/wp-content/uploads/2020/03/ChinaTribunal_JUDGMENT_ 1stMarch_2020.pdf (accessed 7 September 2021).

Cho, Y., Gamo, M.D., Park, G. and Lee, H. (2018) Characteristics of victims of trafficking in persons and determinants of police reports of victims in ASEAN countries. *Asia Pacific Journal of Multidisciplinary Research*, 6(2): 101–12.

Columb, S., Ambagtsheer, F., Bos, M., Ivanovski, N., Moorlock, G., Weimar, W. and ELPAT Working Group on Organ Tourism and Paid Donation (2017) Re-conceptualizing the organ trade: Separating 'trafficking' from 'trade' and the implications for law and policy. *Transplant International*, 30(2): 209–13.

Cousins, S. (2016) Nepal: Organ trafficking after the earthquake. *The Lancet*, 387: 833.

Dawn (2017) Jordanian woman died during illegal transplant in Lahore. *Dawn*, 15 May.

de Jong, J. and Ambagtsheer, F. (2016) Indicators to identify trafficking in human beings for the purpose of organ removal. *Transplantation Direct*, 2(2).

del Mar Lomero-Martínez, M., Sánchez-Ibáñez, J., Lopez-Fraga, M., Dominguez-Gil, B. and Fernandez-Garcia, A. (2017) Trafficking in human organs and human trafficking for organ removal: A healthcare perspective. *Journal of Trafficking and Human Exploitation*, 1(2): 237–56.

Delmonico, F.L. (2009) The hazards of transplant tourism. *Clinical Journal of the American Society of Nephrology*, 4(2): 249–50.

Delmonico, F.L., Chapman, J., Fung, J., Danovitch, G., Levin, A., Capron, A. et al (2014) Open letter to Xi Jinping, President of the People's Republic of China: China's fight against corruption in organ transplantation. *Transplantation*, 97(8): 795–6.

Efrat, A. (2013) The politics of combating the organ trade: Lessons from the Israeli and Pakistani experience. *American Journal of Transplantation*, 13(7): 1650–4.

Evans, R. (2017) Pakistani police rescue 24 from organ trafficking gang. *BBC*. Available from: https://www.bbc.co.uk/news/health-38722052 (accessed 29 August 2021).

Fatima, H., Fatima Qadir, T., Moin, A. and Bilal Pasha, S. (2017) Pakistan: A transplant tourism resort? *Journal of Public Health*, 40(4): 899.

Francis, L.P. and Francis, J.G. (2010) Stateless crimes, legitimacy, and international criminal law: The case of organ trafficking. *Criminal Law and Philosophy*, 4(3): 283–95.

Gawronska, S. (2021) Illicit organ removal in Nepal: An analysis of recent case law and the adequacy of human trafficking and transplantation frameworks. *Journal of Human Trafficking*, 1–22.

Gentleman, A. (2008) Kidney thefts shock India. *New York Times*, 30 January. Available from: www.nytimes.com/2008/01/30/world/asia/30kidney.html (accessed 28 August 2021).

Ghods, A.J. and Mahdavi, M. (2007) Organ transplantation in Iran. *Saudi Journal of Kidney Disease and Transplantation*, 18(4): 648–55.

Gill, J., Madhira, B.R., Gjertson, D., Lipshutz, G., Cecka, J.M., Pham, P.T. et al (2008) Transplant tourism in the United States: A single-center experience. *Clinical Journal of the American Society of Nephrology*, 3(6): 1820–8.

Government of Pakistan (2007) Transplantation of human organs and tissues ordinance. Available from: https://pakistanlaw.pk/statutes/9277/transplantation-of-human-organs-and-tissues-ordinance-2007 (accessed 13 July 2022).

Goyal, M., Metha, R.L., Schneidermann, L.J. and Sehgal, A.R. (2002) Economic and health consequences of selling a kidney in India. *Journal of the American Medical Association*, 288(13): 1589–93.

Greenbaum, J., Stoklosa, H. and Murphy, L. (2020) The public health impact of coronavirus disease on human trafficking. *Frontiers in Public Health*, 685.

Huang, J., Mao, Y. and Millis, J.M. (2008) Government policy and organ transplantation in China. *The Lancet*, 9654(372): 1937–8.

Huang, J., Zheng, S.S., Liu, Y.F., Wang, H.B., Chapman, J., O'Connell, P. et al (2014) China organ donation and transplantation update: The Hangzhou Resolution. *Hepatobiliary & Pancreatic Diseases International*, 13(2): 122–4.

Huang, J., Millis, J.M., Mao, Y., Millis, M.A., Sang, X. and Zhong, S. (2015) Voluntary organ donation system adapted to Chinese cultural values and social reality. *Liver Transplantation*, 21(4): 419–22.

Ilyas, M., Alam, M. and Ahmad, H. (2009) The Islamic perspective of organ donation in Pakistan. *Saudi Journal of Kidney Diseases and Transplantation*, 20(1): 154.

Indian Society of Organ Transplantation, 1994 The Transplantation of Human Organs Act (THOA) 1994. https://legislative.gov.in/sites/default/files/A1994-42.pdf (accessed 13 July 2022).

International Summit on Transplant Tourism and Organ Trafficking (2008) The Declaration of Istanbul. *Transplantation*: 1013–18.

Interpol Analytical Report (2021) *Trafficking of Human Beings for the Purpose of Organ Removal in North and West Africa*. Available from: file:///C:/Users/tgsta/Downloads/2021%2009%2027%20THBOR%20ENGLISH%20Public%20Version%20FINAL%20(1).pdf (accessed 29 March 2022).

Keyue, X. (2020) World's first double-lung transplant for COVID-19 infection succeeds in China. *Global Times*, 1 March. Available from: https://www.globaltimes.cn/content/1181228.shtml (accessed 7 September 2021).

Lomero-Martínez, M., Sánchez-Ibáñez, J., Fernández-García, A. and López-Fraga, M. (2017) Trafficking in human organs and human trafficking for organ removal: A healthcare perspective. *Journal of Trafficking and Human Exploitation*, 1: 237–56.

Madrid Resolution on Organ Donation and Transplantation (2011) National responsibility in meeting the needs of patients, guided by the WHO principles. *Transplantation*, 91(Suppl 11): S29–S31. Available from: https://journals.lww.com/transplantjournal/Fulltext/2011/06151/The_Madrid_Resolution_on_Organ_Donation_and.4.aspx (accessed 7 September 2021).

Merrill, J.P., Murray, J.E., Harrison, J.H. and Guild, W.R. (1956) Successful homotransplantations of human kidneys between identical twins. *JAMA*, 160: 277–82.

Moazam, F., Zaman, R.M. and Jafarey, A.M. (2009) Conversations with kidney vendors in Pakistan. *Hastings Center Report*, 39(3): 29–44.

Mudur, G. (2004) Kidney trade arrest exposes loopholes in India's transplant laws. *British Medical Journal*, 328(7434): 246.

Naqvi, S.A.A., Ali, B., Mazhar, F., Zafar, M.N. and Rizvi, S.A.H. (2007) A socioeconomic survey of kidney vendors in Pakistan. *Transplant International*, 20(11): 934–9.

National Human Rights Commission, Office of the Special Rapporteur on Trafficking in Women and Children (2011) *Trafficking in Persons (Especially on Women and Children) in Nepal, National Report 2009–2010*. Available from: https://www.nhrcnepal.org/nhrc_new/doc/newsletter/NHRC%20Final%20Format%20nov%205.2011.pdf

Nepal Law Commission (1998) *The Human Body Organ Transplantation (Regulation and Prohibition) Act, 2055 (1998)*. Nepal Law Commission (accessed 4 September 2021).

Paul, N.W., Caplan, A., Shapiro, M.E., Els, C., Allison, K.C. and Li, H. (2017) Human rights violations in organ procurement practice in China. *BMC Medical Ethics*, 18(1): 1–9.

Project MUSE (2011) 13 April. Available from: http://muse.jhu.edu/Int (accessed 29 August 2021).

Radcliffe Richards, J. (2012) *Careless Thought Costs Lives: The Ethics of Transplants*. Oxford: Oxford University Press.

Raza M, Skordis-Worrall, J. (2012) Pakistan's kidney trade: An overview of the 2007 'Transplantation of Human Organs and Human Tissue Ordinance': To what extent will it curb the trade? *Journal of Pakistan Medical Association*, 62(1): 85–9.

Rizvi, S.A. and Naqvi, S.A. (1996) Renal replacement therapy in Pakistan. *Saudi Journal of Kidney Diseases and Transplantation*, 7(4): 404.F

Robertson, M.P., Hinde, R.L. and Lavee, J. (2019) Analysis of official deceased organ donation data casts doubt on the credibility of China's organ transplant reform. *BMC Medical Ethics*, 20(1): 1–20.

Rogers, W.A., Trey, T., Singh, M.F., Bridgett, M., Bramstedt, K.A. and Lavee, J. (2016) Smoke and mirrors: Unanswered questions and misleading statements obscure the truth about organ sources in China. *Journal of Medical Ethics*, 42(8): 552–3.

Sarkar, S. (2014) Rethinking human trafficking in India: Nature, extent and identification of survivors. *The Round Table*, 103(5): 483–495.

Sharif, A., Singh, M.F., Trey, T. and Lavee, J. (2014) Organ procurement from executed prisoners in China. *American Journal of Transplantation*, 14(10): 2246–52.

Shrestha, P. (2018) Developing a human transplantation health service in Nepal with ethical and moral medical leadership. In J. Aylott, J. Perring, A.L.N. Chapman and A. Nassef (eds) *Medical Leadership*. Abingdon: Routledge, pp 163–72.

Stammers, T. (2019) Trafficking, tourism and trading: A dark convergence in transplantation. In A.M. Phillips, T.C. De Campos and J. Herring (eds) *Philosophical Foundations of Medical Law*. Oxford: Oxford University Press, pp 237–52.

Stammers, T. (forthcoming) Organ trafficking: Why do healthcare workers engage in it? *Cambridge Quarterly of Healthcare Ethics*.

Todres, J. and Diaz, A. (2021) COVID-19 and human trafficking: The amplified impact on vulnerable populations. *JAMA Pediatrics*, 175(2): 123–4.

Transplantation of Human Organs Act (2008) Available from: http://health.bih.nic.in/Docs/THO-A-Rules-2008.pdf

Transplantation of Human Organs (Amendment) Bill (2011) Available from: http://164.100.24.219/BillsTexts/LSBillTexts/PassedBothHouses/transplnt.pdf (accessed 28 August 2021).

Transplantation Society and International Society of Nephrology (2018) *Declaration of Istanbul on Organ Trafficking and Transplant Tourism*. Available from: https://declarationofistanbul.org/the-declaration (accessed 7 September 2021).

Trey, T., Sharif, A., Schwarz, A., Fiatarone Singh, M. and Lavee, J. (2016) Transplant medicine in China: Need for transparency and international scrutiny remains. *American Journal of Transplantation*, 16(11): 3115–20.

Tyldum, G. and Brunovskis, A. (2005) Describing the unobserved: Methodological challenges in empirical studies on human trafficking. *International Migration*, 43(1–2): 17–34.

United Nations (2000) *Protocol to Prevent, Suppress and Punish Trafficking in Persons, Especially Women and Children*. Available from: http://www.ohchr.org/EN/ProfessionalInterest/Pages/ProtocolTraffickingInPersons.aspx

United Nations Office on Drugs and Crime (2021) Impact of the COVID-19 pandemic on trafficking in persons. Available from: https://www.unodc.org/documents/Advocacy-Section/HTMSS_Thematic_Brief_on_COVID-19.pdf (accessed 7 September 2021).

US Department of State (2020) *Trafficking in Persons Report: Sri Lanka*. Available from: https://www.state.gov/reports/2020-trafficking-in-persons-report/sri-lanka/ (accessed 3 September 2021).

Walsh, D. (2005) Transplant tourists flock to Pakistan, where poverty and lack of regulation fuel trade in human organs. *The Guardian*, 10 February. Available from: http://www.guardian.co.uk/world/2005/feb/10/pakistan. declanwalsh (accessed 29 August 2021).

Xiang, Y.T., Meng, L.R. and Ungvari, G.S. (2016) China to halt using executed prisoners' organs for transplants: A step in the right direction in medical ethics. *Journal of Medical Ethics*, 42(1): 10.

3

Online child sexual exploitation in the Philippines: addressing demand

Imogen Fell and Sasha Jesperson

Introduction

International awareness of online sexual exploitation of children (OSEC) has increased in recent years.[1] In particular, the Philippines is documented as a principal source for the production of online child sexual abuse materials (Hernandez et al, 2018: 306). Environmental and structural factors such as 'poverty, family breakdown and dysfunction, poor parenting and supervision of children' (Gill, 2021: np), are identified as circumstances that have been linked to the prevalence of child sexual exploitation (CSE). Another important way to understand this issue is via the dynamics of international demand for child sexual exploitation materials (CSEM) external to the Philippines and the domestic and international practice and policy efforts to disrupt supply and demand.[2] Based on a dearth of academic literature on demand, the focus of this chapter is to explore how international attention on CSE and OSEC in particular has supported a range of interventions tackling exploitation in the country, in this case the Philippines, but neglects to engage with the location of the perpetrator, a challenge unique to OSEC. The chapter also critiques the Trafficking in Persons (TIP) report, published annually by the US State Department, arguing that instead of focusing solely on the response of each country where exploitation occurs, it also needs to engage with international demand.[3] Throughout this chapter, the term local is used to distinguish responses in the Philippines from those directly implemented by international donors. It refers to being Philippine based. While OSEC is understood as one aspect of CSE, the TIP report takes a more expansive view. The report focuses on 'trafficking in persons', which is defined as 'sex trafficking in which a commercial sex act is induced by force, fraud, or coercion, or in which the person induced to perform such an act has not attained 18 years of age' (US Department of State, 2021). Thus, OSEC is included as a component part of the phenomena and response reviewed annually by the TIP report. Lastly, the chapter considers the implications on policy in the UK, specifically the Online Safety Bill, where OSEC has been prioritised, but questions remain whether such actions will deter demand and impact CSEM sourced from the Philippines.

The rise of online sexual exploitation

In the Philippines, both offline and online forms of CSE are a pressing issue where the nation has been rendered a hub for OSEC. Based on law enforcement data, the US Department of State (2020) reported the Philippines as one of the leading sources of OSEC, highlighting that 'traffickers sexually exploit children, individually and in groups, in live internet broadcasts, in exchange for compensation wired through a money transfer agency by individuals most often in another country, including the United States, Australia, Canada, and the United Kingdom'. Increasingly, globalised networks and technological advancement have increased the risks posed to children but also driven the global agenda to protect children from online forms of sexual exploitation. A key reason for its rise includes technological advances that increase accessibility to children through online platforms. The spread of high-speed internet has fuelled a surge in Filipino children at risk of sexual exploitation. Perpetrators do not physically need to be in the same location as victims, which complicates investigations and responses.

UNICEF (2016) puts into perspective the scale and impact of OSEC, highlighting the number of rising cases and low conviction rates of OSEC and online abuses against children, and signals the importance of protecting children's rights, as specified in the 1989 UN Convention on the Rights of the Child. Global awareness of the issue has grown, as indicated by the Sustainable Development Goals introduced in 2015, where target 16.2 calls for a unified global initiative to 'end abuse, exploitation, trafficking and all forms of violence and torture against children' (United Nations, 2015). Accordingly, there has been significant international attention focused on CSE, and specifically OSEC in the Philippines, but this has not necessarily resulted in an effective response.

Demand is a key aspect of the United Nation's Protocol to Prevent, Suppress and Punish Trafficking in Persons introduced in 2000, referred to as the Palermo Protocol. It states that 'State Parties shall adopt or strengthen legislative or other measures, such as educational, social or cultural measures, including through bilateral and multilateral cooperation, to discourage the *demand* that fosters all forms of exploitation of persons, especially women and children, that leads to trafficking' (UN General Assembly, 2000, italics added). Accordingly, the demand side is recognised as a key element in the international response to exploitation, but it is not given the attention it requires.

Demand refers to the 'supply and demand' concept often linked with human trafficking whereby 'as long as there is a demand (consumers willing to pay to have sex with children and traffickers motivated by money), then supplies (children) will be recruited' (Miller-Perrin and Wurtele, 2017: 129). Baines (2019: 199) develops this concept further, arguing that 'OSEC conforms to the principles of supply and demand to some degree, but there are different emotional affordances at work, not least sexual gratification in many (but not all) cases'. As explained by Baines, this can make demand difficult to manage and deter because of the human element. One example is that 'individuals may utilise the internet and associated facilities in order to meet sexual needs in an attempt to compensate for deficits in intimacy' (Kloess et al, 2014 135). The unpredictability of online social engagements combined with a paucity of research into perpetrators' behaviour makes prevention efforts focused on demand more complex.

Online behaviours of children have direct implications on how OSEC can be understood better for deterrence purposes. For example, research specific to internet and social media technology in relation to OSEC is especially relevant given the 'huge transformation in the range and speed of communication' associated with globalisation (Stafford et al, 2011). However, there has been little in the way of exploring the implications technological transformation and increased connectivity have had on OSEC. For instance, the agency We Are Social produced a digital report showing the Philippines as the leading country for social media usage in their index. The report stated that Filipino users aged 16 to 64 are averaging four hours and 15 minutes every day (Kemp, 2021). To put the Philippines' social media usage in perspective, the worldwide average is two hours and 25 minutes, which is almost half of Filipino social media usage. These behaviours demonstrate a growing need to understand the use of internet and social media technologies and how this intersects with indicators of OSEC. Social media engagement is a crucial platform for perpetrators of OSEC, but We Are Social's report did not capture younger children. As a result, the full extent of children's direct engagement with social media and therefore risks associated with utilising tech platforms remain unknown. Efforts to understand online behaviours could help support the development of preventative mechanisms for demand reduction, where there is still a distinct lack of critical research into how online and technological practices in the Philippines influence OSEC. Instead, most literature tends to focus on detailing characteristics of OSEC and providing case studies of survivors' experiences.

For Southeast Asian nations, the modern dimensions of technology and globalisation have increased access to children, complicating preventative efforts to protect children from sexual exploitation due to the increased accessibility to the internet and lack of education around web-based exploitation (Terre des Hommes, 2013; Curley, 2014). Hernandez et al (2018: 310) states that OSEC has been 'perceived to be more prevalent in areas known for sex tourism', which poses risks to children in cosmopolitan cities and communities near beaches. Hernandez et al (2018: 310) indicate that offline forms of CSE have influenced the prevalence of OSEC. In addition, historical links with prostitution in Southeast Asia, and the sexualised treatment of women and children has generally led to a normalisation of sexual exploitation in countries like the Philippines (Jeffreys, 1999; Reid and Jones, 2011). In the Philippines, a combination of increased accessibility to children, demand and normalised ideas around sexual exploitation have put children at greater risk of sexual exploitation. One example of normalisation is the false idea maintained by adults who engage children in online forms of sexual exploitation, in which they perceive OSEC to be less harmful to children since there is no physical contact involved (Ramiro et al, 2019: 9). Thus, exploiters perceive OSEC as a less traumatic way to make 'easy money' since it uses minimal resources and children do not come into direct contact with perpetrators. In cases of OSEC involving older children, financial gain is largely the incentive for these groups engaging in self-generated online sexual activities. Among teenagers, Ramiro et al (2019: 7) found peer influence to be a common enabling factor, with research participants expressing that they were more comfortable engaging in exploitation with peers. Evidently, dangers and risks to children in the Philippines are present through local networks and relationships, not only directly between perpetrators and victims but through local facilitation, which contributes to normalised attitudes towards CSEM creation and production.

Understanding the Philippines perspective: methods

The findings in this chapter draw on analysis of 13 semi-structured interviews with frontline practitioners from a number of local non-governmental organisations (NGOs) responding to CSE across well-known 'hotspots' for OSEC in Luzon and the Visayas region (US Department of State, 2020: 409). NGOs were chosen as a source for accessing frontline practitioners because their operations are close to local communities and they are known for being 'flexible innovators, able to promote local participation and reach the poor' (Markowitz, 2001: 40). In the Philippines, NGOs play a crucial role in leading responses to CSE. Based on their importance, NGOs and their frontline practitioners were selected for interviews based on a snowball sampling approach. All interviews were face-to-face with NGO practitioners working in child protection efforts, advocacy and education, and with legal services leading the prosecution of exploiters and partnership engagement with other locally based NGOs in the Philippines. Frontline practitioners included social workers, lawyers and law enforcement coordinators working with Philippine government agencies such as the Philippine National Police. Therefore, engaging with frontline NGO practitioners affords this chapter a comprehensive understanding of the realities experienced by those exposed to the challenges on the ground in the Philippines.

The challenge of international demand in the Philippines

While responses to CSE tend to focus domestically, the findings show that most frontline practitioners interviewed observed from their casework that demand for CSEM outside of the Philippines was a growing problem, which had increased prevalence of OSEC and contributed to changes in victim demographics. On the ground, social workers had observed that the age of children being sexually exploited online was getting lower, a trend associated with rising demand and specific requests from abroad. For example, one participant stated that they were managing a case where the perpetrator or 'customer' had requested CSEM involving a one-year-old child. They explained that in previous years, teenagers were at risk of OSEC but increasingly cases have included infants to meet CSEM demand, resulting in severe trauma and in some cases death. Similarly, another participant stated that they had seen an upward trend in boys being involved in OSEC, whereas previously girls had been the primary victims. Responses have historically been tailored to teenage girls and these demographic changes are challenging for practitioners supporting victims. In this case there is a specific challenge mentioned about to support to remedy the impact of demand on the gender and age of victims.

Increases in the rise of international demand and availability has also altered the chain of perpetration. While standard cases of CSE involve a victim and perpetrator, the distance of the perpetrator from the victim requires an additional layer in the form of a facilitator. Facilitators are locally based adults, often the parents, or family members related to the child who is being exploited, whereas perpetrators are often foreign nationals engaged in watching live-streamed CSE, accessing pornographic images and distributing CSEM. In the findings, lawyers interviewed explained that prosecuting cases of OSEC were often complex as legal cases had to be filed both locally against the local facilitator and internationally against the foreign perpetrator. However, the drivers behind the involvement of facilitators and perpetrators are significantly different. While arresting facilitators is much easier for prosecutors in the Philippines, continued international demand ensures other facilitators will fill the gap, taking advantage of the revenue potential in areas with few other lucrative options.

Frontline practitioners have all seen increased prevalence of OSEC in the Philippines through their work, articulating they had seen supply surge to meet the demand. One interviewee explained: "[the] lack of education plus huge demand outside Philippines, [is difficult as] there's huge demand then there's supply" (interview with a social worker, 2019, Manila). These insights indicate that present efforts to curb demand internationally are not being felt on the ground.

A blindspot in the Trafficking in Persons report

Globally, the TIP report is a widely accepted human trafficking policy tool, which influences funding for anti-trafficking efforts. Under the US Trafficking Victims Protection Act (TVPA), the term 'severe forms of trafficking in persons' is fully defined as: (a) sex trafficking in which a commercial sex act is induced by force, fraud or coercion, or in which the person induced to perform such act has not attained 18 years of age; or (b) the recruitment, harbouring, transportation, provision or obtaining of a person for labour or services, through the use of force, fraud or coercion for the purpose of subjection to involuntary servitude, peonage, debt bondage or slavery. The US-created TIP report is modelled on the US domestic TVPA but has been adopted for the international anti-trafficking response (Chuang, 2014: 613). The TIP report is an example of a shift from 'direct intervention to sponsorship of acts of global governance' by policing international responses to trafficking (Wiss, 2013: 66). The US State Department's monitoring approach seeks to engage states by promoting compliance to strengthening their response to human trafficking, as poor performers are discredited. The TIP report also takes a carrot and stick approach by including the threat to withdraw financial support provided by USAID (Wiss, 2013: 66). Critiqued for being biased, the report has faced scrutiny for being politically swayed in favour of states with strong international relations with the US. Despite this, the TIP report is a widely accepted global policy tool for monitoring and assessing anti-trafficking responses, solidifying its position as pioneering efforts in global responses to OSEC and resulting in its inadvertent use as an international anti-trafficking benchmark.

Historically, the Philippines has had a strong relationship with the US, which generates a desire to comply with the criteria of the TIP report, but funding is also an important driver. The Philippines is currently ranked as a Tier 1 country as it meets the minimum standards set out by the TIP report (US Department of State, 2021: 52). However, challenges in addressing international demand for OSEC have the potential to derail this ranking. The Philippines has been called out for the prevalence of OSEC in the country reports since 2015. The TIP report has provided 'prioritised recommendations' across the prevention, protection, prosecution and partnerships (4Ps) paradigm to remedy this, emphasising gaps in OSEC responses and detailing the level of engagement between international and local actors (US Department of State, 2020: 406). The report has called for increased resources to address OSEC, a recommendation that has been met by the Child Protection Compact Partnership (CPC) between the Philippines and US State Department, to support interventions.

The CPC is welcomed by Philippine officials and agencies as a positive investment for child protection efforts. However, it reveals strategic biases in the TIP report that have become a blindspot. For instance, the CPC bilateral agreement, originally signed in 2017, details the commitment of US$3.5 million by the US State Department and US$800,000 from the Philippine government to 'strengthen' OSEC responses, by adopting a 'victim-centred approach to prosecuting traffickers and ensuring specialised services for child victims' (US Department of State, 2018). International funding, while not explicitly tied, comes with specific conditions to which grantees must adhere, acting as a powerful tool for donors to support OSEC efforts in the Philippines. However, these tend to be to international priorities, leaving the Philippines with limited agency to determine the most appropriate course of action. The power dynamic that this establishes has the effect of overriding local priorities and directing attention to the supply-side instead of examining demand. As a result, local actors are tied to more reactive responses focused on funders' timescales and criteria, and meeting monitoring and evaluation requirements to show impact, rather than focusing on more strategic contextually specific response development.

Within the TIP report, demand is examined in terms of the actions of the government of the Philippines in preventative efforts, rather than addressing the sources of demand. The emphasis is on 'governmental efforts to reduce the demand for commercial sex acts and international sex tourism' (US Department of State, 2021: 52). However, demand for CSEM is primarily located in affluent countries and, thus, outside of the power, capacity and surveillance of the Philippines government to respond. Aside from resource difficulties, barriers that prevent the Philippines government from addressing demand include a dearth of evidence on demand-side behaviours in other contexts required to influence both international and Philippine policy, a lack of control over international demand beyond the Philippine jurisdiction and limited influence over the private sector to deter online engagement between perpetrators and minors. There is very limited engagement with international demand-side responses, and the default position remains focused on addressing supply. Fouladvand (2017: 13) argues that for human trafficking in general, 'supply-side issues have taken precedence once again and demand-side interventions which require increased attention to root causes including economic, social and cultural factors that enable the exploitation of trafficked persons, have been ignored'. Likewise, in the country narrative for the Philippines, there is no significant international effort or response detailed in the TIP report to minimise demand. Instead, the narrative challenges the Philippine government's failure to 'reduce the demand for commercial sex acts' and highlights the number of 'foreign registered sex offenders' travelling to the Philippines (US Department of State, 2020: 408). In other words, the TIP report places responsibility on the Philippine government to initiate preventative mechanisms to counter OSEC demand. Hughes (2005: 7) states that in order to address demand 'defin[ing] and characteris[ing] each component so that policies and laws can be created to address it' are crucial, meaning that more attention on critically examining demand and causal factors is required.

International demand from states such as the UK, US and Australia add to the challenges faced by the Philippines, which struggles to access resources to adequately develop nuanced OSEC responses including efforts to deter demand. The TIP report and the lack of demand-side focus contained in the report highlights a Western bias, where demand has been overlooked in favour of scrutinising the supply-side where CSEM is generated. Furthermore, the TIP report fails to discuss comprehensive responses to demand beyond emphasising the need for local government to lead responses deterring demand. From the local perspective, frontline Filipino practitioners indicate that more international responsibility to reduce demand is necessary to ease the growing pressures experienced on the ground.

Implications of online sexual exploitation of children for UK policy

As an identified demand-side country by the US Department of State (2020), the UK government has a key role in addressing demand. Overall, the UK government has shown a commitment towards anti-OSEC efforts through the UK Home Office, which invested Official Development Assistance (ODA) funds in the 'End Violence Against Children Fund'. The ODA funds provided financial aid of £40 million, which was granted to the United Nations Children's Fund (UNICEF), to implement responses across different sectors as part of the 'WePROTECT Global Alliance's (WPGA) strategy for national action' comprising of 97 countries (UK Home Office, 2020). The WPGA is an independent organisation that seeks to stimulate a global coordinated response, by providing resources to states enabling the creation of preventative tools, the generation of international awareness and detection capabilities, improved reporting of CSE and ensuring financial and technical resources are accessible (WeProtect Global Alliance, 2016: 12). Another important shift towards improving counter-demand efforts is the proposed Online Safety Bill following the publication of the Online Harms White Paper (HM Government, 2020). The Online Safety Bill indicates the UK government is taking measures to introduce legislation safeguarding online activities. Furthermore, it details how government policy is working towards improving tech sector detection, specifying that:

The scale, severity and complexity of child sexual exploitation and abuse is particularly concerning, with private channels being exploited by offenders. In light of this, the regulator will have the power to require companies to use automated technology that is highly accurate to identify illegal child sexual exploitation and abuse activity or content on their services. (HM Government, 2020: 43)

In the White Paper, the UK government notes the vital role for private companies to develop detection practices to identify CSEM and improve the management of public communications and social media specifically in 'private channels' that traffickers can use for exploitation purposes. For instance, the use of 'online instant messaging services and closed social media groups' to address the online risks to children (HM Government, 2020: 10). Therefore, developing robust policy around CSEM and child protection is clearly necessary. The crucial role of governments in the protection and management of online data and information has been recognised (Meltzer, 2014: 96–7). Their role is not only to restrict and monitor information but also to educate internet users, especially families, in protecting themselves from exploitation. On further examination, governments should take on more of an expansive role, rather than limiting the demand response to nations where CSEM is produced. Instead, prioritisation of 'cross-border data flows', sharing access to relevant and appropriate data across borders, should be comprehensively investigated by governments as a viable option (Meltzer, 2014: 100). Moreover, exploring the fine line between data privacy and online child protection should be considered as an area for investment to establish where loopholes and gaps exist that allow perpetrators to continue engaging with CSEM.

Technology allows for reach that goes beyond recognised boundaries and governments need to start further acknowledging the implications of this on their policies and practices. As ECPAT (2009: 4) states, 'technology has facilitated connections that transcend most of the traditional boundaries to community building: geography, culture, time, and jurisdictional boundaries'. The harnessing of such a medium has yet to evolve and is therefore not only a concern for the Philippines alone but requires a transnational approach (Johnson, 2011).

Similarly, International Justice Mission (2020) published a White Paper claiming that demand–side sentencing was not reflective of the domestic sentencing in the UK for sex offenders. Overall, current studies analysing legal practices for human trafficking have acknowledged that the UK has adopted a stricter criminal justice response (Fouladvand, 2017). However, the International Justice Mission's White Paper argued that under the Sexual Offences Act 2003 UK perpetrators were facing and often convicted with shorter sentences, in comparison to Filipino facilitators of OSEC who, because of local legislation, were convicted with stronger sentences in the

Philippines for OSEC offences (International Justice Mission, 2020). In summary, the White Paper called for more proportionate UK sentencing for perpetrators purchasing and engaging with facilitators to request sexual acts for the facilitator to perform on children. Reflecting on the sentencing focus demonstrates an emphasis on prosecution as a punishment, which needs further consideration and critical analysis. For instance, Fouladvand (2017: 13) argues that human trafficking needs to adopt a regulatory approach when dealing with demand by 'encouraging compliance ... through responsibilization [which] offers an alternative to prosecution strategies to reduce re-offending on the one hand and to prevent crime and tackle the root cause of human trafficking on the other'. This calls into question the focus on sentencing and favours the proposed Online Safety Bill, which looks at adopting a regulatory approach to ease the emphasis on supply-side efforts, deterring demand on countries like the Philippines. However, both the Online Safety Bill and the TIP report encounter similar issues, which is that demand for OSEC is treated too individualistically rather than as a collective international issue for all governments and organisations within the technology sector, as shown in the Online Safety Bill. Simply put, efforts to tackle demand require a unified response across governments and specifically in demand-side countries. The Online Safety Bill highlights that progress is being made but efforts to address the global community from demand-side countries are still lacking. Policy and government initiatives responding to OSEC work independently or fund initiatives without considering the broader global picture and the detrimental impact this may have on children in the Global South. A unified response requires unified coalitions and government policy, which complements other nations to bridge gaps across the global response by considering bringing nations like the Philippines, most affected by OSEC, into policy conversations. Therefore, policy needs to consider demand efforts that are not isolated but collaborative where possible across countries, but also across sectors and organisations. Instead, the focus of the Online Safety Bill is centred on each organisation's own deterrence efforts, where they are requested 'to identify illegal child sexual exploitation and abuse activity or content on their services' (HM Government, 2020: 43). This approach indicates that problems may arise with lack of shared classification in identifying CSEM and challenges with the differing capabilities of each organisation. Likewise, the Online Safety Bill presents as a passive blanket approach towards online safety rather than mediated to ensure that online activity is managed according to the level of risk it poses to children globally.

Conclusion

Global efforts to address OSEC and demand for CSEM have been scarce. While demand is mentioned in the TIP report and there is some literature on policy, efforts to tackle demand do not go far enough to effectively respond to the extent where countries like the Philippines can feel the impact. The growth of OSEC has shifted demand away from the location of victims and moved it directly into affluent countries, where perpetrators originate. While threats such as sex tourism persist, OSEC has become much more prevalent and more damaging because of the varied requests of perpetrators even to the extent of changing the demographics of victims. At present, the focus on the supply-side response to demand, as maintained by important tools such as the TIP report, is unlikely to create sufficient impact for OSEC in countries such as the Philippines where victims are recruited and exploited. The UK government has taken some steps in at least identifying the issue of demand stemming from the UK, and developing several mechanisms to respond, such as the Online Safety Bill. However, further prioritisation of the UK government to respond to the lack of demand-side efforts is needed, particularly mechanisms to prevent risks by UK citizens to children globally. Ultimately, the response by the UK government needs to be a unifying one, bringing together where possible demand-side governments, but also the private sectors who provide the technology where CSEM is made available.

Notes

[1] Online sexual exploitation of children 'includes all acts of a sexually exploitative nature carried out against a child that have, at some stage, a connection to the online environment. It includes any use of ICT that results in sexual exploitation or causes a child to be sexually exploited or that results in or causes images or other material documenting such sexual exploitation to be produced, bought, sold, possessed, distributed, or transmitted' (Luxembourg Guidelines, 2016).

[2] Child sexual exploitation material is also known as indecent sexual images and videos of children.

[3] The US State Department's Trafficking in Persons report outlines human trafficking responses internationally, documenting the frontline implementation of interventions to protect children. It has served as an important policy tool informing the international community of responses to OSEC.

References

Baines, V. (2019) Online child sexual exploitation: Towards an optimal international response. *Journal of Cyber Policy*, 4(2): 197–215.

Chuang, J. (2014) Exploitation creep and the unmaking of human trafficking law. *American Journal of International Law*, 108(4): 609–49.

Curley, M. (2014) Combating child sex tourism in south-east Asia: Law enforcement cooperation and civil society partnerships. *Journal of Law and Society*, 41(2): 283–314.

ECPAT (2009) *Research Findings on Child Abuse Images and Sexual Exploitation of Children Online*. Available from: https://www.ecpat.org/wp-content/uploads/legacy/ecpat_journal_sept_2009_full_0.pdf (accessed 31 August 2021).

Fouladvand, S. (2017 Decentering the prosecution-oriented approach: Tackling both supply and demand in the struggle against human trafficking. *International Journal of Law, Crime and Justice*, 52: 129–43.

Gill, M. (2021) Online child sexual exploitation in the Philippines: Moving beyond the current discourse and approach. *Anti-Trafficking Review*, 16: 150–5.

Hernandez, S., Lacsina, A., Ylade, M., Aldaba, J., Lam, H., Estacio, Jr., L. and Lopez, A. (2018) Sexual exploitation and abuse of children online in the Philippines: A review of online news and articles. *Acta Medica Philippina*, 52(4).

HM Government (2020) *Online Harms White Paper: Full Government Response to the Consultation*. UK Government Home Office and Department of digital, culture, media and sport.

Hughes, D. (2005) *The Demand for Victims of Sex Trafficking*. Available from: https://www.academia.edu/3415676/The_Demand_for_Victims_of_Sex_Trafficking (accessed 31 August 2021).

International Justice Mission (2020) *Falling Short: Demand-side Sentencing for Online Sexual Exploitation of Children*. Available from: https://www.ijmuk.org/documents/IJM-SUMMARY-FALLING-SHORT-Demand-Side-Sentencing-for-Online-Sexual-Exploitation-of-Children-October-2020-002.pdf (accessed 31 August 2021).

Jeffreys, S. (1999) Globalizing sexual exploitation: Sex tourism and the traffic in women. *Leisure Studies*, 18(3): 179–96.

Johnson, A. (2011) International child sex tourism: Enhancing the legal response in south east Asia. *The International Journal of Children's Rights*, 19(1): 55–79.

Kemp, S. (2021) Digital 2021: The latest insights into the 'state of digital'. *We Are Social*. Available from: https://wearesocial.com/blog/2021/01/digital-2021-the-latest-insights-into-the-state-of-digital (accessed 26 August 2021).

Kloess, J., Beech, A. and Harkins, L. (2014) Online child sexual exploitation. *Trauma, Violence, & Abuse*, 15(2): 126–39.

Luxembourg Guidelines (2016) *Terminology Guidelines for the Protection of Children from Sexual Exploitation and Sexual Abuse*. Available from: https://www.ilo.org/ipec/Informationresources/WCMS_490167/lang--en/index.htm (accessed 24 November 2021).

Markowitz, L. (2001) Finding the field: Notes on the ethnography of NGOs. *Human Organization*, 60(1): 40–6.

Meltzer, J. (2014) The internet, cross-border data flows and international trade. *Asia & the Pacific Policy Studies*, 2(1): 90–102.

Miller-Perrin, C. and Wurtele, S. (2017) Sex trafficking and the commercial sexual exploitation of children. *Women & Therapy*, 40(1–2): 123–51.

Ramiro, L., Martinez, A., Tan, J., Mariano, K., Miranda, G. and Bautista, G. (2019) Online child sexual exploitation and abuse: A community diagnosis using the social norms theory. *Child Abuse & Neglect*, 96 (9): 104080.

Reid, J. and Jones, S. (2011) Exploited vulnerability: Legal and psychological perspectives on child sex trafficking victims. *Victims & Offenders*, 6(2): 207–31.

Stafford, A., Parton, N., Vincent, S. and Smith, C. (2011) *Child Protection Systems in the United Kingdom: A Comparative Analysis*. London: Jessica Kingsley Publishers.

Terre des Hommes (2013) *Webcam Child Sex Tourism*. Available from: https://www.terredeshommes.org/wp-content/uploads/2013/11/Webcam-child-sex-tourism-terre-des-hommes-NL-nov-2013.pdf (accessed 31 August 2021).

UK Home Office (2020) *Development Tracker: End Violence Against Children (EVAC Fund)*. Available from: https://devtracker.fcdo.gov.uk/projects/GB-GOV-6-03 (accessed 4 October 2020).

UN General Assembly (2000) *Protocol to Prevent, Suppress and Punish Trafficking in Persons, Especially Women and Children, Supplementing the United Nations Convention against Transnational Organized Crime*. UN General Assembly

UNICEF (2016) UNICEF study: 8 in 10 Filipino youth in danger of online sexual abuse. *UNICEF Philippines, Media Centre*. Available from: https://www.unicef.org/philippines/media_25534.html#.WdS2WIbasy4 (accessed 5 October 2017).

United States Department of State (2018) *Trafficking in persons report 2018*. Available from: https://www.state.gov/wp-content/uploads/2019/01/282798.pdf (accessed 15 July 2022).

US Department of State (2020) *Trafficking in Persons Report 2020*. Available from: https://www.state.gov/wp-content/uploads/2020/06/2020-TIP-Report-Complete-062420-FINAL.pdf (accessed 17 August 2020).

US Department of State (2021) *2021 Trafficking in Persons Report*. Available from: https://www.state.gov/reports/2021-trafficking-in-persons-report/ (accessed 31 August 2021).

WeProtect Global Alliance (2016) *The WePROTECT Global Alliance: Our Strategy to End the Sexual Exploitation of Children Online*. Available from: https://www.weprotect.org/s/WePROTECT-Global-Alliance-Strategy.pdf (accessed 6 October 2020).

Wiss, R. (2013) And justice for all? International anti-trafficking agendas and local consequences in a Philippines sex tourism town. *Australian Journal of Human Rights*, 19(1): 55–82.

4

The role of business in the exploitation and rehabilitation of victims of modern slavery

Colleen Theron

Introduction

Business has a role to play in negating the tolerance of slavery and to take active steps to help survivors of trafficking. The UN Guiding Principles (UNGPs) are the global standard for businesses to respect human rights and create an obligation upon business to implement policies and due diligence processes to identify, prevent and remedy (if possible) negative human rights impacts that they may have caused or contributed to. This includes a duty to prevent human trafficking. Legislation like the UK Modern Slavery Act requires a business to take steps to tackle and proactively report on human trafficking and modern slavery in their organisations and supply chains. Effective due diligence allows companies to identify and assess potential and actual human rights abuses in their operations and services, including their supply chains and business relationships. The EU draft Directive on Corporate Sustainability Due Diligence will require businesses within its scope to develop and implement a mandatory human rights due diligence strategy (European Parliament, 2021). It is argued that while businesses will assess risk before entering key business transactions, very few take responsibility for decent work in their supply chains (BHRRC, 2017).

COVID-19 highlighted that business practices impact on people in supply chains. It has posed unprecedented challenges for business and workers in supply chains, particularly those exposed to forced labour and modern slavery. The shutdown of countless factories during the pandemic increased unemployment rates, putting those most vulnerable at greater risk of exploitation. Perpetrators of modern slavery induce victims to rely on them for basic needs such as food and shelter, and circumstances where income generated would be confiscated (GBCAT, 2020). The chapter outlines contributing factors in the exploitation of workers including the role of the businesses, demand for cheap labour, global inequality and poverty. Business leaders representing both the survivor employment programmes – Bright

Future, Holos – and the retail organisations who collaborated with them – the Co-op, Dixons Carphone and Brightwork Recruitment – were interviewed for this chapter, discussing their roles in the rehabilitation of survivors and identifying barriers in this process.

The role of business in the exploitation of victims

The journey from legitimate employment to exploitation can be linked to business in multiple ways. Businesses and their supply chains provide opportunities for millions of people around the world to enter employment and underpin global economies for the purpose of production or service provision. According to the International Labour Organization's (ILO) *World Employment and Social Outlook* report, over 453 million people are employed in global supply chains (ILO, 2021). Despite supporting local economic growth and providing employment, millions of people work in inhumane conditions within global supply chains; paid less than living wage and mistreated at work, fatal accidents are still common. These conditions can arise because of pre-existing social and geographic vulnerabilities and can be exacerbated by businesses' pricing and performance demands, combined with a lack of enforcement of voluntary and legal standards. The issue of labour exploitation is by no means affecting transnational supply chains only, illustrated by numerous case studies in which domestic workforces, sometimes directly employed but often through supplier or subcontractor relationships, allowed companies to unjustly profit from the exploitation of workers (Nolan and Boersma, 2019).

While corporate social responsibility, voluntary frameworks and self-regulation of business practices have been in place for over two decades to ensure that companies positively manage their human rights and environmental impacts, the impact and the effectiveness of these approaches are now recognised as being insufficient to address the exploitation of workers globally in supply chains. The way supply chains are designed and managed is fundamentally linked to labour exploitation (LeBaron, 2021a).

Until recently, state efforts to regulate forced labour in corporate supply chains have predominantly focused upon increasing transparency by mandating corporations to publicly disclose their efforts to address modern slavery in an annual statement. Examples of reporting laws include the UK Modern Slavery Act 2015, Australia Modern Slavery Act 2018 and California Transparency in Supply Chains Act 2010. Among other things, these laws require full disclosure of efforts to identify and mitigate modern slavery risks. A significant shortcoming in these laws is that they do not place any obligation on businesses to take action to address human rights abuses. Businesses can theoretically comply by stating that they have done nothing to address issues. For this reason, commentators have expressed 'uncertainty over the effectiveness of reporting per se to generate change in corporate culture and to materialise human rights due diligence' (Buchmann, 2017: np).

Demands for low-cost labour

Case study: Boohoo

In 2020 a report from Labour Behind the Label revealed widespread labour abuse in Leicester's garment sector. The report led investors to drop Boohoo, contributing to the £1.5 billion fall in Boohoo's market value in one week (Butler, 2020). In 2021, Boohoo was accused of perpetuating modern slavery conditions. Workers in its Leicester factory were being paid less than the minimum wage and, during the pandemic, were required to work without correct personal protective equipment and without social distancing in place. Boohoo has since been exposed to allegations of slavery practices in Pakistan (Dolan, 2020). The exacerbation of poor working conditions was linked to the rise in online retail demand during the COVID-19 pandemic and Boohoo admitted to over-ordering from suppliers, potentially leading to work being outsourced to unchecked subcontractors. Boohoo commissioned a comprehensive review of the Leicester supply chain. A key recommendation from the Alison Levitt QC review was that Boohoo consolidate its supply chain (Levitt, 2020). Boohoo has since banned subcontracting, instructing its Leicester-based suppliers to bring all clothes-making work in-house, buying out or cutting ties with subcontractors (Mustoe, 2021).

Boohoo is an example of a 'fast fashion' brand, a subsection of the garment industry where an increase in the rate of production has resulted in dependency on flexible and responsive systems of production (Bick et al, 2018). Commercial pressure from lead firms drives strategies like greater informal labour subcontracting, which can act a catalyst to forced labour (Crane et al, 2019). Demand for low-cost labour triggered by a procurement contract with a rapid turnaround has been linked to labour exploitation (Gordon, 2017). A business's scale and market power can enable them to impose slim profit margins and quick turnaround times onto suppliers (LeBaron, 2021b) with fluctuations in demand and to increase flexibility while driving down costs (Crane et al, 2019). Further to this, 'low-value-adding' activities are often not carried out by one of the principal actors in the supply chain. As these activities often carry a higher risk of exploitation, certain business models lend themselves to facilitating exploitation by distancing businesses from their risks. The 'labour supply chain' is understood to carry a high risk of forced labour as workers are recruited through informal and sometimes exploitative relationships (Allain et al, 2013).

Recruitment fees, wage theft and debt bondage

Another root cause of trafficked workers entering supply chains are poverty and restrictive mobility (Ramasastry, 2015). Alongside root causes, insufficient due diligence regarding recruitment and outsourcing can allow intermediaries to exploit migrant workers. Workers who would otherwise be unable to migrate engage with unofficial agents in their origin country, who then deduct high fees from the wages of the worker (Miller and Baumeister, 2013). This practice has been well documented leading up to the Qatar FIFA World Cup, where many migrants sought work in Qatar to escape poverty and unemployment in countries such as Nepal, Bangladesh and India (Amnesty International, 2021). It is noteworthy that these victims often originate from regions where they suffer from very limited state protection (UNODC, 2015). Businesses profiting from workers recruited in this way encapsulate LeBaron's assertion that 'rather than a simple consequence of greed or the moral shortcomings of individuals, forced labour in global supply chains is a structural phenomenon that results when predictable, system-wide dynamics intersect to create a supply of highly exploitable workers and a business demand for their labour' (LeBaron, 2021a: 4). Crucially, debt bondage and wage theft have a significant knock-on effect. Wage violations leave workers vulnerable to severe forms of exploitation and trafficking as workers fear leaving jobs, subjected to the control of the intermediaries that they owe money to (LeBaron, 2021b). This is a further way in which global supply chains facilitate trafficking as they extend to regions where there is a steady flow of unprotected workers seeking employment opportunities.

Recruitment fees are one example of how intermediaries cause businesses to facilitate trafficking. A highly publicised example was the case of D J Houghton Catching Services, who supplied workers to Nobel Foods, one of the UK's largest processors of eggs and chickens. The overseer (gangmaster) deducted £40 a week from workers' wages to live in a damp house, charged workers for transportation between worksites, and sometimes stopped payment entirely, forcing workers into a situation of debt bondage (Skrivankova, 2013). This form of exploitation goes further than earning a margin on the revenue from supplying services, as the perpetrators are 'revenue-generating intermediaries' who seek to control workers and take money directly from them in exchange for involuntary ancillary 'services' contingent to employment (Crane et al, 2013).

Businesses must be aware of conditions that make workers in their operations and supply chains vulnerable. Vulnerability is not an inherent quality of people who are exploited, but rather vulnerability is rooted in structural conditions in the economy in which they live and work (Crane et al, 2013). Structural conditions that create a supply of vulnerable workers include gender inequality, limited economic choices for workers, and limited knowledge of relevant rights and protections. Many of these social conditions are associated with global supply chains and developing countries, but businesses in developed countries also employ vulnerable demographics of workers (Cooper et al, 2017).

Case study: Biffa

An example of this can be found in the case of Biffa in which three alleged victims of modern slavery worked sorting rubbish for Biffa Waste Services through Smart Solutions. While under the control of a trafficking gang, they received no wages. A criminal gang lured and trafficked vulnerable Polish victims to the UK promising money, but instead housed them in squalor, putting them to work on farms, waste recycling centres and poultry factories, and controlling their movements.

The case was uncovered as part of Operation Fort, in which West Midlands Police uncovered a criminal gang with an estimated 400 victims, primarily trafficked to the UK from Poland. One of the criminal defendants worked for Smart Solutions and was responsible for registering victims with Smart Solutions and placing them into work.

This case elucidates domestic structural vulnerabilities resulting from a UK economy which emphasises a 'light-touch, employer friendly regulatory framework in which to do business; the use of agency workers; varying employment status set by immigration policy; and sector specific attributes which create a precarious segment of the workforce that is open to exploitation' (Allain et al, 2013: 8; see also Chapter 1, this volume). It highlights the misconception that victims of trafficking are not exploited in developed countries, even though structural conditions in regions such as the UK can also facilitate exploitation.

Biffa's response to the investigation also underlines the prevention and remediation steps that are necessary for businesses to take to protect vulnerable workers. According to a report published by Biffa, training has since been implemented for high-risk employees, and they have deployed additional awareness resources including multilingual newsletters defining modern slavery and outlining how to report concerns (Gentleman, 2021). Where businesses have a vulnerable workforce made up of people who do not speak the local language, may have a distrust of the authorities, and lack social support networks, businesses must ensure that they receive this additional training and can report concerns. Businesses failing to support workers in raising concerns can perpetuate trafficking.

Failure of voluntary measures

Several 'soft law' voluntary frameworks and initiatives exist to address trafficking caused or perpetuated by business activities. For example, in 2015, the United Nations set 17 Sustainable Development Goals (SDGs), a set of goals with the overall objective to end extreme poverty, fight inequality and injustice, and protect our planet. The SDGs and the 169 targets which underpin them were set to be achieved by 2030. SDG 8 on decent work is pertinent to businesses in relation to trafficking. Specifically, SDG 8.7 requires that immediate and effective measures are taken to eradicate forced labour, end modern slavery and human trafficking, and secure the prohibition of child labour. While the effectiveness of the SDGs has been criticised for being broadly framed and non-binding, the SDGs allow businesses to align their governance strategy with international expectations. Many businesses select SDG targets to set goals and measure progress towards addressing modern slavery in their operations and supply chains. For example, Unilever now reports against targets based on the SDGs, specifically, SDG 3 (Good Health and Wellbeing), SDG 5 (Gender Equality) and SDG 8 (Decent Work). Unlike other voluntary frameworks, the SDGs have not been translated into law by national governments and are generally reported against on a purely voluntary basis in organisations' human rights disclosures, such as modern slavery statements (United Nations, 2015).

The UNGPs, adopted in 2011, are a set of guidelines for businesses to prevent, address and remedy negative human rights impacts linked to their operations. They rest on three complementary pillars: the state duty to protect against human rights abuses by corporations; the corporate responsibility to respect human rights; and the need for greater access to effective remedy for victims. The influence of the UNGPs is evident in the widespread adoption of the concept and terminology of due diligence in other subsequent standards such as the updated Organisation for Economic Co-operation and Development's (OECD) *Guidelines for Multinational Enterprises* (OECD, 2011).

How legislation has sought to address business practises

Despite slavery being illegal globally, the number of victims of modern slavery is increasing (UK Home Office, 2020). Because of the failure of multinational enterprises to address human rights abuses across global supply chains, governments across the world have been increasing the disclosure, accountability and transparency requirements by implementing legislation. For example, the UK Modern Slavery Act requires a business to report steps taken to combat modern slavery in their operations and supply chains. Mandatory human rights and supply chain due diligence legislation is growing across Europe to encourage businesses to assess the potential exposure in their supply chain activities and identify if they are causing or contributing to human rights abuses (including modern slavery) or violations of human rights, and to implement appropriate due diligence policies and practices. Among the proliferation of new national laws concerning ethical sourcing and due diligence in supply chains are France's Duty of Vigilance Law 2017, the Netherlands' Child Labour Due Diligence Law, and most recently Germany's Supply Chain Due Diligence Act 2021, all of which align with the UNGPs and require due diligence to be carried out to prevent and remedy several human rights issues, including modern slavery.

Human rights due diligence legislation requires companies to publicly disclose details of their business, supply chains, and efforts to identify and mitigate risks, and mandating that businesses undertake due diligence. Human rights due diligence is defined as 'an ongoing risk management process that a reasonable and prudent company needs to follow to identify, prevent, mitigate, and account for how it addresses its adverse human rights impacts' (UNGPs, nd). Appropriate action will vary depending on the severity and the business's degree of involvement in the impact (Bueno and Bright, 2020).

In 2021, the European Parliament voted in favour of legislation obliging companies to undertake mandatory environmental and human rights due diligence in their value chains. In February 2022, the European Commission published the draft Directive on Corporate Sustainability Due Diligence (the Directive) on the basis that voluntary due diligence standards failed to achieve significant progress in preventing human rights harms and failed to achieve access to justice.

Even so, the SDGs, UNGPs, ILO conventions and the OECD due diligence guidance informed the Directive, meaning the key principles regarding business's approach to preventing forced labour remain largely unchanged, but that stronger state enforcement can be expected. With their enhanced focus on remediation, mandatory human rights due diligence legislation has the potential to have a far greater impact for victims of human rights abuses, as businesses are expected to do no harm and when harm is caused to provide a meaningful remedy to victims (Ramasastry, 2015). In the context of forced labour, meaningful remedy includes a range of measures, from an apology to compensation, protection and working with anti-trafficking initiatives to reintegrate victims back into the labour market.

The failure of voluntary standards to bind companies to address human rights impacts in their operations contributes to the continuation of forced labour in business worldwide. There is, however, an opportunity for business to address their impacts and look forward to support victims after the fact, through survivor reintegration programmes. BSI has developed British Standard BS25700 to provide organisations with guidance to manage modern slavery risk in their operations, supply chains and wider operating environment (BSI, 2022).

The role of business in the rehabilitation of survivors

Some businesses recognise that there are opportunities to advance human rights and actively support anti-slavery practises. Examples that have been cited are:

- demonstrating a commitment to actively preventing human trafficking;
- supporting organisations to make a meaningful impact;
- creating an empathetic environment (GBCAT, 2020: 14).

One way in which a business can demonstrate its commitment to actively preventing human trafficking and modern slavery is to:

- ensure that they are taking steps to identify the risk of modern slavery in their organisation and supply chain;
- create a policy commitment that is also enforceable to address modern slavery;
- develop a supplier code of conduct that sets out the key ethical principles of the business and what is required of its suppliers, particularly to ensure that decent and fair working practices are included (see Ardea, 2020).

Beyond evidencing a commitment to human rights or reporting on how a business is preventing a negative human rights impact or taking steps to prevent incidents, a business can go further and commit to supporting survivors of trafficking. Through their operations and in partnership with other organisations, businesses can deploy opportunities to survivors of trafficking, building critical skills as well as forming new relationships (GBCAT, 2020: 9).

There are several ways that businesses can support the empowerment of survivors, for example, partnering with organisations that support survivors by providing safe and long-term employment. There are a handful of organisations across the globe providing employment to survivors. Meaningful reintegration is complex and expensive. For many trafficked victims, the desire to improve their economic situation and those of their families is often a key contributor to their initial reasons to migrate into high risk of exploitation. Economic activities remain a primary focus after exiting a trafficking situation or as part of a longer-term process (whether in the form of a job or microfinance) (Surtees, 2012).

While trying to provide support through employment to survivors of trafficking, several challenges exist for businesses, such as restrictions on entitlement to work, matching survivors to jobs in areas that may not be accessible by public transport, or that victims are vulnerable to re-trafficking particularly upon the termination of their support. These challenges were typically cited in conversations with business owners and charities providing support to survivors of trafficking. These barriers are discussed in more detail in what follows.

Non-UK case study: corporate culture and inclusivity

As part of the effort to rehabilitate and reintegrate woman workers, Outland employs, at its Cambodian cut and sew facility, survivors of modern slavery as well as other people who have faced exploitation, creating a corporate culture that aligns with the company's broader aim to achieve social justice (University of Nottingham Rights Lab, 2019: 9). The reference to corporate culture is insightful. The corporate culture of a business is often reflected in how a company demonstrates that it is fulfilling its duty to respect human rights as set out by the UNGPs. Where the culture embeds respect for human rights throughout their core business practices, the likelihood of negative systemic impacts on human rights is less than where the culture is focused on pure economic gain.

The *Social Progress and Responsible Business Practice* report published by the University of Nottingham Rights Lab recommends that a company should 'ensure that survivors of slavery are seen and heard by introducing measures to develop survivor-informed support for this group of employees' (University of Nottingham Rights Lab, 2019). It states the necessity of survivor-led measures to support survivors as well as the wider workforce, highlighting that specialist advice is necessary to understand how survivors and non-survivors navigate trust and cooperation, and ways to enhance interactions between employees, from groups such as the Survivor Alliance.

A report by the Nexus Institute highlights that survivors of trafficking achieving a 'successful, sustainable and appropriate job placement' involves overcoming a range of challenges (Surtees, 2012). They identify three types of challenges: those stemming from residual effects of trafficking (for example, stress, anxiety, traumatisation); those linked to the individual trafficked person's situation and characteristics (for example, their educational and professional capacities, confidence level); and those attributable to a broader socioeconomic environment (for example, limited job opportunities, preconceptions of employers).

UK case studies of how business can support the empowerment of survivors

Five individuals were interviewed representing UK businesses and non-governmental organisations (NGOs) that have been working with survivors of trafficking to understand the barriers and opportunities that exist when working with survivors. A summary extract is provided next from conversations with representatives from the Co-op, Bright Futures, Dixons Carphone, Holos and Brightwork Recruitment illustrating the benefits and challenges facing a diverse range of businesses offering employment opportunities for survivors of modern slavery and human trafficking in the UK.

Co-op

In 2017, the Bright Future programme was launched by the Co-op in the UK to offer paid employment to survivors of modern slavery in their food and distribution operations. Developed in partnership with charity City Hearts, the programme now has 68 partners and has provided permanent roles for over 50 survivors to date. Alison Scowen, the Senior Campaigns and Public Affairs Manager at the Co-op, explained how the idea of Bright Future was germinated from a discussion between Stronger Together and City Hearts, who approached the Co-op, and Bright Future was started. The culture of collaboration that they developed and the creativity in developing the programme was crucial to its success. The opportunity to give people a chance to develop skills and progress in the workplace has always been part of the Co-op's approach and is not limited to modern slavery. They also work with ex-offenders and other vulnerable groups.

One of the barriers experienced in the Bright Future programme has been that there are areas where the businesses operate where there is no 'feed of survivors'. In rural areas there is also the challenge that survivors may not have a support network, thereby heightening vulnerability. If survivors have been moved at the outset of their recovery journey, any further changes may intensify vulnerability.

Since it began in 2017, the Bright Future employment programme has achieved a 72 per cent success rate supporting 69 survivors to complete work placements; 50 of these survivors were offered permanent employment with the business partner. The University of Liverpool was commissioned to undertake a review of the programme. It concluded that the programme provides 'a remarkable opportunity for survivors (who are ready and able to do so) to experience decent work, and to enjoy the dignity and personal stability which goes with this' (Balch, 2017: 23).

City Hearts and Bright Futures

City Hearts is a charity founded in 2015 to support traumatised people who have suffered severe exploitation. They offer a range of services from crisis safe houses to long-term support, helping survivors integrate back into society and live independently, which includes pioneering work with the Co-op in developing the Bright Future programme, removing barriers to employment and accelerating survivors towards a brighter future. The programme provides a fast track into work with major companies on a human rights basis.

Phil Clayton, Head of Development at City Hearts, shared his insights on what motivates businesses to get involved in the Bright Future programme. According to Clayton, "a desire to be involved in the recovery of a survivor, to leverage business for good and see a life changed" is a motivating factor. It offers a way to create powerful social value and example how the business is doing good. Restoring life is a powerful draw. He explains that City Hearts has a strong presence among large national businesses which gives it credibility and attracts other businesses looking for an established organisation, with no geographical or demographical restrictions, to engage with around the modern slavery agenda.

Barriers that have been identified by the programme include organisational capacity. The Bright Future system requires engagement at senior level to ensure all departments are involved. The system needs to be embedded in the business; it can require change in HR policy to adapt to the requirements of Bright Future, such as ensuring a permanent direct employment opportunity is available at the end of the placement. In addition, knowing who drives and manages the site placements requires a single point of clear contact which can be a resource barrier.

Benefits in getting involved with the Bright Future programme are multifaceted, including 'restoring life' for someone who has experienced modern slavery. Other benefits to business can include reporting for modern slavery statements and social impact reporting, and reputational and brand recognition as being part of the UK's largest modern slavery collaboration between charities and businesses.

Dixons Carphone

Simon Murray, Group Responsible Sourcing Manager of Dixons Carphone (a member of the Bright Future Co-operative), explained that Dixons Carphone (Dixons) supports survivors of modern slavery by providing them with an employment opportunity. Simon had become aware of modern slavery through several forums and proposed the idea to Dixons to create a survivor programme. The desire to 'do the right thing' has been a key motivator for Dixons to participate in a programme and support survivors.

A critical element of any programme is the opportunity to provide a survivor with 'dignity'. Dixons initially created the opportunity for participants to work in their warehouses. While there were some challenges at the outset of the programme (for example, a candidate who suffered from post-traumatic stress disorder was unable to fulfil their employment obligations), they drew lessons from these experiences. On the whole candidates are committed, with a good work ethic, and many survivors have since been offered permanent positions in the company.

Challenges are similar to those expressed by other businesses – namely the availability of candidates as they rely on safe houses for accommodation, care and travel arrangements, but these are not always located near the business. Candidates who are required to move must be stable as it is likely they would have already been relocated away from their traffickers. The conversation also confirmed the very real challenge COVID-19 presented. It impacted the roles of many then-furloughed staff members, affecting their ability to bring new candidates on board. They also could not arrange interviews if they could not be done online.

As a result of participating in the programme, there is more visibility of modern slavery within the business, raising awareness and promoting company involvement. Simon is positive that Bright Future will expand to more businesses and he also sees an opportunity to expand the model to other countries, for example Norway (which has recently passed legislation addressing modern slavery) is keen to adopt a similar programme.

Holos Kombucha

Holos Kombucha (Holas) is a Sussex-based social enterprise, set to support, equip and encourage survivors of slavery to achieve long-term, meaningful and sustainable employment. We interviewed Naomi Partridge, Holos co-founder, and manufacturer of Kombucha. She had previous knowledge of the impact that employment has on survivors of trafficking through her experience of working with survivors in Cambodia.

Holos set aside 25 per cent of the founders' shares to support survivors of trafficking. They aim to create a blueprint for any size business to consider how they can employ survivors of trafficking. The Holos foundation aims to offer wraparound support during the survivor's working life, to enable survivors to progress onwards successfully into the future. In their first year (2018), Holos had two survivors working with them as part of a placement. Their roles were diverse, involving sales, health and safety, and marketing, and included training. They also obtained a food safety qualification. When COVID-19 hit, it had a direct impact on the business, and they were unfortunately unable to provide positions for survivors. Other challenges include travel to get the survivors to the factory in Sussex, as well as accommodation.

In seeking to address these challenges, Holos is developing integrated support placements which enable survivors to also have accommodation during their employment. As part of the training programme, survivors are offered training focused on vocational needs, for example, food safety qualifications and sales training. For the next group of participants, they will offer communication training within their induction and will be looking to offer other kinds of behavioural training over time based on: job-based needs (as the roles evolve); needs of participants and referral partners; partnership with referral charities; what is already available to participants elsewhere (many are receiving support with their finances already, and so on); and internal resources at Holos and what is manageable.

Brightwork Recruitment

Shan Saba, director of Brightwork Recruitment, got involved with developing a programme through Brightwork to support victims of trafficking. Having undertaken 'tick box' training needed to grow the business in food manufacturing, he had been completely unaware of the horrific reality of modern slavery and felt that as one of the biggest recruitment agencies in Scotland, they needed to do something. They founded the movement Scotland Against Modern Slavery in partnership with the Scottish government, Police Scotland, Migrant Help and many other organisations. He is proud of the fact that having had very little knowledge of modern slavery in business, they now lead their industry in raising awareness in the Scottish business community.

Each instance is classified as a success if Brightwork can provide someone with access to well-paid, long-term work that builds their confidence. They have witnessed several survivors who do not succeed in employment due to their circumstances and they have learned that survivors need far more support and guidance than expected. The complexity of a survivor's vulnerabilities (that perhaps contributed to them getting exploited in the first place) must be considered and they now work with partners to ensure that they have 'buddies' in place to support them through their journey. Businesses need an understanding that the victims do not just need a job, but support and guidance to enable them to grow.

Summary of barriers facing business when setting up programmes to support victims

Several barriers currently exist for businesses in setting up programmes to support victims. In the interviews, the following barriers were identified:

- Where businesses are in rural locations, it is difficult to employ survivors:
  - there is not an obvious 'feed', that is, referrals from NGOs running safe houses; and
  - there is a risk of increased vulnerability among survivors who have already experiencing being moved.
- The impact of COVID-19.

- Getting to grips with post-traumatic stress and other psychological issues facing survivors.
- Organisational challenges.

How business can get started

Despite these challenges, Global Business Coalition against Human Trafficking (GBCAT) set out five steps to be considered by businesses that want to develop opportunities for survivors:

1. Carry out in internal assessment to understand if the business is positioned to support a survivor of trafficking.
2. Determine which departments should be involved.
3. Identify the charities/partners to refer survivors to the business.
4. Ensure monitoring of practises to ensure no exploitation is taking place once someone is placed.
5. Provide survivors with appropriate education on trauma informed approaches (GBCAT, 2020).

Conclusion

Victims of trafficking are more likely to be found in supply chains than ever before, yet many businesses remain unaware of their own supply chain risks. The case studies explored in this chapter highlight that no business can assume there is no risk of modern slavery without a comprehensive analysis of their supply chain's structure and composition. This is likely to become mandatory for many businesses with the growing emphasis on legislation to address due diligence requiring businesses to better understand their supply chains and be able to report on these issues. It is also clear that modern slavery is not a randomly occurring phenomenon, but one that can be linked to several conditions, namely poverty, inequality, lack of transparency and low-cost labour demands. These are well documented, but it remains to be seen whether a greater number of businesses will begin to consider these factors to identify and prevent modern slavery risks within their operations.

It is apparent that across sectors there are businesses taking a proactive stance to create programmes to rehabilitate survivors of trafficking. The programmes vary, but all the businesses, charities or social enterprises participating in this study reported benefits to the survivors of trafficking and to the organisations involved, for example, improving visibility of modern slavery throughout the company, and improved reporting under the modern slavery statement. Survivors enlisted in company programmes reported gaining a sense of dignity as well as the opportunity to develop new skills and gain workplace confidence.

The interview data highlighted the barriers facing the organisations seeking to provide rehabilitation to survivors, such as identifying locations that are suitable for survivors to be moved to, having sufficient internal resources and support, and overcoming COVID-19 challenges. It is hoped that as society at large gains awareness of the issue of modern slavery, increased support will become available to businesses seeking to rehabilitate survivors and develop ways to overcome challenges.

Human trafficking is a heinous and complex crime. The impact of the pandemic paired with increasingly complex and diverse supply chains, cost-squeezing and business models that directly or indirectly facilitate exploitation has led to an increase in the numbers of victims of modern slavery. Despite this, business has always had the ability to harness its global power for good and it is encouraging to see the impact that some businesses are creating by committing to supporting some of the most vulnerable people in our communities. However, if we are to see more survivors being supported there needs to be a cultural change within the global business community. Businesses must demonstrate their commitment to ensuring they will refrain from contributing to actual or potential human rights abuses, and creating a business model to integrate and protect survivors.

Acknowledgements

The author would like to thank Rory Oake and Katie Bunn for their input on this chapter.

References

Allain, J., Crane, A. and LeBaron, G. (2013) Forced labour's business models and supply chains. *Joseph Rowntree Foundation*. Available from: https://www.jrf.org.uk/sites/default/files/jrf/migrated/files/forced-labour-business-full.pdf

Amnesty International (2021) Qatar World Cup of shame. *Amnesty International*. Available from: https://www.amnesty.org/en/latest/campaigns/2016/03/qatar-world-cup-of-shame/

Ardea (2020) The value of supplier codes of conduct: Supporting transparency and improving performance. Available from: https://www.ardeainternational.com/thinking/new-whitepaper-the-value-of-supplier-codes-of-conduct-supporting-transparency-and-improving-performance/

Balch, A.R. (2017) The Co-op's Bright Future programme: An independent Interim Review. *University of Liverpool*. Available from: https://www.antislaverycommissioner.co.uk/media/1176/the-co-op-s-bright-future-programme_an-independent-interim-review.pdf

Bales, K. and Griffin, A (2019) Social progress and responsible business practice: A 759 study on Outland Denim's cut and sew facility in Cambodia. *University of 760 Nottingham Rights Lab*. Available from: https://cdn.shop ify.com/s/files/1/0253/3280/9773/files/2019-Nottingham-Case-Study-Final.pdf?v=1602721167

Barrientos, S., Bianchi, L. and Berman, C. (2019) Gender and governance of global value chains: Promoting the rights of women workers. *International Labour Review*, 158(4): 729–52.

Bick, R., Halsey, E. and Ekenga, C. (2018) The global environmental injustice of fast fashion. *Environmental Health*, 17(1): 92–5.

BSI (2022) BS25700: Organisational responses to modern slavery – guidance. Available from: https://www.bsigroup.com/en-GB/standards/bs-25700/

Buchmann, K. (2017) Neglecting the proactive aspect of human rights due diligence? A critical appraisal of the EU's non-financial reporting directive as a pillar one avenue for promoting pillar two action. *Business and Human Rights Journal*, 3(1): 23–45.

Bueno, N. and Bright, C. (2020) Implementing human rights due diligence through corporate civil liability. *International and Comparative Law Quarterly*, 69(1): 789–818.

Business and Human Rights Resource Centre (2017) Modern slavey in company operations and supply chains: Mandatory transparency, mandatory due diligence and public procurement due diligence. Available from: https://media.business-humanrights.org/media/documents/fb7a2e03e33bcec2611655db2276b4a6a086c36c.pdf

Business for Social Responsibility (2018) *Gender Equality in Social Auditing Guidance*. Available from: https://www.bsr.org/reports/BSR_Gender_Equality_in_Social_Auditing_Guidance.pdf

Butler, S. (2020) Boohoo shareholders demand answers after shares plunge by a third. *The Guardian*, [online] 7 July. Available from: https://www.theguardian.com/business/2020/jul/07/boohoo-shares-concern-fact ory-conditions

City Hearts (2022) *Bright Future – City Hearts*. Available from: https://cit yhearts.global/bright-future

Cooper, C., Hesketh, O., Ellis, N. and Fair, A. (2017) A typology of modern slavery offences in the UK. *Home Office*. Available from: https://www.basw.co.uk/system/files/resources/basw_93136-3_0.pdf

Crane, A., Soundararajan, V., Bloomfield, M., Spence, L.J. and LeBaron, G. (2019) *Decent Work and Economic Growth in the South Indian Garment Industry*. Bath, London and Sheffield: University of Bath, Royal Holloway University and University of Sheffield.

Dolan, A. (2020 Boohoo 'pays Pakistani workers 29p an hour' investigation claims, *Daily Mail*. Available from: https://www.dailymail.co.uk/news/article-9081105/Boohoo-pays-Pakistani-workers-29p-hour-investigation-claims.html

European Parliament (2021) *Corporate Due Diligence and Corporate Accountability*. Available from: https://ec.europa.eu/info/sites/default/files/1_2_183888_annex_dir_susta_en.pdf

French Parliament (2017) *French Corporate Duty of Vigilance Law*.

GBCAT (2020) *Empowerment and Employment of Survivors of Human Trafficking*.

Gentleman, A. (2021) Three victims of trafficking and modern slavery to sue Biffa, *The Guardian*. Available from: https://www.theguardian.com/law/2021/jan/14/three-victims-of-trafficking-and-modern-slavery-to-sue-biffa

Gordon, J. (2017) Regulating the human supply chain. *Iowa Law Review*, 102: 445–504.

Human Rights Watch (2019) *Combating Sexual Harassment in the Garment Industry*. Available from: https://www.hrw.org/news/2019/02/12/combating-sexual-harassment-garment-industry

Inter-Agency Coordination Group Against Trafficking in Persons (2016) *Providing Effective Remedies for Victims of Trafficking in Persons*. Available from: https://www.unodc.org/documents/human-trafficking/ICAT/ICAT_Policy_Paper_3._Providing_Effective_Remedies_for_Victims_of_Trafficking_in_Persons_2016.pdf

International Labour Organization (2014) *Profits and Poverty: The Economics of Forced Labour*, 43–4.

International Labour Organisation (2021) *World Employment and Social Outlook Trends 2021*. Available from: https://www.ilo.org/wcmsp5/groups/public/---dgreports/---dcomm/---publ/documents/publication/wcms_795453.pdf

LeBaron, G. (2021a) The role of supply chains in the global business of forced labour. *Journal of Supply Chain Management*, 57(2): 29–42.

LeBaron, G. (2021b) Wages: An overlooked dimension of business and human rights in global supply chains. *Business and Human Rights Journal*, 6(1): 1–20.

Levitt, A. (2020) *Independent Review into the boohoo Group PLC's Leicester Supply Chain*. Available from: https://www.boohooplc.com/sustainability/supply-chain-review/review-led-by-alison-levitt-qc, PDF Copy: https://www.boohooplc.com/sites/boohoo-corp/files/final-report-open-version-24.9.2020.pdf

Miller, R and Baumeister, S (2013) Managing migration: Is border control fundamental to anti-trafficking and anti-smuggling interventions? *Anti-Trafficking Review*. Available from: 6b342a00355c9d1db6bb04d25aead944942b.pdf (semanticscholar.org)

Mustoe, H. (2021) Boohoo tells suppliers not to subcontract, raising job fears. *BBC News* [online] 8 February. Available from: https://www.bbc.co.uk/news/business-55974075

Nolan, J. and Boersma, M. (2019) *Addressing Modern Slavery*. Sydney: University of New South Wales Press.

OECD (2011) *OECD Guidelines for Multinational Enterprises*. Available from: http://dx.doi.org/10,1787/9789264115415-en

Parliament of Australia (2018) *Australian Modern Slavery Act: Commonwealth Act.*

Ramasastry, A. (2015) Corporate social responsibility versus business and human rights: Bridging the gap between responsibility and accountability. *Journal of Human Rights*, 14(2): 237–59.

SDGs (2021) *The 17 Goals: Sustainable Development*. Available from: https://sdgs.un.org/goals

Skrivankova, K. (2013) Forced labour in the UK. *Joseph Rowntree Foundation*. Available from: https://www.academia.edu/download/39903988/JRF_-_Forced_Labour_in_the_UK.pdf

Surtees, R. (2012) Re/integration of trafficked persons: Supporting economic empowerment. *Vienna, Austria: Nexus Institute*. Available from: nexus_economic-empowerment.pdf (wordpress.com)

Theron, C. (2020) Modern slavery and transparency in supply chains: The role of business. *Ardea International*. Available from: https://www.ardeainternational.com/resources/publications/modern-slavery-and-transparency-in-supply-chains-the-role-of-business/

UK Home Office (2020) *2020 UK Annual Report on Modern Slavery*. Available from: assets.publishing.service.gov.uk/government/uploads/system/uploads/attachment_data/file/927111/FINAL-_2020_Modern_Slavery_Report_14-10-20.pdf/

UK Parliament (2015) *UK Modern Slavery Act 2015.*

UNGP (nd) *Human Rights Due Diligence*. Available: https://www.ungpreporting.org/glossary/human-rights-due-diligence/#:~:text=An%20ongoing%20risk%20management%20process,its%20adverse%20human%20rights%20impacts.

Unilever (2020) *Unilever Annual Report and Accounts 2020*. Available from: https://www.unilever.com/Images/annual-report-and-accounts-2020_tcm244-559824_en.pdf

Unilever (2021) *Respect Human Rights*. Available from: https://www.unilever.com/planet-and-society/respect-human-rights/

United Nations (2015) *Human Rights Due Diligence: UN Guiding Principles Reporting Framework*. Available from: https://www.ungpreporting.org/glossary/human-rights-due-diligence/

United States Senate (2012) *California Transparency in Supply Chains Act.*

University of Nottingham Rights Lab (2019) Social progress and responsible business practice. Available from: https://cdn.shopify.com/s/files/1/0253/3280/9773/files/2019-Nottingham-Case-Study-Final.pdf?v=1602721167

UNODC (United Nations Office on Drugs and Crime) (2015) *The Role of Recruitment Fees and Abusive and Fraudulent Recruitment Practices of Recruitment Agencies in Trafficking in Persons*. Vienna: UNODC. Available from: https://www.unodc.org/documents/human-trafficking/2015/Recruitment_Fees_Report-Final-22_June_2015_AG_Final.pdf

PART II

Being a victim: discourses and representations

Contributions in this section tackle modern slavery and human trafficking as a discourse intersecting with ideologies – around vulnerable migration, of race and racialisation and of victim versus villain – which are echoed in the representation of the victim in the film industry and social media, as well as in legislation and court rooms.

5

Trafficking on film: a critical survey

Jon Hackett

Introduction

In her recent book, *The Truth About Modern Slavery*, Kenway draws on the work of Lakoff in order to characterise the concept of modern slavery in terms of framing:

> Modern slavery as a metaphor for extreme exploitation and as a political frame constructs a way of seeing that makes us blind to things we need to know. By characterising severe exploitation as exceptional and making it into its own category, with its own heroes and villains, its ideal victim types and its solutions, the modern slavery frame hides crucial information. (Kenway, 2021: 9)

Whether or not we agree with this judgement on the adequacy of modern slavery as a concept, we can extend the analysis of framing literally to the moving image. Popular genre cinema in particular has a marked fondness for its own clearly defined heroes and villains. If we consider the prevalence of representations of modern slavery and human trafficking (MSHT) in screen media, then an analysis of the creative choices made during production will extend this attention to framing to types of media that are literally bounded by frames (in the camera and on screen).

Though film and television may seem remote from the immediate concerns of those involved in supporting survivors and victims of MSHT, one might appeal to anecdotal evidence from this author from teaching postgraduate students. Several students, at both master's and PhD level, have stated that their first memory of learning about trafficking derived from the action film, *Taken* (Pierre Morel, 2008). The fact that this rather sensationalist treatment of MSHT nonetheless inspired students to undertake postgraduate study, with a view to a career in the field, underlines the importance of popular culture representations. It also attests to the critical faculty of viewers to negotiate their way through the tropes of popular culture to consider the important social issues at stake in such films.

Film and media representations have a particular role in providing salience for MSHT for a public that otherwise may have limited exposure to or interest in the topic. As Iordanova argues, 'a popular TV sitcom or a Hollywood blockbuster has got a much broader public reach (and influence over minds) than a government "white paper" or a policy initiative that remains known to a handful of specialists' (Iordanova, 2010: 110). Film brings with it the risk of oversimplification and stereotyping; but what it loses in nuance, it gains in reach.

This chapter presents a survey of film representations of MSHT. It begins with the silent-era 'White slave' cycle of films in order to outline the importance of trafficking for cinema at a time when it became established as a mass entertainment industry. The continuities between this and contemporary mainstream examples are highlighted through discussion of *Taken* by Pierre Morel (2008), which has, as just shown, often been seen as emblematic of popular culture representations of human trafficking. In the last part, the chapter aims to bring the literature on films on MSHT up to date through a survey of relevant films available on two streaming services. Netflix is the dominant global streaming service for filmed media; and MUBI is selected as the alternative platform, most associated with world cinema, art cinema and film festival releases, in which migration and trafficking themes have been relatively prevalent.

Moving image, moving bodies

Though what is at stake is massively different, at a conceptual level cinema shares several broad features with human trafficking. They are both transnational phenomena, which involve bodies and identity, migration and mobility. A short discussion of this view from a historical and conceptual level will help to bring out some of these shared aspects.

Cinema is a mass medium and, as such, a phenomenon of sociological modernity. In his 1939 book, *The Rise of the American Film*, Jacobs wrote: 'the movies gave the newcomers, particularly, a respect for American law and order, an understanding of civic organization, pride in citizenship and in the American commonwealth' (cited in Hansen, 1994: 68). For such an advocate, cinema had a socialising, patriotic and pedagogical function. Accounts of early cinema spectatorship underline the fascination of viewers with the technology (Gunning, 1990). Even at its outset, some viewers were disappointed with the lack of sound and monochrome image in early cinema; what no one questioned, however, was cinema's fidelity to human and natural *motion* (Bottomore, 1999). The moving pictures were part of the same '*regime of social motion*' (Nail, 2015: 3, emphasis in original) as increased migration to the city – they were the visual counterpart to the human body in transit.

The links between the two phenomena – cinema and human trafficking – coalesce two decades after cinema's inception, with the mid-1910s cycle of 'White slavery' films. Films such as *Traffic in Souls* (George Loane

Tucker, 1913) and *The Inside of the White Slave Traffic* (Frank Beal, 1913, see Figure 5.1) enjoyed huge popular success, as sensationalist exposés in US urban centres of alleged slavery. Stamp argued that these one-reel films (lasting around a quarter of an hour) were crucial in establishing cinema's dominance as popular entertainment, since these film representations were very popular: 'White slave films announced cinema's "arrival" as a major entertainment form in New York with particular force, for they helped dramatize the widespread conversion of the "legitimate" theatres into moving picture houses in the early teens' (Stamp, 2000: 53).

Furthermore, Stamp (2000) points to the anxieties in the press at the time regarding the female audience for whom such films proved to be so popular, whether this was at the level of 'entertainment' or a curiosity to find out about phenomena generally deemed unsuitable for a female audience. Among media concerns was the apparent enjoyment of women spectators for narratives that, for the press, might be construed as seedy or perhaps even corrupting. Cinema venues themselves became a source of anxiety. Women's unregulated participation in urban life and their free mobility in urban entertainment centres was at the basis of moral panics regarding both screen media, and the 'White slavery' it depicted on screen. Newspapers, according to Stamp, pointed to cinemas themselves as a possible site of encounter between women newly arrived at the city, and would-be male traffickers.

Figure 5.1: *The Inside of the White Slave Traffic* (Frank Beal, 1913)

Progressives, reformers, sociologists and feminists, including Charlotte Perkins Gilman, were all listed in the credit sequence of *The Inside of the White Slave Traffic*. For Diffee, the film's illustrious supporters provided an alibi for spectators whose prime interest might have been voyeuristic: 'Viewers could have their moralism and "eat" their scandal, too' (Diffee, 2005:425). Stamp points to the extra persuasiveness supplied by the photographic apparatus, with the appeal in the films to authentic shooting in locations of actual trafficking; as well as the camera's (apparently) disinterested documentary look, which, as a technology of surveillance, was able to convey objectivity and detail in a way apparently unmatched by prose.

The progress of one-reel cinema in the mid-1910s was therefore closely linked to a successful cycle of alleged exposés of trafficking. For Stamp and Diffee, this cycle of films related to 'White slavery' appeared at a time in which cinema was being standardised into mass entertainment and into a particular narrative form. Cinema was also finding a home in converted entertainment venues (theatres that had become cinemas). On this basis, these early films played an important role in advancing the popularity of the medium at a crucial time. This is important, since it points to some shared concerns between the medium and the social phenomenon.

Cinema as an apparatus and as an exhibition venue provided plenty of analogies with human trafficking at the level of representation (what was on screen in these films) and the anxieties aroused by the mobility and assembly of female bodies in space (the growing cinema audience). These analogies were strengthened by the fact that these films adapted a popular earlier literary and dramatic form, namely melodrama. Melodrama is above all associated with exaggerated emotion, starkly contrasted character types (heroes and villains) and suspense. Singer points out that the term is also associated with notional appeals to female viewers: 'heightened emotionalism and sentimentality: the family melodrama, the woman's film, the weepie, the soap opera, etc.' (cited in Neale, 2000: 181). Melodrama forms the basis of much filmed entertainment and its legacy lives on in blockbuster cinema. We should also note that what we now understand *documentary* to be was largely formulated by criticism in the 1930s (Nichols, 2017: 5). Staging events for the camera rather than spontaneously was acceptable for Flaherty's famous early feature documentaries such as *Nanook of the North* (1922), for instance. Films in the 'White slave' cycle of films might be understood as 'factual' while retaining melodramatic elements – since contemporary audiences did not yet have a clear concept of what separated documentary from fiction film. These melodramatic elements are also present in the key melodrama feature film that was to replace the earlier single-reel films, namely Griffith's 1915 *Birth of a Nation*. This film is now correctly seen as an ode to the Ku Klux Klan, but is one of the most popular films in cinema history; at the film's climax, a virginal heroine is rescued from a villain in blackface by White supremacist saviours. Melodrama tropes live on in contemporary productions, such as the aforementioned *Taken* (Pierre Morel, 2008). There, the protagonist, whose daughter has been abducted by traffickers, is reunited with his daughter for an embrace to the accompaniment of stirring music after dealing with the Orientalised villain (whose deviousness and salaciousness recall the stereotypes analysed by Said, 1978). The term 'White slavery' in itself racialises the categories of victim and (by implication) perpetrator (see Chapter 7, this volume).

My first point here is to underline the thematic elements linking film and human trafficking in both narrative and spectatorial terms. As cinema standardised and consolidated itself as the (then) dominant entertainment form, it did so on the basis of, among other things, single-reel White slavery films (Stamp, 2000; Diffee, 2005), as well as epic multi-reel melodramas of Griffith and others. On screen, the sensationalist spectacle of 'vice' appealed to documentary authenticity and found advocates from activist and academic environments. As with contemporary discourses of MSHT, 'White slave' films often presented racialised narratives of White women ('ideal victims', see also Chapter 9, this volume) at the mercy of perpetrators of other nationalities and ethnicities. Finally, we can note the individualistic nature of the melodrama genre, the implications of which are still pertinent to popular culture representations of human trafficking, such as *Taken*:

> The persistence of melodrama might indicate ways in which popular culture has not only taken note of social crises and the fact that the losers are not always those who deserve it most, but has also resolutely refused to understand social change in other than private contexts and emotional terms. (Elsaesser, 1991:72)

That is to say, in the world of films like *Taken*, a kinetic action hero is required to resolve the social issue of human trafficking, not international legislation, regulation or organising. The solution is sentimental and individual, not social and institutional.

My second point is that film is not an impartial medium that merely turns its attention to phenomena with objectivity. When cinema turns its attention to a particular social issue, it does not reinvent storytelling from scratch. Melodrama, for instance, has proved to be a highly versatile genre across national cinemas throughout the 20th and 21st centuries. Documentary is not a self-evident concept, and its understanding in relation to 'truth' has evolved over time. The genres that are hard-wired into cinema's narrative traditions inevitably provide frames and tropes for phenomena such as MSHT that can limit or skew how it, its perpetrators, survivors and victims, are depicted on screen.

Visual and narrative tropes

Narrative and visual tropes serve as a shorthand for viewers. This is no exception in MSHT cinema. Audiences draw on their recognition from pre-existing examples of oversimplified and stereotyped aspects of characters associated in the popular mind with the perpetrators, survivors and victims of trafficking. There already exists a helpful literature on this topic (Vance, 2012; Kelly, 2014). I will outline only some of these tropes in this section, before proceeding to a survey of selected examples in recent cinema in the next section.

If we are using *Taken* as our paradigm of blockbuster cinema approaches to human trafficking, then we might consult Kelly's thorough analysis of this film in terms of White masculinity as 'avenger of white women's purity against the violent and sexual impulses of racial Others' (Kelly, 2014: 414). According to this reading, the protagonist serves as a protector of a naive female character who leaves the US for a Paris populated by feckless and corrupt Europeans, as well as lascivious and violent Arabs. Here the 'White saviour' type – the father hero, as already mentioned – is saving his own daughter's virginity. Such a template can be extended to other films from the same production stable, such as *Transporter* (Corey Yuen and Louis Leterrier, 2002). A recent action film from South Korea, *Deliver Us From Evil* (Hong Won-Chan, 2020) sees a South Korean hired killer attempting to rescue his daughter from organ trafficking after she is abducted to Thailand (for context on this neglected aspect of trafficking, see Chapter 2, this volume). Here we can see the ethnic differentiation of the action template being spatially reorganised in regional terms. Like the French-produced *Taken* and *Transporter*, *Deliver Us From Evil* reproduces mainstream blockbuster cinema tropes of fighting, abduction, chase and pursuit, as well as sentimentalised parent–child relations, once more with a specific trafficking subplot. The Hollywood-derived fusion of action and melodrama becomes a transnational ('glocal') template adopted by producers in Europe and East Asia, for an international audience.

Another cycle of films, associated more with arthouse styles of cinema, concerns 'Fortress Europe' and migrant and diasporic cinema, with a certain proportion of these involving trafficking plots. These came to prominence in the 1990s, prospered in the first decade of the 21st century, and received scholarly attention (Berghahn and Sternberg, 2010; Loshitzky, 2010). On the whole, these films are produced from outside the US, as part of the international circuit of 'arthouse' cinema which sometimes shares with blockbuster cinema a stock of established stereotyped representations. These include the victim who might be characterised, in Andrijasevic's terms, as 'the figure of a young, innocent and foreign woman tricked into prostitution abroad. She is battered and under continuous surveillance so that her only hope is in police rescue' (Andrijasevic, 2014: 359). Arthouse cinema examples, such as *Lilya 4-ever* (Lucas Moodysson, 2002), feature an innocent 'Natasha' character trafficked by a devious 'loverboy' trafficker. While there are elements in such narratives that undeniably reflect real life experiences, as Andrijasevic points out, they tend to present an 'ideal victim', where the agency of the trafficked women is effaced (see Chapters 6 and 9, this volume). Particularly in relation to the Eastern European cycle of films, it is worth citing Andrijasevic further:

> The simplicity of the narrative pattern is most visible in the fact that the plot never varies: the deception is followed by coercion into prostitution; subsequently, the plot moves into the tragedy of sexual slavery, which in turn is resolved through the rescue of the victim by the police, an NGO or a benevolent client. (Andrijasevic, 2014: 366)

Other scholars echo Andrijasevic's standpoint. Critiques of this type of MSHT narrative emerge from intersectional feminist analyses, which have focused on this question (for example, Doezema, 2000; see also Chapter 10, this volume). Rodríguez-López characterises the narrative frames that drive human trafficking narratives on screen in terms of 'sexual exploitation, immigration, and organized crime' (Rodríguez-López, 2018: 62). This might exclude other frames, such as those informed by social justice or intersectional feminism; as well as those striving for the impartial gaze of observational or ethnographic documentary, however hard in practice that might be to achieve. Rodríguez-López also highlights the marginalisation of characters who do not fit the 'ideal victim' stereotype. Vance points out that the films nod towards a 'rescue' resolution, often guaranteed by the state (Vance, 2012). This is the case for the *Human Trafficking* miniseries, which was permitted for screening in public events – as long as a member of the US State Department were present at the event (Torchin, 2010: 233). Both of these authors underscore that what is at stake in the representations of MSHT on screen transcends cinema – since it informs the public sphere and thereby, influences policy, however indirectly. As Rodríguez-López states: 'The misinterpretation of the definition of trafficking, based on the influence of media representations and social perceptions, can sometimes carry more weight than legal provisions, causing law enforcement efforts to be still mainly focused on sex trafficking, while resources for victims of nonsexual trafficking remain scarce' (Rodríguez-López, 2018: 66). Vance concurs: 'these representations have serious consequences for law and policy, as well as for the public that cares about human rights issues' (Vance, 2012: 200).

In considering the overrepresentation of sex trafficking as opposed to forced labour or organ trafficking, we might productively allude to another classic analysis of the 'male gaze' in cinema, Mulvey's (1975). According to

Mulvey, mainstream cinema (specifically Hollywood studio-era cinema) tends to identify the gaze of character, director, camera and spectator in film and posits them as all notionally male. Although later spectatorship studies have complicated this binary schema, it nonetheless brings out the voyeuristic aspects of the gendered display that can be recuperated in representations of sex trafficking. The spectacle of scantily clad trafficked women in nightclubs, or the protagonist's daughter Kim in harem regalia during a slave auction in *Taken*, might offer time-honoured titillating objects to the gaze of the notional male viewer that Hollywood typically sees as its core audience (Mulvey, 1975).

A key challenge for filmmakers in representing MSHT is capturing broader structural contexts in an audiovisual medium, on screen. We have identified the individualistic hero narratives that inform melodrama and popular genre cinema; more tricky is to construct film narratives that draw in wider contextual factors and how these compromise the agency of individual (social) actors (for these contexts see the Introduction to this volume). As Vance comments: 'The typical anti-trafficking video replays images of women in the brothel and their sinister clients and traffickers, but how does one insert the World Bank, structural readjustment plans, or enforced free-trade policies as characters in this seemingly realist depiction?' (Vance, 2012: 202). For film to do this effectively would require a sort of 'cognitive mapping' (Jameson, 1991: 51), which would allow us to track spatially complex transnational phenomena that frequently defy public comprehension.

Survey of recent cinema

Many of the examples discussed in the previous sections have been considered in the academic literature. This occurred particularly a decade ago when the 'Fortress Europe' cycle of films prompted an academic interest in film narratives of migration, human trafficking and other transnational phenomena (Berghahn and Sternberg, 2010; Loshitzky, 2010). The concern in this section is to survey some recent examples to bring the analysis up to date. Inevitably, given the constraints of an individual chapter, the survey is selective and brief.

Though the majority of films discussed will relate specifically to MSHT, there will be mention of films about migration, asylum seekers and refugees more generally, as the phenomena are interrelated (see Chapter 6, this volume). If we accept the arguments of Kenway (2021) and O'Connell Davidson (2015) that MSHT need to be seen within wider contexts, such as those of migration and labour exploitation, this choice will be justified. The cycle of 'Fortress Europe' films was perhaps more characteristic of the first decade of the century, where distribution of European cinema in theatres was healthier in the UK. These European films treated the migrant experience extensively and were released at a time when UK cinemas were more receptive to national cinemas other than mainstream Hollywood productions. All is not lost in the cinemas: Ben Sharrock's British film *Limbo* (2020) obtained a theatrical release, for example. It is a film about asylum seekers stranded on a Scottish island, which demonstrates the potential of films about migration, trafficking and related themes. The film won the Grand Prix at the Brussels International Film Festival before securing cinema release and distribution on the MUBI platform.

Film Festivals have indeed become an important distribution circuit for world cinema, including cinema that deals explicitly with transnational themes of migration, diaspora, refugees and MSHT. If such films are made by identifiable *auteurs* (noted creative individuals, most likely film directors), then they face a good chance of a festival screening; this might in turn lead to the film being picked up by a distributor for release in cinemas or on streaming services. There are specific festivals, such as the London Migration Film Festival, Human Rights Watch Film Festival, in the UK, or screening strands such as the Human Rights Day at the Sarajevo Film Festival, all of which might see screenings for films on MSHT. Short films might be screened on festivals run on a smaller scale, such as the RENATE (Religious in Europe Networking Against Trafficking and Exploitation) Film Festival. Streaming services also offer opportunities for filmmakers to get their films seen. Theatrical screening remains, however, the unparalleled method for raising awareness of new films and guaranteeing lucrative releases in subsequent windows, such as streaming, home video or television. MUBI in the UK is the prime arthouse cinema distributor and would likely be the port of call for world cinema aficionados. Amazon Prime also streams a selection of art cinema releases. Netflix might be more focused on popular genre cinema – and especially television and serial drama. However, there too, some noted films on MSHT and vulnerable migration have been released recently.

The selection that follows considers some recent films available via the Netflix and MUBI platforms. Although a fairly arbitrary selection, these have been chosen first due to the inventory available on the platforms and, second, given the contrasting nature of films (crudely, popular versus art cinema) associated with the two platforms. In line with the scope of this chapter, this is not intended to be exhaustive or representative of the streaming services in their entirety. This selection involves films that were available on these platforms at the time of writing, in August 2021.

Netflix

Atlantique (*Atlantics*, Mati Diop, 2019, see Figure 5.2) competed for the Palme D'Or at Cannes Film Festival, where Diop became the first Black woman director to vie for this prize. Diop is French-Senegalese and the film is shot in the suburbs of Dakar. Migration is a key theme in the film and it utilises the supernatural to figure and memorialise drowned refugees. The Atlantic

Figure 5.2: *Atlantique* (*Atlantics*, Mati Diop, 2019)

Source: Screenshot taken by the author

of the title is featured heavily in the film's cinematography, evoking Paul Gilroy's *Black Atlantic* (1993), albeit from within a Francophone culture. The film's poignant and suggestive use of haunting and the supernatural brings to mind Gordon's arguments in *Ghostly Matters*, that '[h]aunting is a constituent element of modern social life' (Gordon, 2008: 7), and applies it skilfully to the contemporary phenomenon of migration in Dakar.

Sudabeh Mortezai is an Austrian-Iranian filmmaker. Her 2018 film *Joy* is available on Netflix. The film is a gritty representation of the eponymous character from Nigeria, trafficked into debt peonage that is paid off through sex work in Austria. The film presents the grey zone between complicity and victimhood with the madam, who is a previously trafficked woman. The film highlights the lack of alternatives to Joy's life, which might lead to her being re-trafficked in the future. Nonetheless, solidarity between the women in the brothel, within limits, is evident and poignant. One of a number of Nigerian films recently receiving distribution on Netflix, *Òlòtūré* (Kenneth Gyang, 2019), exemplifies the 'New Nollywood' style pioneered by Kunle Afolayan that features glossy production values (see Agina, 2020). This is an involving film, which presents a slightly paternalist narrative of a naive female journalist under cover, over her head in investigating human trafficking; a male colleague desperately tries to rescue her from her predicament. The film does escape some of the Orientalising pitfalls of Western attempts to represent MSHT, also thanks to the involvement of the almost exclusively Nigerian cast and crew. *Òlòtūré* is impressive for its refusal to marginalise trafficked women in a popular culture narrative, since they receive decent characterisation, dialogue and screen time. This is remarkable despite the fact that the plot does reduce their agency by the later stages. Towards the end of the film, the journalist joins the other women trafficked in a situation that is entirely orchestrated by the traffickers.

It remains, in this section, to mention other films on the Netflix platform that feature MSHT as a narrative device with which to deliver the action and mystery/thriller genres (Purse, 2011). This aligns them with a film such as *Taken*, discussed earlier. Here, the trafficking plot is rather subservient to the spectacle of combat, athletic stunts and car chases. Reviews of these films in the mainstream press will often cite the 'important message' implied by the inclusion of a wider social issue. The films are, at the same time, evaluated in terms of their delivery of familiar generic pleasures, involving mystery, suspense and fight scenes. Generally, the familiar criticisms of these films are: that they risk trivialising the issue at hand; they pretend to provide magical solutions delivered by kinetic action heroes; and they tend to reduce the agency of those trafficked by rendering them helpless and in need of rescue. This does not however entirely negate their worth in bringing attention to MSHT; but the understanding the audience will derive from such material is limited. As stated earlier, what is lost in nuance is gained in reach, on this dominant platform – so even if narratives are problematic, they contribute to the visibility of MSHT in the public sphere, nonetheless.

One example of action-based films is *I Am All Girls* (Donoval Marsh, 2021), a South African film, in which human trafficking features as part of a mystery/police procedural narrative. The film features some interesting characterisation – albeit with some stock types such as the driven workaholic, rogue cops, the steady boss who wishes to keep a check on his headstrong subordinates. The rather lurid plot involves complicity between child traffickers and politicians during the apartheid-era regime in South Africa. Another example is *Furie* (Lê Văn Kiệt, 2019, see Figure 5.3) that

Figure 5.3: *Furie* (Lê Văn Kiệt, 2019)

Source: Screenshot taken by the author

features a debt collector (the athletic Veronica Ngô) who needs to rescue her daughter, who has been abducted by organ traffickers. Ngô herself acknowledges the influence of *Taken* on the film narrative (Lee, 2019); the result was the highest grossing domestic film ever at the Vietnamese box office. Finally, *Darc* (Nick Powell, 2018) is an independent US action thriller, with the protagonist of the film rescuing the kidnapped daughter of an Interpol agent abducted by the Yakuza (an organised crime trope). The focus on suspense, action and revenge might leave little room for nuance in these particular film examples, although the first two are noteworthy in terms of their crossover to international audiences. *I Am All Girls* and *Furie* do have the virtue of bringing popular cinema from South Africa and Vietnam to audiences who may never have been exposed to films from these countries. I am pointing this out also to avoid over-contrasting Netflix too rigidly (as the mainstream, 'popular' streamer) with MUBI (as the 'international', arthouse one).

MUBI

MUBI might be seen as intuitively a more likely platform on which to view more complex representations of MSHT on screen, given its prevalent focus on international arthouse cinema, sometimes perceived as less formulaic. MUBI currently hosts documentaries such as *El Sicario: Room 164* (Gianfranco Rosi, 2010) and *Overseas* (Yoon Sung-A, 2019). The first of these features an anonymous former assassin who worked for a Mexican drug cartel while serving on the police force. The interviews take place in the hotel room (room 164), in which the subject of the interview carried out killings and torture, which he recounts during the course of the film. The gang trafficked in drugs, but was involved in prostitution too, and some of the violence the gangster recounts was inflicted on women. *Overseas* (Yoon Sung-A, 2019) features Filipino women who migrate in order to enter domestic service abroad. This film represents the preparation that the women undergo, which frankly acknowledges the abuse that they might receive in their service. The dangers are explained during the training by women who have previously entered this line of work. Interviews with the women reveal that they will be leaving their children and families behind in order to undertake these positions. The spectre of domestic servitude is clearly entertained by the film. In one revealing scene, the women are taught self-defence in order to repel unwanted sexual advances by potential employers. In this film, as with Rosi's, the viewer's awareness that we are watching documentary, rather than fictional narratives, adds to the credibility of the representations on screen, given the conventional (albeit questionable) belief that documentary is more truthful than fiction film.

Figure 5.4: *Purple Sea* (Amel Alzakout, 2020)

Source: Screenshot taken by the author

To reconnect with migration, discussed in the section on Netflix, an example on the MUBI platform is the Finnish director Aki Kaurismäki's films dealing with this theme. His 2017 film, *Toivon tuolla puolen* (*The Other Side of Hope*) is one of these. The film features a Syrian asylum seeker and Iranian refugee as well as the Finnish businessman who befriends the former. As with many of his films, it mixes quirky comedy with serious subject matter. Although trafficking is not explicitly addressed in the film, migration themes make this interesting from the perspective of the transnational phenomena on screen addressed in this chapter.

Finally, and perhaps most interesting of all, MUBI have recently offered the film *Purple Sea* (Amel Alzakout and Khaled Abdulwahed, 2020, see Figure 5.4) on the platform. This is a film whose production history is a story in itself, since it derives from mobile phone footage shot by the director Amel Alzakout when the smugglers' boat for her own Mediterranean crossing capsized. This left her floating in the sea along with the other migrants. Alzakout is a Syrian artist, and her film, just over an hour long, is more akin to experimental or 'artist's' cinema. However, the film is also an example of the trend for 'migrant media', whereby the accessibility of devices means that migrants themselves can capture their experiences and produce their own representations (Hegde, 2016). Alzakout's harrowing footage, which is often submersed, recording legs suspended in the ocean, is combined with her own prose and poetry, with a simultaneous immediacy (the 'now' of the life-threatening event) and temporal dilation through reminiscence and hope for the future. As Rossipal, discussing this and other films, has recently observed:

Instead of reproducing spectacular crisis images, these filmmakers offer grounded and intimate perspectives on migration in the Mediterranean region. By attuning the viewer to alternative ways of seeing and listening, they enact what I would term a 'poetics of refraction,' a slowed-down and angled articulation that enacts a careful attention to mediation and materiality. (Rossipal, 2021: 35)

The long takes derived from a mobile phone tied to the filmmaker's wrist provide footage that tends towards both ethnographic natural history documentary and poetic abstraction, were it not for the constant reminder of the horrendous event it records for the filmmaker. In this way, it entirely avoids the reductive tropes of mainstream migrant and MSHT cinema while foregrounding the physical, embodied experience of the migrant-filmmaker.

Conclusion

This has inevitably been a brief survey of MSHT on screen, informed by historical and representational perspectives, while attempting to provide a snapshot of relevant recent film releases on streaming services. I am wary of providing a linear narrative of putative improvement from an early and then 'mainstream' cinema to a more recent set of examples that are more 'progressive'. Some of the analysis of popular action films, especially those on Netflix, indicates continuities of current cinema with the *Taken* template. The survivor-produced films are an important and fascinating recent phenomenon; however, the 'mainstream' type persists and thrives alongside the more 'progressive' type of which the former are examples. There are sometimes opportunities for more nuanced and authentic representations in cinema, but they are often cyclical. For instance, the European migrant cinema of a decade ago was received as a generally progressive cinema as regards migrants (Berghahn and Sternberg, 2010; Loshitzky, 2010). However, such cinema is at the mercy of popular taste for European films as opposed to those of the Hollywood mainstream. It has been increasingly difficult for them to obtain distribution to English-speaking audiences since then.

For film studies, MSHT narratives are often of interest for those who study transnational cinema, European cinema or who perhaps have an interest in film festivals, and in the non-theatrical circuit or 'useful cinema' that is used for informational rather than entertainment purposes (Acland and Wasson, 2011). It has often been left for academics more closely researching MSHT as such to propose the wider significance of media representations more generally, but here I will finish with some brief proposals for practice and policy.

At the level of pre-production and development, filmmakers and screenwriters should develop projects that elucidate the *structural* bases that contribute to MSHT, tracking the wider spatial contexts of migration and exploitation that feed into it. Making these links clear in an accessible way helps audiences to perceive the complexity of issues that are otherwise easily oversimplified into stereotyped narratives and characterisations. To incorporate such contextual information in screen narratives is to participate in a process of 'cognitive mapping' (Jameson, 1991: 51). Jameson's argument is that contemporary postmodern culture almost defies representation to track the complexity of global capitalism. Films that attempt to link conventional spectatorial involvement in character, plot and emotion with attention to the complex and global contexts in which MSHT take place would be in the service of public awareness.

Regulators might contribute to this more structural representation of MSHT via including guidance on the representation of MSHT as well as the standard MSHT policies expected of public organisations. The British Film Institute (BFI) includes diversity requirements as part of bids from filmmakers for funding; the BFI (or in the EU, Eurimages and MEDIA) might consider whether separate guidance should be issued for representations of MSHT, as well as wider representations of migrants, asylum seekers and refugees, even if these do not constitute formal requirements for funding bids. The National Union of Journalists in the UK and the United Nations High Commissioner for Refugees have issued guidance on reporting on migration; given the prominence of vulnerable migration and MSHT in contemporary cinema, guidance might be extended to screen media too. Film Festivals, from the London Migration Film Festival to the RENATE Film Festival, as well as strands such as Human Rights Day at the Sarajevo Film Festival, might be supported by those interested in the field, as a way to promote public awareness.

Compared with some of the more immediate concerns presented in this volume, an attention to film and media representations of MSHT will understandably seem a less urgent concern. Even so, it is to be hoped that a case has been made, in this chapter, for the relevance of the cinema discussed here and an attention to the contexts in which MSHT are mediated and discussed, and the wider impact that popular culture representations may have towards public awareness and the public sphere. The salience of these issues – and perceptions of them – for the public, in turn feeds into policymaking and the urgency with which the issue is treated by government and civil society. If this is the case, then particular interventions at the level of film narratives produced, and at the level of the institutions that foster and distribute cinema, might contribute to supporting a welcoming climate for survivors and victims of MSHT.

References

Acland, C.R. and Wasson, H. (eds) (2011) *Useful Cinema*. Durham, NC: Duke University Press.

Agina, A. (2020) *Toolkit: Southern Nigerian Cinema*. London: SOAS & European Commission. Available from: https://screenworlds.org/resour ces/southern-nigerian-cinema/ (accessed 21 August 2021).

Andrijasevic, R. (2014) The figure of the trafficked victim: Gender, rights and representation. In M. Evans, C. Hemmings, M. Henry, H. Johnstone, S. Madhok, A. Plomien and S. Wearing (eds) *The SAGE Handbook of Feminist Theory*. London: SAGE, pp 359–73.

Berghahn, D. and Sternberg, C. (2010) *European Cinema in Motion: Migrant and Diasporic Film in Contemporary Europe*. Basingstoke: Palgrave Macmillan.

Bottomore, T. (1999) The panicking audience? Early cinema and the 'train effect'. *Historical Journal of Film, Radio and Television*, 19(2): 177–216.

Diffee, C. (2005) Sex and the city: The white slavery scare and social governance in the progressive era. *American Quarterly*, 57(2): 411–37.

Doezema, J. (2000) Loose women or lost women? The re-emergence of the myth of white slavery in contemporary discourses of trafficking in women. *Gender Issues*, 18(1): 23–50.

Elsaesser, T. (1991) Tales of sound and fury: Observations on the family melodrama In M. Landy (ed) *Imitations of Life: A Reader on Film and Television*. Detroit, MI: Wayne State University Press, pp 68–91.

Gilroy, P. (1993) *The Black Atlantic: Modernity and Double Consciousness*. London: Verso.

Gordon, A. (2008) *Ghostly Matters: Haunting and the Sociological Imagination*. Minneapolis: University of Minnesota Press.

Gunning, T. (1990) The cinema of attractions: Early film, its spectator and the avant-garde. In T. Elsaesser (ed) *Early Cinema: Space, Frame, Narrative*. London: BFI, pp 56–62.

Hansen, M. (1994) *Babel and Babylon: Spectatorship in American Silent Film*. Cambridge, MA: Harvard University Press.

Hegde, R. (2016) *Mediating Migration*. Cambridge: Polity.

Iordanova, D. (2010) Making traffic visible, adjusting the narrative. In W. Brown, D. Iordanova and L. Torchin (eds) *Moving People, Moving Images: Cinema and Trafficking in the New Europe*. St Andrews: St Andrews Film Studies, pp 84–117.

Jameson, F. (1991) *Postmodernism, or The Cultural Logic of Late Capitalism*. Durham, NC: Duke University Press.

Kelly, C.R. (2014) Feminine purity and masculine revenge-seeking in *Taken* (2008). *Feminist Media Studies*, 14(3): 403–18.

Kenway, E. (2021) *The Truth About Modern Slavery*. London: Pluto.

Lee, J.-L. (2019) Action star Veronica Ngo kicks butt on and off screen. *Korea JoongAng Daily*, [online] 6 November. Available from: https://koreajo ongangdaily.joins.com/2019/11/06/movies/Action-star-Veronica-Ngo-kicks-butt-on-and-off-screen-The-Vietnamese-actors-film-Furie-is-a-huge-hit-all-around-the-world/3069929.html (accessed 21 August 2021).

Loshitzky, Y. (2010) *Screening Strangers: Migration and Diaspora in Contemporary European Cinema*. Bloomington and Indianapolis: Indiana University Press.

Mulvey, L. (1975) Visual pleasure and narrative cinema. *Screen*, 16(3): 6–18.

Nail, T. (2015) *The Figure of the Migrant*. Stanford: Stanford University Press.

Neale, S. (2000) *Genre and Hollywood*. London and New York: Routledge.

Nichols, B. (2017) *Introduction to Documentary*. Bloomington, IN: Indiana University Press.

O'Connell Davidson, J. (2015) *Modern Slavery: The Margins of Freedom*. Basingstoke and New York: Palgrave.

Purse, L. (2011) *Contemporary Action Cinema*. Edinburgh: Edinburgh University Press

Rodríguez-López, S. (2018) (De)constructing stereotypes: Media representations, social perceptions, and legal responses to human trafficking. *Journal of Human Trafficking*, 4(1): 61–72.

Rossipal, C. (2021) Poetics of refraction: Mediterranean migration and new documentary forms. *Film Quarterly*, 74(3): 35–45.

Said, E. (1978) *Orientalism*. New York: Pantheon.

Stamp, S. (2000) *Movie-Struck Girls: Women and Motion Picture Culture after the Nickelodeon*. Princeton: Princeton University Press.

Torchin, L. (2010) Traffic jam: Film, activism, and human trafficking. In W. Brown, D. Iordanova and L. Torchin (eds) *Moving People, Moving Images: Cinema and Trafficking in the New Europe*. St Andrews: St Andrews Film Studies, pp 218–36.

Vance, C.S. (2012) Innocence and experience: Melodramatic narratives of sex trafficking and their consequences for law and policy. *History of the Present*, 2(2): 200–18.

Filmography

Atlantique (Atlantics). 2019. [Film]. Mati Diop. dir. France, Senegal & Belgium: Les Films du Bal, Cinekap, Frakas Productions, Arte France Cinéma & Canal+.

Birth of a Nation. 1915. [Film]. D.W. Griffith. dir. USA: David W. Griffith Corp.

Darc. 2018. [Film]. Nick Powell. dir. USA: Hollywood Media Bridge, Inner Media & Julius R. Nasso Productions.

Deliver Us From Evil. 2020. [Film]. Hong Won-Chan. dir. South Korea: Hive Media Corp.

El Sicario: Room 164. 2010. [Film]. Gianfranco Rosi. dir. USA & France: Robofilms & Les Films d'Ici.

Furie. 2019. [Film]. Lê Văn Kiệt. dir. Vietnam: Studio 68.

I Am All Girls. 2021. [Film]. Donovan Marsh. dir. South Africa: Nthibah Pictures.

Inside of the White Slave Traffic, The. 1913. [Film]. Frank Beal. dir. USA: Moral Feature Film Co.

Joy. 2018. [Film]. Sudabeh Mortezai. dir. Austria: FreibeuterFilm & Österreichischer Rundfunk.

Lilya 4-ever. 2002. [Film]. Lucas Moodysson. dir. Sweden & Denmark: Memfis Film, Film i Väst, Sveriges Television, Zentropa Entertainments, Svenska Filminstitutet & Det Danske Filminstitut.

Limbo. 2020. [Film]. Ben Sharrock. dir. UK: Film4 Productions, Creative Scotland, British Film Institute & Caravan Cinema.

Nanook of the North. 1922. Robert J. Flaherty. dir. USA: Revillon Frères.

Òlòtūré. 2019. [Film]. Kenneth Gyang. dir. Nigeria: EbonyLife Films.

Overseas. 2019. [Film]. Yoon Sung-A. dir. Belgium & France: Clin d'oeil Films, Centre de l'Audiovisuel à Bruxelles, Clin d'Oeil, Iota Production, Les Productions de l'Oeil Sauvage & Michigan Films.

Purple Sea. 2020. [Film]. Amel Alzakout & Khaled Abdulwahed. dir. Germany: ZDF/Arte.

Taken. 2008. [Film]. Pierre Morel. dir. France: EuropaCorp, M6 Films, Grive Productions, Canal+, TPS Star & M6.

Toivon tuolla puolen (The Other Side of Hope). 2017. [Film]. Aki Kaurismäki. Finland & Germany: Sputnik, Bufo & Pandora Film.

Traffic in Souls. 1913. [Film]. George Loane Tucker. dir. USA: Independent Moving Pictures Co. of America.

Transporter, The. 2002. [Film]. Corey Yuen & Louis Leterrier. dir. France: EuropaCorp, TF1 Films Production, Current Entertainment & Canal+.

6

Discursive representations of 'invisible migrants' in British social media

Thi-Diem-Tu Tran and Karen Sanders

Introduction

Human trafficking and undocumented migration[1] are closely intertwined. Although the two phenomena have different political implications (Väyrynen, 2003), there are clear intersections between these phenomena. In this chapter, we approach trafficking, and modern slavery, from the viewpoint of the broader British public debate on undocumented migration. In the most general terms, undocumented migration refers to either unlawful residence, unauthorised employment or border crossing, without valid travel documents (Vollmer, 2014). In light of increased border controls that manage migration flows worldwide, more migrants are forced to turn to the services of smugglers who facilitate their unlawful move across borders (Jesperson et al, 2019 and Chapter 1). Human trafficking and people smuggling constitute different legal categories.[2] In reality, however, both practices often intersect, as undocumented migrants frequently engage in exploitative work during their journey in order to be able to pay for their further migratory movement.

Modern slavery and human trafficking (MSHT) can occur at different points along a migrant journey which makes individuals susceptible to exploitative work conditions and hence puts them into the category of MSHT. One of the drivers of human trafficking is the demand for cheap and illegal labour (Arlacchi, 2011). Employment without authorisation reflects a connection between low-paid work in the informal economy, exploitation and a sense of the powerlessness of undocumented migrants living in illegality (Lewis and Waite, 2019). Given that little regulation of the labour force exists in the informal economy, migrants who work in this economy may be more at risk of being exploited by unscrupulous employers. The absence of a work permit could exacerbate their disadvantaged position, for example, in cases where employers impose poor work conditions or threaten migrants with denouncing them to officials. The fear of being detected by authorities can also prevent migrants from negotiating higher incomes or better work conditions. Put differently, the 'invisibility' of undocumented migrants in the receiving society can enhance their vulnerability of becoming victims of potential traffickers who facilitated their entry into the destination country in the first place (Forgione, 2011). Undocumented migrants usually have little chance of being granted asylum, for example due to strict legislation, and may turn to organised crime gangs to find work (Väyrynen, 2003; also Chapter 8, this volume). This interdependence between criminal groups and migration highlights the fact that undocumented migrants could be susceptible to a range of violations of human rights and MSHT risks, including forced labour (see also Chapter 7, this volume).

In relation to the UK, studies have shown that the exceptional vulnerability faced by migrants partly results from the policy measures introduced by the Conservative government targeting specifically the group of undocumented migrants (Lewis and Waite, 2019). Everyday border practices have been part of the so-called 'hostile environment policy' in the context of the Immigration Acts of 2014 and 2016 that are explicitly directed at undocumented migrants in the area of banking, unauthorised work, housing and healthcare (Lewis and Waite, 2019). Under these laws, authorities are allowed to imprison migrants for illegal work, close bank accounts of foreigners with uncertain migration status and penalise landlords for renting accommodation to foreigners without a residence permit (Gadd and Broad, 2018). Several other scholars (Broad and Turnbull, 2018; Skrivankova, 2019; Van Dyke, 2019) emphasise the tensions between restrictive immigration and counter-trafficking policies in the UK, especially with the introduction of the offence of 'illegal working' in 1996. This offence reinforces the power imbalance between employers and migrant workers by making it a criminal offence to employ an immigrant who does not have the right to work or stay in the country.

The political focus on combating undocumented migration resulted in a criminalisation of those trafficked migrants in the area of forced labour (see Chapter 8, this volume). It has also created a paradox between addressing the needs of trafficked people and controlling undocumented migration. In other words, stricter immigration laws in destination countries that target undocumented migration are criticised for creating a 'lucrative market for traffickers' who feel impelled to use more drastic measures in order to 'overcome the barriers that are needed for making a profit' (Väyrynen, 2003: 6). Similarly, others have stressed that the UK government consistently fails to address these elements of their immigration policy that create trafficking risks for vulnerable workers (McQuade, 2019). More specifically, the political construction of a 'threat of illegal migrants' fails to acknowledge that undocumented migration can be a source of trafficking itself, as it 'causes increasing of criminal activity, breach of competitive market, and destroying respect to human right and civil society' (Mehdiyev, 2011: 87). Again, this is largely due to the fact that the illegal status of migrants makes them more vulnerable to exploitation by traffickers. Roberts (2019: 151) poignantly argued that 'the UK government's deliberate creation of an environment that is "hostile" to "illegal workers" is one example of how, while rightly declaring outrage at those who abuse and enslave others, the UK has created a space in which criminals can more easily exploit people with insecure immigration status'. People with insecure immigration status are potentially a highly vulnerable and invisible group (see Chapter 7, this volume); nevertheless, we find that this group has been very visible in British media coverage.

Little knowledge exists on public views towards undocumented migrants and how people regard the state's responses, with most previous research limited to newspaper analyses. These studies emphasised a widespread negative portrayal of migrants as cultural and security threats (Allen, 2016; Gray and Franck, 2019). Social media presents an additional rich source to traditional media (see Chapter 5, this volume), but its potential to unveil the public discourse on undocumented migration remains largely untapped. As other scholars have recognised, social media form a key platform for the expression of public opinion and people participate in this public discourse by sharing, liking or re-posting (Anstead and O'Loughlin, 2015; Vollmer and Karakayali, 2017). They are, then, vital for contemporary discourse research.

This chapter is concerned with the analysis of the discourse on undocumented migration, as a complex socioeconomic phenomenon that is closely linked to MSHT. Data source is the social media website Facebook between 2015 and 2018 in the British context. This time period covers the heightened public interest in migration following the so-called 'migration crisis' in Europe. The selected period is significant as migration became a paramount public concern after the arrival of the unprecedented number of 1.2 million migrants in 2015 (Rea et al, 2019). Moreover, migration was a crucial factor influencing the outcome of the British European Union (EU) referendum in 2016, which decided that the UK would leave the EU. Both events are expected to have caused an increasing interest in migration among the online press and social media users/commenters.

In the following parts of the chapter, we will first present our data source and analytical methods; then discuss our analysis chronologically by highlighting how the discursive representation of undocumented migrants changed from 'intrusive' migrants (2015) to significant threats for the British population (2016), and finally to unwanted but insignificant strangers (2017–18).

Social media discourse on undocumented migration: data source and analysis

Studies show that people in the UK increasingly use social media in their daily lives in general, including for news consumption (Nielsen, 2017; Jigsaw

Research, 2019). In the UK, Facebook ranked second as the most popular social media website in 2020, with over 35 million users (Statista, 2021). A survey conducted in 2016 highlighted that 28 per cent of British people get their news from Facebook (Nielsen, 2017). Indeed, it has been shown that Facebook is one of the most widespread online social media platforms with regard to news and information consumption in general (Housley et al, 2014; Ernst et al, 2017). Despite the fact that the British media landscape is changing in the face of the aforementioned rise of digital developments, the mainstream newspapers still occupy a leading position in public debate and policy narratives (Allen, 2016; Allen and Blinder, 2018).

In recognition of the importance of both traditional newspapers and social media, our study has incorporated the analysis of digital version of news articles published by British newspapers on their Facebook accounts. The Facebook account of each newspaper was examined and the articles on undocumented migration were searched using the available search engine on the account's page. This chapter is based on a study where 244 online newspaper articles and 22,967 corresponding comments published on Facebook have been gathered and analysed (Tran, 2021). These two Facebook datasets were selected to acquire a rounded view of the interrelationship between newspapers' media coverage of undocumented migration and public opinion. Both datasets were systematically sampled and checked for appropriateness to make sure that they fulfil the criteria of interest for this study. These consisted in references to undocumented migration in the British and European context published between 2015 and 2018. Following Allen (2016), the ten newspapers selected represent a range of different types of publication (broadsheets, tabloids and midmarket papers), of political affiliation (left-wing, centre and right-wing) of the British press and all have a wide circulation. Although British newspapers are not explicitly affiliated with a political party, they are tilted to various ideological orientations (Allen and Blinder, 2018):

- left-wing – *Daily Mirror, Guardian, Independent*;
- centre – *Financial Times*; and
- right-wing – *Express, Daily Mail, Daily Star, Sun, Telegraph, Times*.

Qualitative and quantitative methods were used to analyse both online newspaper articles and corresponding comments of social media users. This study used Critical Discourse Analysis which is an interpretive and explanatory analytical approach that explores the relationship between discourse and reality in a particular context (Regmi, 2017). Critical Discourse Analysis assumes that power relations operate and are perpetuated in a tacit way in society and can be investigated through the analysis of different forms of discourses. Furthermore, this study uses quantitative analytical methods located in corpus linguistics, which aim at identifying word patterns as well as frequencies in textual data and in doing so strengthens the legitimacy of the research and complements the qualitative Critical Discourse Analysis.

The invader during the 'migration crisis'

The majority of the migrants who reached and travelled through Europe during the European 'migration crisis' did not possess authorised travel documents (Rea et al, 2019). Both media attention and political responses across Europe depicted the arrival of this type of migrant as a 'crisis' situation in 2015. As a consequence, this event was in essence represented as a time of intense difficulty for European societies (Dines et al, 2018). Findings of this study show that the general macro-structure of the British news reportage of undocumented migration reflected this sociopolitical context and predominantly featured the discourse of 'chaos' and 'crisis' in 2015. In particular, the absence of a coordinated migration policy at EU level was expressed in a media perception of political 'chaos', which painted a picture of an uncontrollable group of undocumented migrants who attempted to enter the UK at all costs. In this light, it is noticeable that the online British press analysed in this study paid special attention to the entry of undocumented migrants into the UK by focusing on the topics of 'smuggling' and 'trafficking'. Issues around the trafficking and smuggling industry were particularly raised in tandem with allegedly rising numbers of migrants. Migration facilitators – interchangeably referred to by the media as 'smugglers' and 'traffickers' – were mostly held responsible for the arrival of undocumented migrants in 2015.

The negative press depiction of undocumented migrants was adopted by the responding social media users with an overall focus on the discourse of the foreigners' unlawful entry. The perceived rise in the number of undocumented migrants to the UK was seen by commenters as worrying and linked to the notion 'we are full'. 'Us' and 'Them' as identity categories were frequently constructed to emphasise the inability of the British society to accept more migrants arguing that too many of 'Them' were already in the country. Negative outgroup representation that focuses on portraying foreigners as an uncontrollable and undesirable social group is a typical feature of populist discourses on undocumented migrants (Moffitt, 2016; also Chapters 5 and 7, this volume). Furthermore, among the social media comments analysed, the argument prevailed that migrants were accepted if they came through legal routes. The group of 'legal migrants' was described, in several comments, as superior to the group of 'illegal migrants' who were charged for circumventing immigration laws and disparaging the efforts of their 'legal' counterparts. The notion of the 'bad illegal migrant' was strongly associated with economic migrants, who were attributed negative features and intentions. Social media commenters mainly argued that most undocumented migrants were economic migrants who were not in need of asylum as they did not remain in the so-called 'first safe country'. This is based on the logic that individuals who seek asylum should have stayed in the country that they first passed through in which it was safe for them to apply for refugee status.

Overall, varying definitions and levels of acceptance of refugees and asylum seekers were identified in this study. The analysis shows that social media users tended to associate undocumented migrants with not only one specific migrant group, but with various migrant groups, such as asylum seekers or refugees. However, it is notable that victims of trafficking were not explicitly considered as a potential subgroup of undocumented migrants by the British newspapers and Facebook commenters. However, the right-wing newspapers generally pointed out the issue of undocumented migrants being taken advantage of in several accounts. For example, the media adopted a critical stance towards British landlords by arguing that a new tenancy law, as part of the Immigration Act 2016, also aimed at cracking down on rogue British landlords. The latter were believed to exploit vulnerable migrants by profiting from their undocumented situation. The following news excerpt illustrates the critical attitude of the press towards British landlords: 'A new Immigration Bill, which will be outlined in next week's Queen's Speech, will include tougher powers for councils to tackle unscrupulous landlords and to help honest landlords evict illegal migrants quicker' (*Daily Mail*, 2015). This argumentation is in line with left-wing newspapers' reportage, which expressed disapproval of unwelcome consequences of this new law for migrants. By incorporating the voices of lawyers, charities and the British National Landlord Association, the left-wing press stressed that this new policy would drive migrants into the hands of even more exploitative landlords. The use of negative attributions for British landlords directed readers' attention towards a critical view of their own ingroup by suggesting that landlords were biased and tended to prefer White tenants. In a similar vein, social media commenters expressed opposition towards British landlords who were referred to as 'worse than the worst criminals', in the words of a commenter. The discourse about British landlords potentially capitalising on the vulnerability of undocumented migrants reflects the fact that this migrant group usually lives on the margins of society, seeking to remain undetected (Thorbjørnsrud, 2015). In line with what we have already argued in the introduction to this chapter, undocumented migrants are more dependent on social networks and informal markets in order to find housing and employment. This dependency entails the risk of exploitation and other forms of abuse, putting them in a precarious situation without access to civil rights (Benhabib, 2004).

The enemy: the European Union referendum and the fixation on criminals

In 2016, the key political event in the British context was the outcome of the EU referendum which determined the UK's exit from the EU. In the second part of the campaign, Brexit advocates began to focus on issues of immigration, demanding to take back control in this area of policy where they felt the EU had failed them (Baston, 2017). British governments frequently expressed the desire to tackle migration in anti-immigration agendas that fuelled fears of being swamped by migrants of different cultures (Bennett, 2018). The British Conservative Party promised, in 2010, to reduce the level of net migration to the tens of thousands by 2015, when the then Home Secretary Theresa May introduced the aforementioned 'hostile environment policy' (Allen and Blinder, 2018). In fact, most Britons thought that May would not fulfil her commitment and reduce the net migration rate to tens of thousands in the following five years (Ipsos MORI, 2017). In this sense, an Ipsos MORI study concluded that the EU referendum partly reflected the loss of patience among the public in relation to unachieved immigration targets.

In line with this, our study found that the right-wing British press dominated the news coverage in 2016 and tended to represent migrants in connection with their unlawful entry into the UK as a problem. The discourse of unlawful entry of migrants considered mostly the perspectives of politicians and citizens who were quoted arguing that smugglers and gangs took advantage of loose border controls and deliberately exploited the British coasts. In this regard, the general issue of human trafficking was raised by the media and accentuated along with the increasing numbers of those entering illegally in the previous few years. Although human trafficking was linked to the rise of undocumented migration, the press did not discuss any details or specific concerns about those trafficked. Instead, the news coverage continued to be unsympathetic towards undocumented migrants by drawing on reports about foreigners already residing in the UK and by focusing on crime-related issues. Newspapers frequently reproduced negative stereotypes of migrants as benefit frauds or criminals. For example, the media stressed that organised gangs were very adaptive and succeeded in their illegal cross-border activities to smuggle arms and people including potential terrorists. This finding created an overall picture of an illegitimate outgroup that incited outrage and resentment among the readers against the migrants. This was based on the argument that the British government failed to prevent their unauthorised entry.

Similar to the right-wing newspapers, security concerns were raised by commenters of the newspapers' Facebook pages particularly, again, in terms of fears related to the arrival of potential terrorists among undocumented migrants. In line with the content of the newspaper articles, a considerable number of comments were concerned with the control of undocumented migration and the failure to fulfil this task:[3]

> The Cameron government are doing absolutely nothing to increase border control staff to protect us.

> Who is to be blamed in that case? Not only the murderer but also the law; the Government and the Immigration authorities. UK an open arm country for criminals because the law over here protects them. Call it free movement. Who knew who knows what filthy diseases they are bringing here probably deliberately infected then sent here Who let them in?

These comments expressed the desire for more restrictive policy measures with the aim of reducing the number of migrants. Among the social media comments, repeated calls were made demanding the government to care for and protect its own citizens first, while arguing that those states where migrants entered European territory first should have accepted them: 'Who makes rules where people who pay into a system don't always get the help they need yet illegal immigrants milk the country and get away with everything. France, they are in your Country … the first safe Country they arrived at … they are your responsibility.'

All newspapers across the political spectrum continuously represented the government in a negative fashion. Even though with different foci, the left- and right-wing newspapers voiced strong criticisms about the migration policy and overall handling of migration-related issues by the British government:

> The Home Office does not know how many migrants are working illegally in the UK and previous estimates vary considerably. In 2009 the London School of Economics put the figure at between 373,000 and 719,000, while Migration Watch UK suggested that it was more than 1.1 million. (*The Times*, 2016)

> Don't help the state bully migrants – boycott the school census. … Today brought confirmation of what we at the Against Borders for Children campaign have suspected for months: the government is trying to make schools part of its agenda to create a 'hostile environment' for migrants accused of entering the country illegally. (*The Guardian*, 2016)

The government's management of issues associated with undocumented migration was strongly criticised, in particular the lack of prevention of unlawful entry of migrants and the perceived neglect of its duty to represent the interests of British nationals. Although some articles also aimed to re-establish public confidence in the government's ability to tackle undocumented migration, all newspapers analysed in this study held the government accountable for failing to gain control over undocumented migration into the UK: 'NHS spent £181,000 treating just one illegal immigrant; Leading cancer specialist claims migrants are putting "unsustainable" strain on NHS' (*Telegraph*, 2016). Previous research confirms that the political responses to undocumented migration are chiefly concerned with border surveillance and control (Green and Grewcock, 2002; Väyrynen, 2003). In doing so, migration, and undocumented migration in particular, are securitised and ultimately presents migrants as a danger for the receiving state and its people. Green and Grewcock (2002) point out that undocumented migrants are constructed as a threat to the receiving country and the sinister image of a 'trafficker' is being used by policymakers to justify penalties and restrictive measures aiming to deter undocumented migration.

Human trafficking in the UK context must, therefore, be understood within a public and political environment that is hostile towards immigration as a potential facilitator of trafficking (McQuade, 2019). Despite the fact that trafficking in human beings and undocumented migration are interlinked, the policy landscape in the UK strongly separates trafficking from undocumented migration by showing compassion for innocent victims of trafficking and criminalising the 'undeserving' undocumented migrant (Lewis and Waite, 2019).

The insignificant stranger: post-European Union referendum years

In this study, 2017 and 2018 are jointly referred to as the 'post-EU referendum' period. In this period, news coverage primarily represented undocumented migrants as 'insignificant strangers'. The number of new migrants arriving in the UK and EU continuously declined in these years with the political and public attention equally shifting away from undocumented migration. The year 2017 saw a stark decrease in the number of migrants entering the EU resulting from its political agreement with Turkey (Salter, 2017). This deal required the return of individuals from Greece to Turkey who arrived in Greece irregularly. In the meantime, the EU promised, *inter alia*, financial support for the Turkish government for the provision of humanitarian aid for refugees in Turkey. The decline in the number of migrants in Europe is reflected in the significantly lower number of published newspaper articles on undocumented migration in this year. The media interest in undocumented migration diminished. The left-wing newspaper, *The Guardian*, dominated the news coverage on undocumented migrants in 2018. The remaining news reports published on Facebook were covered by right-wing papers which continued to feature predominantly anti-immigration topics and, to a lesser degree, the plight of migrants. An interesting finding is that a number of themes that were already prevalent in the British press in 2015 and 2016 continued to attract media attention in 2017. Within a persistent antipathetic representation of migrants and a macro-argument that illegal entries require a robust state response, the themes included crimes associated with undocumented migrants, unlawful entry, weak border controls and the plight of migrants. However, it must be noted that the statistics given by the newspapers were not as alarmist and the British press was generally more sympathetic towards migrants compared to the previous two years.

The right-wing newspapers frequently depicted nationals as empathic and understanding towards undocumented migrants, characterising the outgroup as scared and desperate. Several other news articles featured the plight of migrants by providing details about the nature of the smuggling industry in relation to what groups are involved, what methods migrants use for hiding and the harsh travel conditions in lorries. Furthermore, acting in the interest of migrants, the *Express* featured accounts of non-governmental organisations (NGOs) and officials who blamed the British government for jeopardising the safety of minor migrants in Calais. This discourse was based on the argumentation that the British government changed a law which made it impossible for these migrants to be accepted as refugees in the UK: 'But some unaccompanied minors have returned to Calais, which is just 33km from Britain, after learning they would not be allowed to enter the UK under a change to immigration law which permits the country to take in vulnerable unaccompanied child refugees' (*Express*, 2017). In this way, a sense of urgency to protect the outgroup's rights was generated by claiming that the British government's move represented a failure to protect 'a handful' of minor migrants. The right-wing press emphasised that these children were at high risk of falling into the hands of traffickers. Although this representation clearly reflects a mistrust towards the British government and their values on the rights of minors, the press did not explicitly discuss the structural causes of the vulnerability of undocumented migrants and the risk of becoming trafficked due to their 'insecure migration status', as discussed.

Left-wing newspapers mainly covered instead hardships experienced by undocumented migrants ranging from life-threatening journeys and difficult living conditions to unjust treatment by government representatives. A number of comments reacting to the humanitarian news discourse showed a similar sense of solidarity with the outgroup. For example, they emphasised the vital contribution of migrants to Europe's economy: 'It needs more and more immigrants to keep their societies alive. Without migration, European societies and economies would bleed to death.' Furthermore, negative ingroup representation was used by commenters to criticise other social media users for stereotyping all migrants as criminals, or to condemn

British employers for exploiting these non-nationals by paying them low wages. Some arguments adopted the perspective of undocumented migrants by accusing British citizens and companies of exploiting undocumented migrants. These comments stressed that the Conservative government did not have measures in place to stop this exploitation. Migrants were repeatedly perceived as vulnerable human beings, who struggled to survive and did not deserve to be taken advantage of. The internal diversity within the ingroup was further expressed in accounts in which British employers and landlords were frequently designated as greedy and perceived as wealthy nationals. They were believed to exploit undocumented migrants for financial gain, as shown for the data of the year 2015. However, it is striking that the vulnerability of undocumented migrants to trafficking remained absent among commenters.

McQuade (2019) argues that the public and media discourse on trafficked people, which primarily aims at supporting victims of trafficking, tends to be centred around the notion of an innocent victim that strongly focuses on minors and women. This victim discourse is problematic for various reasons. First, it can exclude other trafficking experiences that do not fit this category, for example, trafficked men who work as cannabis gardeners (McQuade, 2019). As a result of this one-dimensional discursive focus, men are less identified and protected as victims of trafficking. The complex realities of trafficked people are generally overlooked. Second, Gadd and Broad (2018) point out that the 'politics of pity' neglects the difficulties that migrants face in general, such as uncertain migration status, violation of human rights and access to legal protection. In addition, this rhetoric creates a notion of 'deservingness' of certain groups and tends to view others, such as undocumented migrants, as less deserving of help, as they allegedly engaged in unlawful entry themselves. In other words, this binary discourse starkly delineates innocent victims of trafficking who are worthy of human rights from a larger group of culpable undocumented migrants who are regarded by definition as 'lawbreakers' and complicit in their struggles (Gadd and Broad, 2018, see also Chapters 7 to 9, this volume).

Conclusion

This study found that the sociopolitical context played a pivotal role in the news coverage on undocumented migration and the responding online comments. Contrary to popular opinion (YouGov, 2018), the British media reportage and readers' respective evaluations on Facebook were not entirely negative towards undocumented migration. They, however, consistently rose and fell with the changing sociopolitical environment over the selected time span. There was a shift in the social media construction from the undocumented migrant representing a 'significant enemy' to an 'insignificant stranger' in 2017 and 2018. Particularly in 2015 and 2016 (that is, those years in which the topic of undocumented migration was most salient in the news compared to the following two years), the British press orchestrated the theme of undocumented migration as a pressing security-related concern. This was also a crucial time in which migration in general was a top political issue with regard to the European 'migration crisis', as well as the EU membership referendum in the UK.

The pejorative social representation of undocumented migrants in the news was strongly mirrored by the comments of social media users. The most noticeable way social media users referred to migrants was in the form of strong disapproval by insulting migrants or supporting their deportation. Additionally, undocumented migrants were collectively compared to the ingroup – that is the British citizens – as unwanted competitors when it comes to access to accommodation and jobs. Overall, the comments revealed a strong sense of urgency to protect the ingroup, which was seen as more important than safeguarding the human rights of undocumented migrants.

Although some newspaper articles briefly mentioned that migrants could turn to traffickers in their despair, the vulnerability of undocumented migrants and the specific risks of becoming trafficked were not sufficiently considered by the online British press and the commenters. In fact, the analysis of the online press coverage on Facebook in relation to undocumented migration, and the corresponding readers' comments, highlighted that there is a stark 'silence' over trafficked people in the online discourse on undocumented migration. Within the broad pejorative social representation, the online British press expressed some empathy towards undocumented migrants. However, migrants' vulnerability resulting from their 'illegality' was not explicitly considered as a potential risk for trafficking and ongoing abuse.

Even though the British immigration enforcement efforts still aim at disrupting the lives of undocumented migrants, there is little evidence that these measures are successful in identifying them or reducing their number (Düvell et al, 2018). From this standpoint, the political strategy of combat is believed to be counterproductive and ultimately nourishes undocumented migration that it initially intended to reduce. Furthermore, the logic behind such policy seems to assume that those who adopt irregular methods of travel are less likely to be in real need of protection. This understanding runs the risk of obfuscating the detrimental effects of strict border controls, namely that migrants continue to migrate but under more dangerous conditions, which in turn makes them reliant on smugglers and traffickers (IOM, 2013; Huot et al, 2016). As a result, individuals in urgent need of protection continue to be subject to potential exploitation and violence (Castles, 2004; Aliverti, 2012).

On the one hand, we therefore argue that it is crucial for British policymakers to reconsider the UK government's hostile approach to undocumented migration and ensure that migration policies do not create an underclass of non-citizens (Düvell et al, 2018). Migration policies should also avoid fuelling limited and hostile public understandings of undocumented migration. On the other hand, we suggest that media outlets could reassess their portrayal of undocumented migration. This is often pejorative, and the press should ensure that trafficked migrants are recognised as one of the most vulnerable groups among undocumented migrants. Moreover, we also encourage NGOs and other organisations that support victims of MSHT to emphasise, in public debates, that there is a thin line between undocumented migration and trafficking in practice. It is necessary to point out that the everyday exclusion of undocumented migrants – exclusion from civic rights and access to state services and exclusion from the territory in the form of deportation – render them 'invisible' individuals. Conversely, it could also lead to victims of trafficking being treated as unwanted undocumented migrants first, and then remain undetected and unprotected workers.

Acknowledgements

We would like to thank Sasha Jesperson and Carole Murphy for their helpful comments at various points in the development of the first author's PhD research on which this book chapter is based.

Notes

[1] It must be noted that the term 'illegal' has been the subject of controversial debate since it frames the migrant as an 'illegal human being' and signifies criminality (Vollmer, 2014). For the purposes of this chapter, we have chosen to use the term 'undocumented' to highlight the vulnerability of this group regarding their limited access to rights and protection.

[2] In legal terms, people smuggling is defined as a crime against the state as it takes place without legal permission across national borders and with the consent of those being smuggled. In contrast, human trafficking is understood as a crime against the individual who is being exploited against their will in their country of origin or in another country (for a more detailed discussion see Jesperson et al, 2019). It is important to clarify that human trafficking may be domestic as well as international; even if we only consider cross-national cases of trafficking, they are not a subset of undocumented migration. As shown in this chapter, trafficking and undocumented migration share demonstrated links, with similar push and pull factors that leave migrants vulnerable to victimisation. However, there are numerous cases of trafficking where migrants are documented.

[3] It must be noted that the selected comments in this chapter are presented as they appeared in the original posts and thus might include spelling, grammatical or other phrasing errors. Details about the comments such as publication date or location of post are not included to protect the identity of the commenters.

References

Aliverti, A. (2012) Exploring the function of criminal law in the policing of foreigners: The decision to prosecute immigration-related offences. *Social and Legal Studies*, 21(4): 511–27.

Allen, W.L. (2016) *A Decade of Immigration in the British Press*. Oxford: Centre on Migration, Policy, and Society (COMPAS), University of Oxford.

Allen, W.L. and Blinder, S. (2018) Media independence through routine press-state relations: Immigration and government statistics in the British press. *International Journal of Press/Politics*, 23(2): 202–26.

Anstead, N. and O'Loughlin, B. (2015) Social media analysis and public opinion: The 2010 UK general election. *Journal of Computer-Mediated Communication*, 20(2): 204–20.

Arlacchi, P. (2011) Time has come to abolish the new slavery. In M. Coen (eds) *Human Trafficking, Smuggling and Illegal Immigration*. Amsterdam: IOS Press, pp 36–43.

Baston, L. (2017) Western and Southern Europe: United Kingdom. In D.S. Lewis and W. Slater (eds) *The 2017 Annual Register: World Events 2016*. Michigan: ProQuest, pp 10–23.

Benhabib, S. (2004) *The Rights of Others: Aliens, Residents, and Citizens*. Cambridge: Cambridge University Press.

Bennett, S. (2018) New "crises," old habits: Online interdiscursivity and intertextuality in UK migration policy discourses. *Journal of Immigrant and Refugee Studies*, 16(1–2): 140–60.

Broad, R. and Turnbull, N. (2018) From human trafficking to modern slavery: The development of anti-trafficking policy in the UK. *European Journal on Criminal Policy and Research*, 25(1): 119–33.

Castles, S. (2004) Why migration policies fail. *Ethnic and Racial Studies*, 27(2): 205–27.

Daily Mail (2015) 20,000 living in rabbit-hutch rooms in just one borough! *Daily Mail* [online] 22 May. Available from: https://www.dailymail.co.uk/news/article-3091950/20-000-live-rabbit hutch-rooms-just-one-borough-Number-living-multiple-occupation-70-times-estimate.html (accessed 23 August 2021).

Dines, N., Montagna, N. and Vacchelli, E. (2018) Beyond crisis talk: Interrogating migration and crises in Europe. *Sociology*, 52(3): 439–47.

Düvell, F., Cherti, M. and Lapshyna, I. (2018) *Does Immigration Enforcement Matter (DIEM)? Irregular Immigrants and Control Policies in the UK*. Oxford: Centre on Migration, Policy, and Society (COMPAS), University of Oxford.

Ernst, N., Engesser, S., Büchel, F., Blassnig, S. and Esser, F. (2017) Extreme parties and populism: An analysis of Facebook and Twitter across six countries. *Information Communication and Society*, 20(9): 1347–64.

Express (2017) Britain has FAILED to protect migrants and FUELS human trafficking, French official claims. *The Express* [online] 6 January. Available from: https://www.express.co.uk/news/world/749782/child-migrants-risk-human-trafficking-Calais-Britain-immigration-laws (accessed 23 August 2021).

Forgione, F. (2011) Mafia export. In M. Coen (ed) *Human Trafficking, Smuggling and Illegal Immigration*. Amsterdam: IOS Press, pp 157–61.

Gadd, D. and Broad, R. (2018) Troubling recognitions in British responses to modern slavery. *British Journal of Criminology*, 58(6): 1440–61.

Gray, H. and Franck, A.K. (2019) Refugees as/at risk: The gendered and racialized underpinnings of securitization in British media narratives. *Security Dialogue*, 50(3): 275–91. doi: 10.1177/0967010619830590.

Green, P. and Grewcock, M. (2002) The war against illegal immigration: State crime and the construction of a European identity. *Current Issues in Criminal Justice*, 14(1): 87–101.

The Guardian (2016) Don't help the state bully migrants: Boycott the school census. *The Guardian* [online] 1 December. Available from: https://www. theguardian.com/commentisfree/2016/dec/01/bullying-migrants-boyc ott-school-census (accessed 23 August 2021).

Housley, W., Procter, R. and Edwards, A. (2014) Big and broad social data and the sociological imagination: A collaborative response. *Big Data & Society*, 1(2): 1–15.

Huot, S., Bobadilla, A., Bailliard, A. and Rudman, D.L. (2016) Constructing undesirables: A critical discourse analysis of 'othering' within the Protecting Canada's Immigration System Act. *International Migration*, 54(2): 131–43.

IOM (2013) *The Essentials of Migration Management: A Guide for Policy Makers and Practitioners volume I, II, III.* Available from: https://docplayer.net/13791 561-Essentials-of-migration-management.html (accessed 18 July 2021).

Ipsos MORI (2017) Most think Theresa May will not achieve her target to cut net migration to the 'tens of thousands'. *Ipsos MORI*. Available from: https://www.ipsos.com/ipsos-mori/en-uk/most-think-theresa-may-will-not-achieve-her-target-cut-net-migration-tens-thousands (accessed 16 April 2019).

Jesperson, S., Henriksen, R., Barry, A.-M. and Jones, M. (2019) *Human Trafficking: An Organised Crime?* London: Hurst & Company.

Jigsaw Research (2019) News consumption in the UK: 2019. *Ofcom*. Available from: https://www.ofcom.org.uk/__data/assets/pdf_file/0027/ 157914/uk-news-consumption-2019-report.pdf (accessed 20 July 2021).

Lewis, H. and Waite, L. (2019) Migrant illegality, slavery and exploitative work. In G. Craig, A. Balch, H. Lewis and L. Waite (eds) *The Modern Slavery Agenda: Policy, Politics and Practice in the UK*. Bristol: Policy Press, pp 219–42.

McQuade, A. (2019) Modern slavery in global context: Ending the political economy of forced labour and slavery. In G. Craig, A. Balch, H. Lewis and L. Waite (eds) *The Modern Slavery Agenda: Policy, Politics and Practice in the UK*. Bristol: Policy Press, pp 29–46.

Mehdiyev, F. (2011) Human trafficking in and around Russia. In M. Coen (ed) *Human Trafficking, Smuggling and Illegal Immigration*. Amsterdam: IOS Press, pp 85–96.

Moffitt, B. (2016) *The Global Rise of Populism: Performance, Political Style, and Representation*. Stanford: Stanford University Press.

Nielsen, R.K. (2017) Where do people get their news? The British media landscape in 5 charts. *Medium*. Available from: https://medium.com/oxford-university/where-do-people-get-their-news-8e850a0dea03 (accessed 14 March 2018).

Rea, A., Martiniello, M., Mazzola, A. and Meuleman, B. (eds) (2019) *The Refugee Reception Crisis in Europe: Polarized Opinions and Mobilizations*. Brussels: Université de Bruxelles.

Regmi, K.D. (2017) Critical discourse analysis: Exploring its philosophical underpinnings. *Méthod(e)s: African Review of Social Sciences Methodology*, 2(1–2): 93–107.

Roberts, K. (2019) Human trafficking: Addressing the symptom, not the cause. In G. Craig, A. Balch, H. Lewis and L. Waite (eds) *The Modern Slavery Agenda: Policy, Politics and Practice in the UK*. Bristol: Policy Press, pp 145–66.

Salter, J.-P. (2017) The European Union. In D.S. Lewis and W. Slater (eds) *The 2017 Annual Register: World Events 2016*. Michigan: ProQuest, pp 367–77.

Skrivankova, K. (2019) The UK's approach to tackling modern slavery in a European context. In G. Craig, A. Balch, H. Lewis and L. Waite (eds) *The Modern Slavery Agenda: Policy, Politics and Practice in the UK*. Bristol: Policy Press, pp 243–60.

Statista (2021) *Social Network Penetration in the United Kingdom (UK) 2020*. Available from: https://www.statista.com/statistics/284506/united-kingdom-social-network-penetration/ (accessed 23 August 2021).

The Telegraph (2016) NHS spent £181,000 treating just one illegal immigrant. *The Telegraph* [online] 21 March. Available from: https://www.telegraph.co.uk/news/nhs/12199883/NHS-spent-181000-treating-just-one-illegal-immigrant.html (accessed 23 August 2021).

Thorbjørnsrud, K. (2015) Framing irregular immigration in Western media. *American Behavioral Scientist*, 59(7): 771–82.

The Times (2016) 'One million' migrants in UK illegally. *The Times* [online] 3 August. Available from: https://www.thetimes.co.uk/article/a-million-migrants-in-uk-illegally-twn2mhjh7 (accessed 23 August 2021).

Tran, T.-D. (2021) Shifting views on irregular migration during a time of socio-political change: A critical analysis of press and social media discourses in the UK, 2015–2018. Unpublished PhD thesis, St Mary's University, London.

Van Dyke, R. (2019) The UK's response to modern slavery: Law, policy and politics. In G. Craig, A. Balch, H. Lewis and L. Waite (eds) *The Modern Slavery Agenda: Policy, Politics and Practice in the UK*. Bristol: Policy Press, pp 47–74.

Väyrynen, R. (2003) *Illegal Immigration, Human Trafficking, and Organized Crime.* United Nations University, World Institute for Development Economics Research, Discussion Paper No. 2003/72.

Vollmer, B.A. (2014) *Policy Discourses on Irregular Migration in Germany and the United Kingdom.* New York: Palgrave Macmillan.

Vollmer, B.A. and Karakayali, S. (2017) The volatility of the discourse on refugees in Germany. *Journal of Immigrant and Refugee Studies*, 16(1): 1–22.

YouGov (2018) *Where the Public Stands on Immigration.* Available from: https://yougov.co.uk/topics/politics/articles-reports/2018/04/27/where-public-stands-immigration (accessed 17 July 2021).

7

Racialising and criminalising vulnerable migrants: the case of human trafficking and modern slavery

Neena Samota and Debbie Ariyo

Introduction

The 'racial other' – on the move, at the border or in detention – is without rights and liberty compared to the White citizen. In the context of mass mobility and social change, it will be helpful to demonstrate how racism and concepts of race are used to justify enforcement policies that continue adversely to affect non-White populations. Recent academic literature not only draws out practices of detention and border controls that criminalise certain types of migrants, but equally problematises the absence of race and racism in migration research. In the UK and European social context, where stark racial inequalities persist, the focus in migration research has shifted from race and ethnicity to social cohesion and integration policy (Erel et al, 2016). These contemporary debates are bound with the broader realm of citizenship characterised by practices of inclusion and exclusion of individuals by the state. Studying the connections between race, migration and borders helps make the point that racism persists and does not differentiate between racialised citizens and migrant non-citizens. Nation-state sovereignty is based on the right to police borders. But borders facilitate and 'preserve racial and colonial hierarchies' (Parmar, 2020). While race remains relevant in shaping migrant experiences, the intersecting dimensions of gender, age, nationality and economic status equally shape the migrant experience both at and inside the border.

This chapter aims to engage critical race theory (CRT) and postcolonial scholarship in criminology to show how experiences of Black children and women are not prioritised in addressing modern slavery and human trafficking (MSHT). This issue adversely affects men too, but the scope of this chapter does not permit engagement with it. Our contribution aims also to show that strategies of support from statutory and charitable organisations fail to draw attention to race and forms of racialisation. The passage of the UK Modern Slavery Act in 2015 promised tough justice for offenders charged with modern slavery offences. The Act committed the UK government and criminal justice agencies to stamp out slavery and address the sexual exploitation, domestic servitude and forced labour of adults and children trafficked into the UK (see Chapter 8, this volume). This coincided with a rapid growth in charitable organisations specialising in tackling modern slavery in the UK (Gadd and Broad, 2018). These organisations have gradually increased their role in multi-agency work with statutory partners in making referrals to the National Referral Mechanism, the UK system of assistance to potential and confirmed victims of MSHT. The charitable sector, however, lacks racial and ethnic diversity; this was highlighted in an action plan for the sector published by the Black and Minority Ethnic Anti- Slavery Network (BASNET) (2021). Another research report, *Home Truths* (Lingayah et al, 2020), illustrated the problem of race equity in the charity sector where racism remains a significant and unresolved problem. Outcomes on recruitment, retention and progression are worse in charities compared to the statutory and private sectors. The report recommended that diversity, equity and inclusion strategies should be embedded across the charity sector to address its diversity deficit and help reorientate charity work towards building a racially just society. This context, throughout the chapter, will help to draw out the centrality of race and racism in shaping the vulnerability of victims of MSHT.

We first expand on the theoretical groundings of this chapter. Secondly, drawing from the advocacy work of the charity AFRUCA, we present the case study of 'Jane', the pseudonym of a MSHT survivor. Details of the case have been provided by the second author who set up AFRUCA – Safeguarding Children, in 2001, following the death of Victoria Climbié, an eight-year-old Ivorian girl who was trafficked to the UK. Jane's case is used to illustrate the experiences of racism and the processes of racialisation that further marginalise young Black children and women like her. We draw out three themes for further analysis from an interview conducted with Jane in September 2021 in London. They are:

- exclusion and under-protection from mainstream narratives of safeguarding;
- not being believed by authorities when accounting for experiences of exploitation; and
- the pains of cultural oppression and dehumanisation.

Following the case study, we apply CRT to these three themes to frame the marginalisation faced by those who experience trafficking and exploitation in the UK. The discussion is further grounded in the conceptual framework of 'crimmigration' (the convergence of criminal law and immigration law): it utilises scholarship on policing migration in the UK to illustrate how criminalisation, race and gender intersect to oppress Black children and women. The chapter concludes by arguing that state and anti-trafficking charities should extend engagement within home and diasporic communities to widen the net of support for victims and survivors of MSHT. In devising culturally appropriate treatment and intervention for support, care and recovery, the statutory and mainstream charitable sectors must first address their own racial disparities. These sectors must improve engagement with Black, Asian, minority ethnic charitable and grassroots organisations, as well as diasporic communities.

Critical race theory and crimmigration

This chapter suggests that the practices of criminology and sociology fail to adequately address race when studying mass mobility, immigration and criminal justice. It also suggests that criminology, as an interdisciplinary field, can use CRT as a useful framework to understand criminalisation of migration within wider sociological processes (Sanchez and Romero, 2010). To do this also means to engage with the problematic relationship between criminology and colonialism. Postcolonial criminological scholarship (Agozino, 2004; Cunneen, 2013; King, 2017) helps to examine the colonial roots of structural racism in criminal justice institutions. To better understand contemporary forms of law enforcement and criminal justice policy and practice, the link to historic governance practices of colonial populations remains relevant.

A detailed elaboration of race relations is beyond the scope of this chapter, but remains essential to offer insights and signposts in recognising the complexity of racialisation and its intersection with immigration and criminalisation today. In a critical evaluation of race, ethnicities and the criminal justice system in the UK, Samota (2021) discusses how imperial powers, over three centuries, colonised different continents and established mechanisms to control and discipline indigenous populations with European ideas of punishment, penal law, justice and rule of law. These mechanisms were used to suppress powerless and marginalised populations in their own lands while disregarding their existing cultures and ways of life. In time, this domination was extended to enslave indigenous people and included the transatlantic slave trade. Scholarship on the legacy of slavery (Reece and O'Connell, 2016) shows that while colonialism was instrumental in creating race and racial categories, modern slavery continues to shape contemporary forms of disadvantage and dehumanisation of Black people (Samota, 2021). This resulted in the establishment of a racially ordered system: one that facilitates the progressive accumulation of advantage for privileged White people on the move, but also restricts, controls and punishes the racial other through immigration controls, surveillance and governance of migration.

In the period after the Second World War, Britain encouraged migration from the old and new Commonwealth countries to fill its postwar labour shortage. Those who arrived from the Caribbean, Africa and the Indian subcontinent experienced political and social rejection. A moral panic developed in the 1970s, stoked by politicians' speeches, that saw racial diversity as a threat to Britain's identity as a White nation. In response, the successive Immigration Acts of 1962, 1968 and 1971 brought restrictions on immigration, and the British Nationality Act 1981 removed the right of citizenship from those having acquired it through registration or naturalisation. Attempts to restrict movement through informal controls, using arbitrary mechanisms for discrimination (determining citizenship and residence rights), eluded scrutiny as they were not explicitly based on race. The problems faced by the Windrush generation in the UK today is a legacy of postwar immigration and nationality laws which have become increasingly hostile to the non-White and non-British migrant. This trend continues with the UK's Nationality and Borders Bill, currently (2022) being debated in parliament (see Introduction, this volume). This has raised several concerns: protection for migrant and asylum-seeking children and the undermining of rights of trafficked persons, which further increase the risks of exploitation, statelessness and deprivation of citizenship. This demonstrates how the racialised politics of citizenship is established and ongoing.

The distinct processes of crime control and migration control are intertwined in Western liberal democracies. As already discussed, a state's decision to include or exclude citizens and non-citizens has shifted over time and has generated debates over what constitutes a desirable or undesirable immigrant (see Chapter 6, this volume). Although overt forms of racism have receded, and race is one of the protected characteristics under the Equalities Act 2010, informal and covert forms of racism continue. The concept of crimmigration, popularised by Stumpf in 2006, is a useful starting point to understand how the application of criminal law is used to sift the desirable from the undesirable. While criminal and immigration streams are distinct legal domains, they both deal with the relationship between the individual and the state. Their gatekeeping role determines who belongs to society and who does not.

Research that explicitly connects the racialisation of immigration policy and practice to penal regimes and practices is emerging. It demonstrates how crimmigration facilitates criminalisation based on race in the context of movement across national boundaries. The seemingly neutral rhetoric and legal processes penalising criminal activity are deployed to frame non-citizens as possible security risks and of concern. This helps to mark undesirables. Recent scholarship (Aas and Bosworth, 2013; Aas, 2014; Bosworth et al, 2018) has drawn attention to criminalisation, policing of borders, punishment, deportation and social exclusion. Bowling's work (Bowling, 2013; Bowling and Westenra, 2018) explores how race shapes immigration policing, results in 'global apartheid' and inflicts border harms on migrants. Equally insightful is Dembour's (2015) work on immigration and the controversial nature of developing case law that allows – or does not – the unprivileged migrant to be within European borders. While Dembour's analysis does not deal with racism, it powerfully asserts that migrants are routinely denied human dignity and treated in discriminatory ways and therefore their human rights are frequently violated.

Drawing on the sociology of the state (Goldberg, 2008; Garner, 2015) and applying CRT to migration control (Romero, 2008), this chapter argues that in MSHT discourse, race remains implicit rather than explicit. While there are studies focused on trafficking as a gender issue, there is little discussion on how race and social marginalisation are stronger risk factors for trafficking. Evidence on policing of immigration and crime in the UK, and elsewhere in Europe, invokes race in ways that classify certain communities as suspect. Furthermore, the same communities experience harsh and dangerous conditions when fleeing persecution, seeking asylum and also in exercising their legitimate right to movement. MSHT are the new frontiers in creating victims, suspects and offenders (see, for example, Chapters 5, 8 and 9, this volume). Racialisation and racism are concepts that enable the interrogation of these overlapping categories.

AFRUCA and the case of Jane

Jane

In 2010, after delivering an anti-trafficking awareness raising session at a Nigerian church in North London, we received a telephone call from the church pastor a few weeks later to report a case of child trafficking in his church. He was worried about a 12-year-old girl who had been trafficked by some of his church members and he wanted her rescued. He also did not want it known that he had reported the case, due to the backlash he felt this would bring. We made a referral in writing to the responsible local authority, with follow-up phone calls. However, unbeknown to us, no action was taken by the statutory agency.

In 2015, five years later, a young woman was referred to our child protection service by another charity. We provided her with a range of services to help address the effect of her experiences of trafficking for forced labour, benefit fraud and sexual exploitation. The young person really struggled with the impact of her experiences. The path towards healing was slow and gradual but there was progress nonetheless.

In 2020, through a Freedom of Information Act request, we discovered that this young person was the same person referred to us by the church pastor in 2010. The local authority had failed to act to protect and rescue her, despite our referral and persistent follow-up. As a result, she was enslaved and exploited for a further five years. The young woman had also tried to escape and reported her case to the police who had failed to take any action against her traffickers, leading to her remaining enslaved for further years.

In February 2000, the news of the death of Victoria Climbié, an eight-year-old Ivorian girl who was trafficked to the UK, hit the nation. As more details of Victoria's short life and her death unfolded, it became apparent that she was trafficked into the UK to access state benefits and had suffered multiple forms of abuse. Despite frequent contacts with various agencies, her status as a child victim of trafficking was never detected.

In 2001, as a direct consequence of the death of Victoria and a deep concern for the safety of other newly arrived children in the UK, the second author of this chapter set up the charity AFRUCA – Safeguarding Children. It soon became apparent that cases like that of Victoria were not few and far between. There were other instances of children and young people trafficked into the UK for different forms of exploitation who could have been safeguarded and protected had the responsible agencies taken timely action. One such involved a young girl, here called 'Jane', whose case study is presented in the 'AFRUCA and the case of Jane' box and further explored in what follows.

Over the next 20 years, AFRUCA worked with more than 600 children and young people who were trafficked into the country for different purposes, notably sexual exploitation and domestic slavery. Most have been female, from Nigeria and other West African countries. Many of these young people experienced extensive abuse and trauma at the hands of their traffickers. AFRUCA's aim has been to provide succour and support to enable young people to recover from their traumatic experiences and rebuild their lives. It has provided a range of services, including one-to-one and group psychotherapeutic support, a befrienders support programme that pairs survivors with vetted community members, residential programmes that bring service users together to network and learn new skills, direct one-to-one support from case workers, and an arts-based skills-building programme that uses drama and music as a form of healing (see Chapter 12, this volume, in relation to experimental ways with post-MSHT healing).

A core feature of AFRUCA's work is the adoption of a culturally specific approach to ensure services are appropriate to the cultural needs of our users. This is facilitated by the engagement of staff from similar cultural and linguistic backgrounds who understand the cultural nuances involved in country-specific MSHT features. This approach has two aims: first, to build trust with the young people by taking into account their specific needs. The second aim is to counter a victim's possible negative perception of their cultural self-worth that could arise from the fact that traffickers are usually also from their culture.

The issues identified through Jane's case study are significant in understanding the dynamics of abuse, exploitation and trafficking of migrant children and women who are Black and whose vulnerabilities are not alleviated, but rather reproduced, through the operation of the criminal justice, social work, asylum and immigration systems (see also Introduction, this volume). The scope of this chapter does not permit a discussion of the social context of globalisation, poverty and attitudes towards sexual and gender-based violence and abuse. It interrogates, however, the failure to account for race and the problem of racism in the operation of these systems.

Hynes (2015) notes the gaps in the current discourse on trafficking and child protection in the UK, one of which is the failure to engage with the culturally distinct contexts from which children arrive in the UK (see also Chapter 8, this volume). To develop holistic responses to this form of exploitation it is essential to contextualise the constellations of vulnerabilities and protective factors for victims of MSHT. Similarly, Ariyo (2021) argues that attitudinal and definitional problems associated with human trafficking prevention, protection and recovery need to be addressed through effective engagement with, and inclusion of, diasporic communities in the UK. At present, support services for victims of trafficking are contracted to mainstream charitable organisations. Ariyo argues that these programmes do not employ diaspora engagement approaches to either of the distinct tasks of prevention and victim recovery. While Ariyo's research study (2021) aims to explore innovative community approaches to address the stigma, denial and isolation experienced by victims of child trafficking from Ghana and Thailand, it also proposes diaspora engagement as a preventive mechanism to dismantle the supply at source and demand in destinations like the UK.

The case study of Jane thus brings us back to note that problems in identifying trafficked children are influenced by several factors. These include migration controls that maintain racial and colonial hierarchies, asylum and immigration policies and the broader political context of control and deterrence. The cases of Victoria Climbié and Jane both show that, despite the Laming Inquiry Report, responses to tackle vulnerability of Black children (Garrett, 2006; Hynes, 2015) remain stuck between two approaches. One approach is that in which state agencies use coercive interventions in their approach to Black families, criminalising them in the process; and the other in which culturally relativist positions are used to justify a lack of support in protecting the best interests of children.

The following discussion uses these three themes that map experiences of racialisation and criminalisation in Jane's case-study journey of victimisation through to recovery:

- exclusion and under-protection from mainstream narratives of safeguarding;
- not being believed by authorities when accounting for her experiences of exploitation; and
- the pains of cultural oppression and dehumanisation.

Theme 1: Exclusion and under-protection

The trafficking of children and young people is a global social problem. In reviewing existing evidence and research (Samota, 2021), it is clear that discriminatory practices disproportionately stigmatise and criminalise young people from minority groups when they come into contact with the criminal justice system. More specifically, in relation to policing experience, children and young people from ethnic minority groups tend to be over-policed through the practice of stop and search and are more likely to be under-protected by police when they have been victims of crime (again more on this can be found in Chapter 8, this volume). Such disparate experiences continue in risk assessment and meeting culturally specific needs of offenders and victims from ethnic minority groups.

Jane's experience of feeling unprotected as a young Black female and victim of MSHT and sexual exploitation sheds light on how the intersections of race, age and gender heightens her vulnerability. Research in the US (Glover, 2008; Butler, 2015; Constance-Huggins et al, 2021) shows that Black girls, who face adverse childhood experiences including neglect, abuse, low educational outcomes, low self-esteem and poverty, are at greater risk of trafficking compared to their White counterparts.

> 'I felt like it was a crime to be Black, young and female. I used to watch the news and see how they used to talk about children like Madeleine McCann. Her case triggered a lot of things in me as I was still with my abusers when she went missing. Her story was on the news every day. I felt there was something wrong with me that no one was looking to rescue me from my abusers. There was no one in the news like myself being reported like that.' (Jane, September 2021, London)

In reflecting on her experience here Jane cannot help but compare her situation to the intensive search for Madeleine McCann who went missing in 2007. An official inquiry from the police was also launched, several years later, to investigate Madeleine's disappearance. Attempts to locate the missing White girl, while Jane was still being abused, forced her to think about her status. A key CRT tenet of Whiteness as privilege is discernible in Jane's reflection that "no one was looking to rescue me" and that "I felt like it was a crime to be Black".

Between 2010 and 2015, there were many missed opportunities by statutory authorities to recognise and support Jane as a victim of MSHT. Her experience not only bears out previous findings from research (Butler, 2015) that risk factors of child sex-trafficking disproportionately affect Black girls, but also that they become victims of sex-trafficking at a younger age compared to White girls. Here, CRT helps to explain the failure of statutory authorities to apply a more nuanced approach to recognise and understand the specific role of culture, race and racism in shaping Jane's experiences. The quote from Jane demonstrates how existing racial disparities and the prioritisation of mainstream narratives marginalise the lived experiences of Black children and women.

Theme 2: Not being believed

Accounts of not being believed by authorities in trafficking and exploitation cases are commonplace and well documented in policy and research reports and official inquiries and reviews. Garrett (2006) argues that a child's race, ethnicity and sense of communal belonging is integral to their sense of self. Jane's experience suggests that her self-esteem, confidence and agency have all been compromised.

> 'I used to think there was something wrong with me as a Black woman with all my experiences and it seemed no one believed me. It messes up with your sanity. It made me doubt myself and what I had been through at the hands of those people. When you are trying to get out of it and you are dealing with people who are supposed to be in a position to help and support you and they depend on you to do their job, forgetting you have already endured so much in your life, they re-traumatise you. The constant and repeated questioning makes you relive your experiences because you are being re-abused by a professional meant to help you.'
> (Jane, September 2021, London)

Jane's comments demonstrate her attempt to understand relationships in practice and in making sense of the social world around her. She tries to reconcile her underlying belief of what she should expect to happen with what in fact happens: "they re-traumatise you". This also reflects a lack of knowledge about her rights and protections to some extent. There is evidence of what Glover (2008) describes as 'double-consciousness', borrowing from W.E.B. DuBois, to refer to the importance of status and identity in a racially ordered society. As Jane is not a British citizen, her minority status makes her unsure about her rights. It also makes her recognise the limitations she experiences as a young Black woman when she feels "re-abused" by a professional meant to help her (see Introduction, this volume). In the immigration and asylum context there is evidence of professionals mistrusting and disbelieving accounts given by individuals in determining their migration status (Hynes, 2015). Such gaps are notable in social services as well. In critiquing the Laming Report on the death of Victoria Climbié (Secretary of State for Health and the Secretary of State for the Home Department, 2003), Garrett (2006) notes the lack of engagement with 'race' and the absence of contextualising the migration context in the inquiry. This is indicative of the neoliberal order in which White privilege is bolstered while migrants are viewed with suspicion and become the focus of punitive policy and media discourses.

A culture of disbelief and suspicion (again, see Chapter 9, this volume) is also perceptible in police investigations of trafficking cases involving children. In the case of *OOO* v *The Commissioner of Police for the Metropolis* (2011), four young Nigerian women, who had been trafficked into the UK as children and forced to work as unpaid servants, were awarded damages from the Metropolitan Police Service. Despite contacting the police on several occasions, they did not receive support or assistance. The High Court, in 2011, found the police in breach of Articles 3 (prohibition of torture) and 4 (prohibition of slavery and forced labour) of the European Convention on Human Rights. The second author Ariyo, who gave evidence at the hearing, noted that the version of events provided by the traffickers and exploiters was taken as truth over the claims of the young people. Lack of appropriate police investigation was due to this culture of disbelief. Jane's case is no different. If police perform their legal duty to safeguard ethnic minority victims of modern slavery, then legal action and court settlements will be unnecessary.

Both cases – Jane's and the four women in the court case – facilitate an understanding of the migrant experience in a country that has a history of racialising and excluding based on race, class, gender and citizenship. CRT's critique of liberal notions of equality can be applied to show how a culture of disbelief and hostile environment policies converge to obscure the daily organisational practices that systematically criminalise already racialised subjects.

Theme 3: The pains of cultural oppression and dehumanisation

Many countries afford special legal status to youth in determining the consequences of their behaviour and their level of responsibility and culpability. These legal and moral principles help protect children from criminalisation and safeguard them from harsh punitive sanctions. Removing considerations of childhood innocence, as a mediating factor in youth behaviour, is the phenomenon of 'adultification', which is well recognised in youth work. Race and gender in relation to this phenomenon is not as well researched, but there is evidence that adultification is more likely to apply to Black girls and boys.

According to Goldberg (2008), race should be made explicit in all public affairs of the state. The author warns that, if discussions of race disappear from the 'socioconceptual' landscape, then racisms get pushed out of existence. Goldberg notes that racism is a mode of 'racially driven subjection and exclusion, debilitation and humiliation, preference satisfaction and privilege' (Goldberg, 2008: 1715). How racial groups are framed and constructed affects how they are treated by the state and public services. When this is applied in the context of MSHT and exploitation, the negative social construction of Black girls leads to their treatment as adults, and they are dehumanised and not believed. Research (Butler, 2015; Constance-Huggins et al, 2021) shows that this process of adultification of Black girls excludes them from the universal notions of childhood innocence and heightens their vulnerability to MSHT and abuse.

Jane's account that follows encapsulates both cultural oppression and being dehumanised because of her race. When racialisation and criminalisation marginalise communities at societal level, it allows proliferation of bias and prejudicial behaviours. By dehumanising people through prejudice and discrimination, we make them blameworthy and leave them more susceptible to risk of victimisation.

'There should be better ways of asking questions of victims like myself. Asking someone at the start of getting help or escaping their abuser questions like what does your abuser look like undressed or does your abuser have a birth mark – all these questions are traumatising, and it is really sad a police officer can deem it fit to ask these questions of someone who has been abused.

The justice system, the legal system does not work for victims of trafficking who look like me. It looks like the system is put there against people like me. It seems the police are only interested in prosecuting the perpetrator and they do not care about the welfare of the victims.' (Jane, September 2021, London)

Jane's understanding of the system that "does not work for victims of trafficking who look like me" is evidence that race, experiences of racism and forms of criminalisation are insufficiently incorporated into child and victims safeguarding (Chapter 8, this volume). The interrogation and investigative techniques used by statutory and non-statutory organisations enhance the risk of perpetuating oppression and vulnerability. The need for healing and recovering for Jane also requires appropriate trauma-informed therapy and support. There is a deficit here too. Culturally appropriate and community-based trauma therapy for Black women and young people from other ethnic minority groups should be offered to victims and survivors. This issue is not widely discussed or understood (Pearce et al, 2009). Jane's account and previous inquiries and reports expose a contradiction between the ideal of equality and fairness and the reality that some groups are disadvantaged and seen as undeserving.

Conclusion

In this chapter, we have used CRT to unpick the social and legal construction of race and the attributing to groups of racially determined traits. We drew on both the conceptual and practical benefits of the CRT framework. The concepts of anti-essentialism and intersectionality are both important to CRT scholars. The former proposes that individuals comprise an accumulation of identities rather than a fixed one; the latter proposes that different features of individual identity intersect to produce different experiences for minority ethnic groups (see also Chapter 10, this volume, in relation to intersectionality and gender). For CRT theorists, racism is a normal feature of social relations. Formal equality laws marginalise and obscure wider social, political and economic inequalities. For the disciplines and practices of criminology and sociology, therefore, CRT is an important methodological framework that makes race salient by incorporating personal narratives and experiences of the marginalised and oppressed. It offers a toolkit to help understand, question and challenge racial oppression. In the UK, CRT is established in the study of education, but it can also prove useful in understanding racial disparities, ethnic disproportionality and unequal outcomes in criminal justice, social work, immigration and MSHT.

In relation to MSHT, the authors emphasise the importance of engaging with race and the processes of racialisation that individuals encounter in their daily interactions. Jane's case illustrated well that the fear of criminalisation undermines the development of social capital and feelings of trust and confidence. Vulnerability to racism and criminalisation has implications for individual wellbeing as well as for the wellbeing of communities in which they live. In light of this, we invite policymakers, researchers and practitioners in the statutory and charitable organisations involved in the MSHT sector to engage with these issues in order to improve policy and practice. With this in mind, BASNET, of which the authors are founders and members, have produced a race equality, diversity and inclusion action plan for the sector to improve approaches towards racial justice in the sector.

In nine distinct areas, BASNET offers recommendations to improve practice for stakeholders. They are targeted at a range of partners from modern slavery, human trafficking and migration-related sectors that work with victims who have experienced racialisation and criminalisation. To address these racial disparities requires the delivery of holistic solutions across the different systems in a systematic way.

1. Modern slavery policy and data collection should record and monitor decision-making outcomes by race, ethnicity, gender, age and nationality.

Such quantitative data help to contextualise race and place, and help address over- and under-representation.

2. Research strategies, approaches and methodologies should be informed by people affected by MSHT including those from ethnic minority backgrounds. Research outcomes should help inform strategies to address structural racism.

3. Law enforcement personnel should improve their knowledge of cultural factors affecting and shaping MSHT.

4. Identification and service provision for survivors should recruit specialists who engage in reflective processes in their engagement with victims and survivors to eliminate bias. Knowledge of service users will help plan for bespoke care and considerations relating to culture, faith and ethnicity.

5. Local authorities should provide access to care and support such that victims are prioritised and safeguarded. Care and support environments should be sensitive to race and cultural needs so that victims are not subjected to further marginalisation and oppression.

6. The immigration and law sectors should enable the establishment of an independent office to deal with racism complaints and other malpractices by legal practitioners. Legal aid funding and support should automatically be provided to victims.

7. Health provision should be available to victims and survivors, regardless of status, so they have access to specialist culturally sensitive and trauma-informed services.

8. All stakeholders should engage affected communities through working groups that encourage dialogue and help influence policy formulation. This includes victims, survivors, carers and grassroots organisations.

9. Charities should review their composition and staffing at all levels to increase representation and diversity and proactively encourage and develop leaders from ethnic minority groups. Charities that engage in direct or indirect service provision to victims and survivors should comply with the public sector equality duty.

The authors have tried to show that statutory and charitable organisations operating in the MSHT sector run the risk of perpetuating racialisation by retaining historic and general associations between race, migration and criminality rooted in everyday thinking. They rather should be at the forefront of breaking this association. To move forward, professional practitioners in the sector should better recognise the nuanced processes that reproduce racialised othering. Critical self-reflection by practitioners, utilising CRT as a tool, for example, will go a long way in reorienting their work in building a racially just society.

Acknowledgements

We would like to thank Runa Lazzarino for her comments on previous drafts of this chapter. We are also grateful to BASNET members and those who participated in drafting the race equality, diversity and inclusion plan for the sector. Their time, personal experiences and solutions for improving services to victims and survivors are invaluable. We are extremely grateful to 'Jane' for sharing her experiences for the case study presented in this chapter.

References

Aas, K.F. (2014) Bordered penality: Precarious membership and abnormal justice. *Punishment and Society*, 16(5): 520–41.

Aas, K.F. and Bosworth, M. (eds) (2013) *The Borders of Punishment: Migration, Citizenship, and Social Exclusion*. Oxford: Oxford University Press.

Agozino, B. (2004) Imperialism, crime and criminology: Towards the decolonisation of criminology. *Crime, Law and Social Change*, 41: 343–58.

Ariyo, D. (2021) *Diaspora Communities as Safety Nets in Protecting Child Victims of Trafficking*. The Winston Churchill Fellowship Trust. Available from: https://media.churchillfellowship.org/documents/Ariyo_D_Report_2019_Final.pdf

BASNET (The UK BME Anti-Slavery Network) (2021) *Promoting Racial Equality, Diversity and Inclusion*. Available from: https://bmeantislavery.org/wp-content/uploads/2021/07/BASNET-Race-EDI-Action-Plan.pdf

Bosworth, M., Parmar, A. and Vasquez, Y. (eds) (2018) *Race, Criminal Justice, and Migration Control: Enforcing the Boundaries of Belonging*. Oxford: Oxford University Press.

Bowling, B. (2013) The borders of punishment: Towards a criminology of mobility. In K.F. Aas and M. Bosworth (eds) *The Borders of Punishment: Migration, Citizenship, and Social Exclusion*. Oxford: Oxford University Press.

Bowling, B. and Westenra, S. (2018) A really hostile environment: Adiaphorization, global policing and the crimmigration control system. *Theoretical Criminology*, 24(2): 163–83.

Butler, C.N. (2015) The racial roots of human trafficking. *UCLA Law Review*, 62(6): 1464–516.

Constance-Huggins, M., Moore, S. and Slay, Z.M. (2021) Sex trafficking of black girls: A critical race theory approach to practice. *Journal of Progressive Human Services*, DOI: 10.1080/10428232.2021.1987755

Cunneen, C. (2013) Colonial processes, indigenous peoples, and criminal justice systems. In S.M. Bucerius and M. Tonry (eds) *The Oxford Handbook of Ethnicity, Crime, and Immigration*. Oxford: Oxford University Press, pp 386–407.

Dembour, M. (2015) *When Humans Become Migrants.* Oxford: Oxford University Press.

Erel, U., Murji, K. and Nahaboo, Z. (2016) Understanding the contemporary race-migration nexus. *Ethnic and Racial Studies*, 39(8): 1339–60.

Gadd, D. and Broad, R. (2018) Troubling recognitions in British responses to modern slavery. *British Journal of Criminology*, 58(6): 1440–61.

Garner, S. (2015) Crimmigration: When criminology (nearly) met the sociology of race and ethnicity. *Sociology of Race and Ethnicity*, 1(1): 198–203.

Garrett, P.M. (2006) Protecting children in a globalized world: 'Race' and 'place' in the Laming report on the death of Victoria Climbie. *Journal of Social Work*, 6(3): 315–36.

Glover, K. (2008) Citizenship, hyper-surveillance and double-consciousness: Racial profiling as panoptic governance. In M. Deflem (ed) *Surveillance and Governance: Crime Control and Beyond Sociology of Crime, Law and Deviance.* Bingley: Emerald Group Publishing, pp 241–56.

Goldberg, D.T. (2008) Racisms without racism. *Publications of the Modern Language Association of America*, 123(5): 1712–16.

Hynes, P. (2015) No 'magic bullets': Children, young people, trafficking and child protection in the UK. *International Migration*, 53(4): 62–76.

King, S. (2017) Colonial criminology: A survey of what it means and why it is important. *Sociology Compass*, 11(3), https://doi.org/10.1111/soc4.12447

Lingayah, S., Wrixon, K. and Hulbert, M. (2020) *Home Truths: Undoing Racism and Delivering Real Diversity in the Charity Sector.* London: Voice4Change England and ACEVO.

OOO v Commissioner of Police of the Metropolis [2011] EWHC 1246.

Parmar, A. (2020) Borders as mirrors: Racial hierarchies and policing migration. *Critical Criminology*, 28(2): 175–92.

Pearce, J.J., Hynes, P. and Bovarnick, S. (2009) *Breaking the Wall of Silence: Practitioners' Responses to Trafficked Children and Young People.* London: NSPCC and University of Bedfordshire.

Reece, R.L. and O'Connell, H.A. (2016) How the legacy of slavery and racial composition shape public school enrollment in the American south. *Sociology of Race and Ethnicity*, 2(1): 42–57.

Romero, M. (2008) Crossing the immigration and race border: A critical race theory approach to immigration studies. *Contemporary Justice Review*, 11(1): 23–37.

Samota, N. (2021) Race, ethnicities and the criminal justice system. In S. Case, P. Johnson, D. Manlow, R. Smith and K. Williams (eds) *The Oxford Textbook on Criminology*, 2nd edn. Oxford: Oxford University Press, pp 273–309.

Sanchez, G. and Romero, M. (2010) Critical race theory in the US sociology of immigration. *Sociology Compass*, 4(9): 779–88.

Secretary of State for Health and the Secretary of State for the Home Department (2003) *The Victoria Climbié Inquiry: Report of an Inquiry by Lord Laming*. Cm 5730. London: HMSO.

8

Victims perpetrating a crime: a critique of responses to criminal exploitation and modern slavery in the UK

Craig H. Barlow

Introduction

In April 2015, the UK government's much-anticipated Modern Slavery Act received Royal Assent. This had been a key component of the Modern Slavery Strategy (HM Government, 2014). The implementation and impact of the Act was reviewed 12 months later (Haughey, 2016). The review described the evolution of understanding, responses and practices by all agencies, but also identified uncertainties and constraints on investigators and the need for strategic development and improved statutory systems. Haughey recommended that the government provided effective training for professionals in relation not only to the legislation, but to investigation and identification, recording and presentation of evidence of exploitation in modern slavery offences.

The later Independent Review of the Act (Field et al, 2019) found uncertainty and confusion among key stakeholders was still prevalent. The review made 80 recommendations and stated that: 'the recommendations made in Caroline Haughey's 2016 Review of the Modern Slavery Act relating to training and the need for specialist advocates in modern slavery cases should now be implemented' (Field et al, 2019: 72). Haughey's identification of the training issue three years before was an early warning: despite a statutory framework that included definitions of slavery, servitude, forced and compulsory labour and trafficking, a lack of understanding of the phenomenon was hampering the application of this legislation and undermining the government's Modern Slavery Strategy. As both a researcher and practitioner, I have found that this has been most acute in the context of criminal exploitation (CE) (Barlow, 2019), despite the stated ambition of the UK government to lead the world in the fight against modern slavery (May, 2016; Gadd and Broad, 2018).

The nature and extent of the problem of CE has emerged over the past 12 years from within the research by, for example, Anti-Slavery International

(2014), ECPAT UK (2010) and the National Crime Agency (2015). Furthermore, illustrations of lived experiences of children and vulnerable people within mainstream news reports (Anti-Slavery International, 2014; Hirsch, 2015; see also Chapter 6, this volume), investigative documentaries (BBC, 2011, 2019) and films (Chapter 5, this volume) and local analyses (Knowsley Council, 2015; Dadabho, 2017) have given ample echo to the problem. Between April 2019 and October 2021, I undertook more than 60 assessments or provided case management advice for the courts, lawyers, social workers and police officers concerning both victims and perpetrators of modern slavery. At the time of writing, the UK government is yet to formulate an effective response to exploitation through CE.

While no definition of CE is set out in law (Setter, 2019; Turner et al, 2019), there is a statutory defence under section 45 of the Act concerning victims that have been forced to commit certain crimes. What constitutes 'exploitation', and where CE sits in relation to slavery, servitude and forced or compulsory labour and trafficking, is largely a matter of interpretation of the law. This results in widespread inconsistency in how CE and its victims are defined, described and identified (Field et al, 2019; Turner et al, 2019).

In this chapter, I argue that the criminal justice system (CJS) that should be prosecuting perpetrators of modern slavery is at odds with the civil justice system's duties to safeguard children and vulnerable adults. I begin the chapter with a broad overview of relevant conventions and protocols in relation to human trafficking. The evolution of definitions is described to explain some of the key concepts that underpin the UK response. In the following two sections, I argue that the Act and the whole UK strategy for modern slavery are seriously undermined by failing to integrate civil legal and criminal legal instruments, as well as statutory safeguarding systems and investigative procedures to address the problem as an output of systematic abuse and organised crime. Policies and safeguarding responses are critically evaluated to identify how implementation of existing tools and increased professional training can be improved by developing theory-informed practice. This chapter is rooted in my research using complex systems theory to develop a theoretical model, as well as in my practice experience as a professional investigator and expert witness to the criminal and civil courts.

'Modern' slavery: the emergence of the new construct

Numerous protocols, treaties and instruments for tackling forms of human trafficking have been developed since the historical abolition of slavery. While various definitions and instruments have been accepted or rejected in different jurisdictions, their relevance to the development of UK responses warrants consideration. In simple terms, the achievement of the abolition of the slave trade created an immediate opportunity for the emergence of an illicit trade in human beings. This trade and efforts to control it have led to evolving patterns of slavery, servitude, forced labour and exploitation in diverse contexts. What constitutes slavery today has therefore stubbornly resisted any neat description or definition.

From the Slavery Convention to the European Human Rights Convention

The term modern slavery risks creating assumptions that slavery in the 19th and 21st centuries are more similar than they really are. Phenomena that we can refer to as 'slavery' have changed and adapted through time; they are influenced by politics, cultural, social, moral or religious values, and other phenomena such as migration, war, colonialism and natural disaster. An understanding of the dynamics of modern slavery cannot be achieved without recognising these contexts (Lee, 2011).

The foundation for the prevention and suppression of the slave trade across the world and in colonial jurisdictions was the 1926 Slavery Convention. Crucially it defined slavery as 'the status or condition of a person over whom any or all of the powers attaching to the right of ownership are exercised'. Considerable progress was made by the International Labour Organization, which sought to build upon the 1926 Convention with the Forced Labour Convention of 1930, providing another pivotal definition of forced or compulsory labour: 'all work or service which is exacted from any person under the menace of any penalty and for which the said person has not offered himself voluntarily' (International Labour Organization, 1930). This definition introduced limitations to what constituted forced or compulsory labour but also made illegal the exaction of forced or compulsory labour a criminal offence (Article 25). Forced labour, and then later slavery and servitude, became a law enforcement and criminal justice issue.

The Universal Declaration of Human Rights (UDHR) of 1948 has been the keystone of the international human rights movement, incorporating both the 1926 Convention and the 1930 Forced Labour Convention. It clearly states in its article 4 that: 'No one shall be held in slavery or servitude; slavery and the slave trade shall be prohibited in all their forms' (United Nations, 1948). The Convention for the Protection of Human Rights and Fundamental Freedoms (the European Convention on Human Rights) came into force in 1953 and was the first instrument to give effect to certain of the rights stated in the UDHR and make them binding on signatories and established the European Court of Human Rights. Article 4 of the 1953 Convention went further than the 1948 Declaration of Human Rights, extending the statement of the UDHR Article 4:

1. No one shall be held in slavery or servitude;
2. No one shall be required to perform forced or compulsory labour.

The European Convention on Human Rights guidance (Council of Europe, 2005) on how to interpret Article 4 clarifies and explains that forced or compulsory labour includes any *work* or *service* and is not limited to manual labour (and therefore potentially incorporates forced criminal activities). 'Force' refers to control or constraint on the victim and compulsory refers to the imposition of 'any penalty'. That may include physical violence or restraint but may also include more subtle forms such as psychological coercion (which might include 'grooming' behaviour), or threats of violence or threat to denounce the victim to police or other authorities.

The Palermo Protocol and human trafficking

The development of human rights through these conventions has resulted in many of the fundamental principles that guide legislation, policy and practice in safeguarding people from exploitation, oppression and violence in the 21st century. However, the most recent international counter-trafficking tool, the Palermo Protocol, frames trafficking of women and children as an output of organised crime. By foregrounding the problem in terms of organised crime, responses have been those of law enforcement and prosecution which are concerned less with the rights and needs of victims than with establishing whether a crime has been committed, and if so by whom. All too often those who work within the CJS are uninformed about the causes and consequences of trafficking, and the appropriate rights-based legal responses (Jordan, 2002), a problem highlighted by both Haughey (2016) and the Independent Review (Field et al, 2019).

The Palermo Protocol provides the most widely accepted definition of human trafficking. It was one of three protocols that supplemented the United Nations Convention Against Transnational Organised Crime 2000. That this comprehensive and highly influential tool sits within that Convention is significant. The definition of human trafficking describes the transport of people, through whatever means, for the explicit purpose of exploitation, be that in the form of slavery, forced labour, servitude or some other form of exploitation. It extends the concept of 'force' to the recruitment and transportation *prior* to the exploitative activity. This effectively makes modern slavery a spectrum of exploitative activity that incorporates chains or networks of agents that variously gain from the exploitation (for example, as recruiter, transporters, facilitators).

Just as the Convention of 1926 overtly criminalised forced labour within any jurisdiction in which it occurred, the UN 2000 Convention and the Palermo Protocol situated human trafficking within the context of serious and organised crime. The Palermo Protocol has been criticised for its separation of trafficking from smuggling as somewhat binary, failing to clearly set out or accommodate the overlaps between illicit migration, smuggling and trafficking (Di Nicola, 2011; see Chapter 6, this volume). As Lazzarino and Greenslade also mention (Chapter 9, this volume), the Protocol's emphasis on women and children has gendered the problem of human trafficking and exploitation and contributed to a disproportionate emphasis in criminological research and policy on sexual exploitation of women and girls, at the expense of male victims and other contexts such as labour exploitation (Gozdziak and Vogel, 2020). Furthermore, this tool prioritises, as mentioned, a criminal justice response to human trafficking as an activity of organised crime over safeguarding victims (Schoaps, 2013).

The limits of the criminal justice approach to criminal exploitation

Instead of innovating new approaches to tackling human trafficking, the UK has emulated Europe and the UN by conceptualising what it has chosen to call modern slavery as primarily a criminal justice matter (Gadd and Broad, 2018), not a human rights one. This neglects the adaptive nature of the problem and the complex relational dynamics between victim, perpetrator and the context in which the exploitation occurs over time. The reductive, linear analysis applied by the UK CJS to the cases of CE is inadequate to address the experiences of a person who is both a victim and a perpetrator of a crime (Brotherton and Waters, 2013; Barlow et al, 2021).

What constitutes organised crime is widely contested (von Lampe, 2019) in terms of its aetiology, structure and activities, and the phenomenon is influenced by policing models in different countries and contexts (Sergi, 2017). Furthermore, whether victims are coerced and controlled to commit crimes is rarely easy to discern. The Convention Against Transnational Organised Crime defines an organised crime group or network in this way:

- A structured group of three or more persons;
- Existing for a period of time and acting in concert with the aim of committing one or more serious crimes or offences, in order to obtain, directly or indirectly, a financial or other material benefit. (United Nations Office on Drugs and Organised Crime, 2004)

While the Modern Slavery Act 2015 and the Serious Crime Act 2015 provide definitions, the complexities of such cases are not accounted for within this legal framework. The process of modern slavery is multifaceted, driven and shaped by relationships between victim, exploiter and their shared physical, social, economic and political environments (Di Nicola, 2011; Barlow, 2017). For professionals, to be able to identify, investigate and evaluate slavery, they must be able to understand its complexity. This requires theory which enables patterns of exploitation to be thought about and analysed (Barlow, 2019). Theory must inform policy and practice (Fairfax, 2017), which can be developed and nurtured through training and education. The benefit of theory-informed practice has been demonstrated in the context of both child safeguarding (Firmin, 2017) and public health approaches to the problem of child exploitation and modern slavery (Barlow, 2017, 2019), and gang violence (Harding, 2014).

The Palermo Protocol's definition of human trafficking and Article 4 of the 1953 Convention suggest that patterns of CE are consistent with human trafficking and forced and compulsory labour. A victim is recruited, transported, harboured and controlled for the purpose of undertaking criminal activity (labour and services). However, the line between victim and perpetrator becomes blurred due to the duality of the person's situation. As a result, the CJS's reductive linear analysis of criminal evidence and actions of the defendant is unconcerned with why the offence was committed, only whether it was committed and by whom. Victims of CE are a heterogeneous group who often defy assumptions about who is or is not a victim of exploitation (Gadd and Broad, 2018; Gregoriou & Ras, 2018) and occupy both victim and perpetrator spaces simultaneously (Pitts, 2007). This leaves criminal investigators and prosecutors with a dilemma: prosecute the obvious offence or investigate whether there is a modern slavery offence? The former is relatively easy, the latter much harder and requires knowledge, understanding and experience of the complexities and dynamics of modern slavery.

In my experience, this knowledge varies greatly and decision-making regarding prosecution of potential victims of trafficking is wildly inconsistent. When law enforcement agencies and criminal justice processes concentrate on prosecuting victims, rather than intervening to protect them and pursue the perpetrators, they become a part of an environment that remains conducive to exploitation. This system simultaneously fails to protect victims and make no impact whatsoever on perpetrators' criminal operations. Tackling modern slavery means recognising that organised crime is a safeguarding issue. Strategic responses must be predicated upon human rights and safeguarding principles that lead to better responses to trafficking, modern slavery and organised crime.

Criminal exploitation in the UK

Victims, offenders and organised groups

Having sketched the legislative backdrop in the previous section, I now expand more on CE. I frame CE as a pattern of abuse that emerges as an output of complex systems and relational dynamics between victims and motivated offenders, within a shared environment that is conducive to the exploitation over time. Obtaining victims for CE is not difficult for lone offenders, joint enterprise offenders or organised crime groups (OCGs).

However, I and other specialist practitioners have found that patterns may vary across regions and by crime type. Globally, particularly vulnerable groups (including migrants, as well as the street homeless, people in destitution, those with very low levels of education, affected by alcoholism and other addictions, those suffering from domestic violence, children with disabilities, neglected and abused children, and so on) have all been identified as especially vulnerable to exploitative predators (Shelley, 2010; Surtess, 2005). Research relating to youth violence and gang involvement (Pitts, 2007; Cottrell-Boyce, 2013), recruitment of children and adults to CE (Densley, 2012; Harding, 2020) and sexual exploitation identifies similar patterns of victimology in the UK (Beckett and Warrington, 2014). The controller of the victim of exploitation may, in some instances, be considered the first-order beneficiary, or user, of the victim. Nonetheless, there may be a system of second-order beneficiaries who act as facilitators, suppliers of the victim or the suppliers of licit goods and services. Modern slavery may be the lucrative tip of a criminal iceberg, its earnings funding both criminal and legal activities and creating the opportunity for cooperative activities between criminals (Sergi, 2017; Barlow, 2019).

Not all such exploitation will be a product of organised or networked abuse and exploitation. Nevertheless, the danger of organised crime arises because the vast profits acquired from the sale of illicit goods and services – be that drug dealing, forced begging, ATM distraction theft, pickpocketing – are reinvested in further activities and enterprises that are both licit and illicit, benefiting from the corruption of economic and political domains (Cressey, 1969). The different degrees of organisation of CE offer various potential opportunities for intervention to stop or disrupt it by integrating criminal and civil law and open new opportunities for investigation, arrest and prosecution, for example, with greater use of Child Abduction Warning Notices, Slavery and Trafficking Prevention Orders, Sexual Offence Prevention Orders, Harassment Orders, and so on. These are applied on the civil standard of evidence. Integrating civil legal and criminal legal instruments, statutory safeguarding systems and investigative procedures is necessary to address the problem of trafficking and exploitation as an output of systematic, networked abuse and organised crime.

The UK strategy against organised crime

Patterns and modalities of exploitation fluctuate over time in response to the needs of illicit markets, the motivations of criminals and the conductivity of the environment to any criminal enterprise (Barlow, 2019; Barlow et al, 2021). While the current discourse on CE in the UK is dominated by exploitation within the so-called county lines model of drugs distribution,[1] criminally exploited children (and vulnerable adults) have historically been coerced into crimes, such as acquisitive crimes, counterfeit DVD selling, cannabis cultivation, benefit fraud and sham marriages (Serious Organised Crime Agency, 2012; Anti Slavery-International, 2014). Although the UK's Serious and Organised Crime Strategy of 2018 does not give much consideration to exploitation of children and vulnerable adults in general, or in relation to CE specifically, it recognised the intersection between street gangs and organised crime. The salience of this relationship has been described and explained through important and influential work on youth gangs recruiting children for exploitation, such as that by Pitts (2008) and Harding (2020).

The UK government's strategy seeks to prevent serious and organised crime partly with interventions that stop or disrupt the routes by which people are drawn in and the mechanisms by which they are maintained in organised crime. This part of the strategy has drawn upon two particularly important pieces of research, but it has simplified them (Kleemans and de Poot, 2008; Francis et al, 2013). Both studies clearly demonstrate the heterogeneity of traffickers and exploiters engaged in organised crime and their victims, but the government strategy does not reflect this variety, citing only the following factors as putting people at risk for being drawn into organised crime:

- having family or social links to organised crime;
- a criminal history resulting in prison sentence and consequent proximity to organised criminals.

While identifying the systemic relevance of gangs, families and prisons to organised crime as Kleemans and de Poot demonstrate (2008; see Chapter 1, this volume), the strategy does not explicitly adopt a systemic model of intervention. For example, the strategy identifies the importance of the Troubled Families programme,[2] the Ending Youth Gang Violence programme[3] and interventions that aim to divert people from involvement in organised crime. Nonetheless, an assumption of a linear causality and an attitude that situates the problem with the victims remains. Consequently, ever increasing target-hardening, reductive approaches are adopted as interventions (Cottrell-Boyce, 2013). Professionals fall into victim-blaming when victims fail to disengage from their exploiters.

This victim-blaming approach is reinforced by the conflation of CE in the context of drug distribution with the wider issue of youth gangs and youth violence within the government's Serious Violence Strategy and Ending Gang Violence and Exploitation Strategy (Cottrell-Boyce, 2013). Simplistic linear analysis neglects the complex processes of exploitation. It fails to address the emergence of patterns of exploitation over time so that children may be targeted and victimised from a young age and on into adulthood (Barlow, 2019). The rigidity of statutory definitions of 'child' and criminal liability mean that, when a victim of CE passes the age of 18, the statutory landscape changes dramatically and accordingly safeguarding policies and systems as well as presumptions about victimhood and criminal liability.

While the scale and scope of the problem of CE has been studied for several years, very little has been produced to assist professionals within the spheres of child and vulnerable adult safeguarding, community safety, law enforcement or the civil and CJS to understand the aetiology of the problem of CE (Barlow, 2019).

Criminal exploitation and 'the Section 45 defence'

International law, conventions and standards concerning the human rights of trafficked people should prevent detention, prosecution and punishment of trafficked people for crimes that they have committed as a direct consequence of being trafficked (Piotrowicz and Sorrentino, 2016). Failure to consider whether defendants are potential victims of trafficking to prevent unfair punishment through the CJS breaches obligations under Article 26 of the Council of Europe's Convention Against Trafficking of Human Beings, 2005. The Convention requires states to 'provide for the possibility of not imposing penalties on victims for their involvement in unlawful activities, to the extent that they have been compelled to do so' (Council of Europe, 2005).

Before 2015, in the UK, Court of Appeal cases demonstrated the ways in which victims have been arrested, charged and prosecuted for offences that occurred as a direct consequence of being forced to do so and the victim having no alternative due to being trafficked. For example: victims of trafficking for sexual or labour exploitation, who were given false identity documents by their traffickers, the possession of which is a criminal offence (for example, as in the case R-v-O [2019] EWCA Crim 1389). Similarly, Vietnamese boys who were trafficked for forced labour in cannabis factories, were convicted for the production of drugs (case R-v-N and R-v-LE [2012] EWCA Crim 189). In drafting the Modern Slavery Act 2015, the UK introduced a statutory defence in Section 45 (s.45) ('the Section 45 defence') a recognition in law of the UK's international obligations to not punish such individuals. s.45 differentiates between adults, that is, over 18 years of ages – s.45(1) and children, that is, under the age of 18 – s.45(4). The defence for adults provides that a person is not guilty of an offence if:

(a) they performed the act because they were compelled to do so (s.45(1) (a-b));
(b) the compulsion was attributable to slavery or relevant exploitation (s.45(1)(c));

(c) a reasonable person in the same situation and sharing the person's relevant characteristics would have no realistic alternative to doing the act (s.45(1)(d)).

Compulsion (s.45(2)) may arise from a third party (such as threats or the exertion of violence by traffickers) or from circumstances (for example, having been transported into the country on false documents by the traffickers). It is attributable to slavery/exploitation if it is a direct consequence of the person being, or having been, a victim of slavery or relevant exploitation (s.45(3)) (Mennim and Wake, 2018). The problem with s.45, I suggest, is the way in which the processes of modern slavery are (mis)understood by lawyers and the judiciary. The emphasis on compulsion has been criticised for its failure to recognise that in the context of an exploitative relationship, abusers utilise such a range of coercive methods to achieve total dominance of the victim that they do not even need to be present for the victim to feel that they have no realistic choice but to commit the criminal act (Jordash QC, 2020).

Some law enforcement professionals and others in the CJS worry that the s.45 defence might be used by children and adults, on the advice of their solicitors, as a 'get out of jail free card'. The Independent Review of the Modern Slavery Act (Field et al, 2019) found no evidence to indicate this as a reality. In fact, people continue to be detained and prosecuted for criminal offences, when the defence has been raised as prosecutors seek to establish that there is no nexus between the exploitation and the offence for which the defendant is indicted (Modin, 2019). Having conducted many assessments of defendants that have sought to rely on the s.45 defence, I have found that in a minority of cases the defence has been raised incorrectly or deceitfully. Of the 60 assessments that I referred to earlier, this has been the case in fewer than ten. In only one case was the defence being raised cynically. In others, it simply was not the appropriate defence. Detecting a false claim is, in my experience, easy if the investigator or assessor understands the nature of trafficking and modern slavery, its nuances, dynamics and processes.

The Crown Prosecution Service (CPS) guidance[4] states that prosecutors should consider all the circumstances of the case, including the seriousness of the offence and any direct or indirect compulsion arising from their trafficking situation (Crown Prosecution Service, 2021). Nevertheless, all decisions in the case remain with the prosecutor, and this seems problematic (Brotherton and Waters, 2013). Though the element of compulsion is obviously not relevant in relation to children, there is still the 'reasonable person' test which has also been criticised. In 2016, the Group of Experts on Action against Trafficking in Human Beings referred to several cases where child victims had been convicted and imprisoned for drug related offences in the context of cannabis cultivation, instead of being recognised as potential victims of trafficking (GRETA, 2016).

There is a widespread professional and academic consensus that responses to CE and the application of s.45 is inconsistent between regions, agencies, and professionals (GRETA, 2016; Haughey, 2016; Rosser, 2019). A fundamental lack of awareness of the processes of modern slavery/human trafficking and CE, the dynamics of exploitative relationships, as well as the factors that create and maintain the opportunity to criminally exploit people over time remains. It is this non-linear complexity that is still not recognised, and addressed within a CJS which runs in parallel to the safeguarding and civil justice systems.

Mind the gap: victims of modern slavery falling in-between safeguarding and the criminal justice system

Although criminal and other forms of exploitation are acknowledged as forms of abuse, it is not specifically addressed by current safeguarding legislation. This accounts in part for the parallel, rather than convergent, pathways of the CJS and the safeguarding and civil justice systems (Moore, 1995). Between 2016 and 2019, the number of county lines operations quadrupled according to the National Crime Agency (2019). From January 2016 to September 2020, there were 18 prosecutions for a modern slavery offence where the victim was aged 17 and under. Of those 18 prosecutions, there were seven cases in which there was a conviction for a modern slavery offence (Watson, 2021). So few prosecutions for child trafficking is astonishing when compared with the growth in county lines exploitation in England and Wales in the same period. The criminal justice, health, social care and family justice systems share a common concern that is trafficking and exploitation, but differ in their perception of the results of the exploitation. The CJS identifies a criminal event; the safeguarding community identifies harm to a victim (Moore, 1995). Both can be equally reductive in their analysis, but statutory responses reflect the dominance of the criminal justice approach in both policy (HM Government, 2014, 2015) and practice, emphasising the problem as a crime first and a safeguarding issue second.

The predicament of criminally exploited people is that they are victims who are perpetrating a crime. Investigation therefore needs to be conducted jointly and cooperatively between law enforcement and social care agencies with jointly formulated interventions and safeguarding plans. Crime prevention and safeguarding are symbiotic, the failure to protect means opportunities to investigate and prosecute exploiters are being lost.

Identification of a potential victim of trafficking/modern slavery may lead to a referral to enter the person into the National Referral Mechanism

(NRM, see Introduction, this volume). This brings with it safeguarding duties and victim entitlements. Ironically, if a referral has been made in relation to a child or a vulnerable adult, there is a tacit assumption that they may be a victim of a serious crime. The local authority has statutory duties to make enquiries when a child in their area has been identified as suffering or likely to suffer significant harm (Children Act 1989 s.47). A similar obligation exists in cases where a vulnerable adult, who would be entitled to care services, may be suffering abuse or exploitation (Care Act 214 s.42). Furthermore, the CPS applies a '4 Stage Test' in cases where a suspect may be a victim of exploitation. Stage one involves the CPS supporting police in making 'reasonable enquiries' (Crown Prosecution Service, 2021). These enquires should not begin and end with an NRM referral. They should include proper referral to the local authority and joint investigative strategies that may lead towards, or away, from the suspect as a perpetrator and/or victim of crime.

Early identification and proper engagement between social care and law enforcement is possible if the existing safeguarding protocols are followed. There is nothing in the guidance that places the entire burden of such 'reasonable enquiries' on the police. In fact, safeguarding investigations conducted by social workers, or joint investigations with police officers, are central to joint agency safeguarding protocols. The fact that this is not happening consistently in cases of modern slavery reflects the problem of two systems working in parallel rather than in congruence. Better joint agency investigation and intervention can be facilitated by a range of injunctions available within the Modern Slavery Act and other legislation that require the civil, rather than criminal, standard of proof to be applied, for example, Slavery and Trafficking Risk Orders, Risk of Sexual Harm Orders, Child Abduction Warning Notices.

If a person has been identified through the NRM as a victim of trafficking, a modern slavery offence should be recorded as a crime. The victim is entitled to support and protection. They also have a 45-day 'reflection and recovery period', in which they may receive advice concerning whether they wish to assist police in their investigation of the modern slavery offence. When they are also a suspect in another offence, they are rarely, if ever, interviewed as a victim, while the decision to prosecute proceeds. Arguably, if the accused is recognised as a victim of trafficking/modern slavery and treated as such, even if they may have committed an offence because of the trafficking, there is an opportunity to investigate more serious modern slavery crimes and OCGs. Too few within the CJS have the knowledge and understanding of safeguarding legislation and statutory duties and too few practitioners in safeguarding agencies understand the CJS. Both systems are on parallel tracks and victims are falling through the gap between them.

Conclusion

I have described some international conventions and protocols in relation to human trafficking and slavery to demonstrate the influence upon UK law and policy development. Drawing on complex systems theory to describe and explain the nature of modern slavery in relation to CE, I have criticised current UK policy and practices, within and outside the Modern Slavery Act 2015, as reductive, simplistic and linear. When a crime is an output of CE, the CJS is failing to recognise and address its complexity. Investigators need to understand the victim's relationship with the perpetrators of the abuse and the processes involved. These principles are currently understood and applied in the context of child safeguarding, domestic abuse and safeguarding of vulnerable adults, and are transferable to the modern slavery context. Robust systems exist, they just need to be utilised. It is insufficient to simply recommend more training for the judiciary and professionals. This training must have a sound theoretical footing that informs public policy and the approach taken across all allied agencies and contexts. It requires an integrated, whole systems approach that simultaneously addresses the needs of victims; identifies, disrupts and apprehends perpetrators and their networks; and addresses the local and institutional processes that contribute to an environment that is conducive to modern slavery and CE. The Modern Slavery Act 2015 may not quite be a 'one stop' piece of legislation, but it can intersect well with other civil and criminal legislation. It could be the keystone in the development of better integrated, multimodal systemic investigation, protection and prosecution strategies. This would require a paradigm shift in both the criminal and civil justice systems – which hopefully is not too far to away.

Notes

[1] 'County lines': OCGs/OCNs (Organised Crime Gangs/Networks) move drugs into one or more supply areas. This distribution is coordinated by dedicated mobile phone lines ('deal lines') used to advertise availability of drugs, prices and offers and in order to take orders. The phone number will often have a name, which effectively acts as the dealer's 'brand'. The gangs are usually based in major cities, well away from the market area that they seek to penetrate. Children are recruited as runners to transport drugs to the market areas, carry out the deals and return with the money.

[2] Troubled Families is a programme of targeted intervention for families with multiple problems, including crime, anti-social behaviour, truancy, unemployment, mental health problems and domestic abuse.

[3] The Home Office funded Ending Youth Gang Violence programme to reduce violence through supporting a change in the way that public services respond to gang and youth violence.

[4] This guidance was updated in December 2021.

References

Anti-Slavery International (2014) *Trafficking for Forced Criminal Activities and Begging in Europe: Exploratory Study and Good Practice Examples.* London: Anti-Slavery International.

Barlow, C. (2017) The adapted SIPPS for CSE: Evaluation of a pilot project in a south London borough. *European Review of Organised Crime,* 4(2): 101–27.

Barlow, C. (2019) *Child Criminal Exploitation: A New Systemic Model to Improve Professional Assessment, Investigation and Intervention.* Hull: University of Hull.

Barlow, C., Green, S., Kidd, A. and Darby, B. (2021) Circles of analysis: A systemic model of child criminal exploitation. *Journal of Children's Services.* https://doi.org/10.1108/JCS-04-2021-0016

BBC (2019) *Drugsland: County Lines.* [Film] s.l.: BBC 3.

Beckett, H. and Warrington, C. (2014) *Suffering in Silence: Children and Unreported Crime.* Luton: University of Bedfordshire.

Brotherton, V. and Waters, F. (2013) *Victim or Criminal? Trafficking for Forced Criminal Exploitation: UK Chapter.* s.l.: ECPAT.

Cottrell-Boyce, J. (2013) Ending gang and youth violence: A critique. *Youth Justice,* 13(3): 193–206.

Council of Europe (2005) *Council of Europe's Convention Against Trafficking of Human Beings.* Warsaw: Council of Europe.

Cressey, D.R. (1969) *The Theft of the Nation: Structure and Operations of Organised Crime in America.* New York, Evanston and London: Harper & Row.

Crown Prosecution Service (2021) *Human Trafficking, Smuggling and Slavery.* Available from: https://www.cps.gov.uk/legal-guidance/human-trafficking-smuggling-and-slavery (accessed 28 February 2022).

Dadabho, F. (2017) *County Lines Analysis for Islington.* London: Safer Islington Partnership.

Densley, J.R. (2012) Street gang recruitment signalling, screening, and selection. *Social Problems,* 59(3): 301–21.

Di Nicola, A. (2011) Researching into human trafficking: Issues and problems. In M. Lee (ed) *Human Trafficking.* Willan, pp 61–84.

ECPAT UK (2010) *ECPAT UK Briefing Paper Child Trafficking – Begging and Organised Crime.* London: ECPAT.

Fairfax, H. (2017) Psychometrics in clinical settings. In B. Cripps (ed) *Psychometric Testing: Critical Perspectives.* Chichester: Wiley, pp 175–84.

Field, F., Butler-Sloss, E. and Miller, M. (2019) *Final Report of the Independent Review of the Modern Slavery Act 2015.* London: The Home Office.

Firmin, C. (2017) *Contextual Safeguarding.* Bedford: University of Bedfordshire / Contextual Safeguarding Network.

Francis, B., Humphreys, L., Kirby, S. and Soothill, K. (2013) *Understanding Criminal Careers in Organised Crime,* Research Report 74. s.l.: Home Office.

Gadd, D. and Broad, R. (2018) Troubling recognitions in British responses to modern slavery. *British Journal of Criminology*, 54:6 1440–61.

Gozdziak, E.M. and Vogel, K.M. (2020) Palermo at 20: A retrospective and prospective. *Journal of Human Trafficking*, 6(2): 109–18.

Gregoriou, C. and Ras, I.A. (2018) Representations of transnational human trafficking: A critical review. In C. Gregoriou (ed) *Representations of Transnational Human Trafficking Present-day News Media, True Crime, and Fiction*. Cham: Palgrave Pivot.

GRETA (2016) *Report Concerning the Implementation of the Council of Europe Convention on Action against Trafficking in Human Beings by the United Kingdom: Second Evaluation Round*. s.l.: Council of Europe.

Harding, S. (2014) *The Street Casino: Survival in Street Gangs*. Bristol: Policy Press.

Harding, S. (2020) *County Lines*. Bristol: Bristol University Press.

Haughey, C. (2016) *The Modern Slavery Act Review: One Year On*. London: The Home Office.

Hirsch, A. (2015) Children 'trafficked' around UK by drug dealers. *Sky News* [online]. Available from: http://news.sky.com/story/children-trafficked-around-uk-by-drug-dealers-10375380 (accessed 3 March 2020).

HM Government (2014) *Modern Slavery Strategy*. London: The Stationery Office.

HM Government (2015) Serious Crime Act. Her Majesty's Stationery Office.

HM Government (2018) *Serious and Organised Crime Strategy*. London: Her Majesty's Stationery Office.

International Labor Organisation (1930) ILO Forced Labour Convention, 1930 (No. 29), 28 June.

Jordan, A.D. (2002) Human rights or wrongs? The struggle for a rights-based response to trafficking in human beings. *Gender & Development*, 10(1): 28–37.

Jordash QC, W. (2020) Forced criminality and non-criminalisation of trafficked persons in the international criminal court. In P. Southwell, M. Brewer and B. Douglas-Jones QC (eds) *Human Trafficking and Modern Slavery Law and Practice*. s.l.: Bloomsbury Professional, pp 589–618.

Kleemans, E.R. and de Poot, C.J. (2008) Criminal careers in organized crime and social opportunity structure. *European Journal of Criminology*, 5(1): 69–98.

Knowsley Council (2015) *Child Exploitation: JSNA Report*. s.l.: Knowsley Council.

Lee, M. (2011) *Human Trafficking*. s.l.: Routledge.

May, T. (2016) My Government will lead the way in defeating modern slavery. *The Telegraph*, 30 July.

Mennim, S. and Wake, N. (2018) Court of Appeal: Burden of proof in trafficking and modern slavery cases: R v MK; R v Gega [2018] Crim 667. *Journal of Criminal Law*, 82(4): 282–6.

Modin, A. (2019) Child victims of human trafficking prosecuted despite CPS rules. *The Guardian*, 17 September.

Moore, M.H. (1995) Public health and criminal justice approaches to health. In M. Tonry and D.P. Farrington (eds), *Building a Safer Society: Strategic Approaches to Crime Prevention*. Chicago, IL: The University of Chicago Press, pp 237–62.

National Crime Agency (2015) *NCA Strategic Assessment: Nature and Scale of Human Trafficking in 2014*. s.l.: National Crime Agency.

National Crime Agency (2019) *Intelligence Assessment: County Lines, Drug Supply, Ability Harm 2018*. s.l.: National Crime Agency.

Piotrowicz, R.W. and Sorrentino, L. (2016) Human trafficking and the emergence of the non-punishment principle. *Human Rights Law Review*: 16: 4 669–99.

Pitts, J. (2007) *Reluctant Gangsters: Youth Gangs in Waltham Forest*.

Pitts, J. (2008) *Reluctant Gangsters: The Changing Shape of Youth Crime*. s.l.: Willan.

Rosser, R. (2019, October) *Section 45: Loophole or Lifeline?* Available from: https://www.2bedfordrow.co.uk/section-45-loophole-or-lifeline/

Schoaps, L.L. (2013) Room for improvement: Palermo Protocol and the Trafficking Victims Protection Act. *Lewis & Clark Law Review*, 17(3): 931–72.

Sergi, A. (2017) *From Mafia to Organised Crime: A Comparative Analysis of Policing Models*. s.l.: Palgrave Macmillan.

Setter, C. (2019) Child trafficking in the UK. In G. Craig and A. Balch (eds) *The Modern Slavery Agenda: Policy, Politics and Practice*. Bristol: Policy Press.

Shelley, L. (2010) *Human Trafficking: A Global Perspective*. New York: Cambridge University Press.

SOCA (Serious Organised Crime Agency) (2012) *UKHTC: A Baseline Assessment on the Nature and Scale of Trafficking in 2011*. London: SOCA.

Surtess, R. (2005) *Other Forms of Trafficking in Minors: Articulating Victim Profiles and Conceptualizing Interventions*. s.l.: Nexus Institute to Combat Human Trafficking.

Turner, A., Belcher, L. and Pona, I. (2019) *Counting Lives: Responding to Children Who are Criminally Exploited*. s.l.: The Children's Society.

United Nations (1948) *Universal Declaration of Human Rights*. New York: United Nations.

United Nations Office on Drugs and Organised Crime (2004) *United Nations Convention Against Transnational Organised Crime and the Protocols Thereto*. Vienna: United Nations.

von Lampe, K. (2019) Definitions of organised crime. Available from: http://www.organized-crime.de/organizedcrimedefinitions.htm (accessed 7 October 2020).

Watson, L. (2021) Personal communication [interview], 23 August.

PART III

Caring: practices and resilience

The voices of survivors as service users and practitioners as service providers come to the forefront in this section, where experiences and practices of assistance are articulated in light of key concepts – such as gender, trauma, resilience, resistance and creativity – and tools to understand which caring approach is more effective are discussed.

9

Subject-making in ambiguous systems: trafficking aftercare in the UK and beyond

Runa Lazzarino and Anne-Marie Greenslade

Introduction

This chapter revolves around modern slavery and human trafficking (MSHT) aftercare systems, drawing on the voices of frontline practitioners and survivors, in the UK and beyond. Our aim is to highlight where key aspects of aftercare systems become challenges and compromises for survivors. To frame the tortuous experience of survivors navigating the ambivalent terrains of the system, we hold onto the concept of 'subjection' (Butler, 1997). As the 'process of becoming subordinated by power' and 'becoming a subject' (Butler, 1997: 2), subjection is a useful tool to capture the continuous negotiations survivors have to engage in with aftercare systems.

The chapter is divided into six sections. As a start, we expand the theoretical grounding of the chapter, introducing the notions of vulnerability and trauma. We also present our critique of MSHT as a discourse, deepening the criminological versus victimological divide, and its implications in aftercare. The context of the research studies underpinning this chapter is also outlined. The following four sections focus on aspects of post-MSHT life, casting light onto specific challenges/compromises for survivors. First, we discuss the process of self-identification and how this conflicts with the way MSHT victims/survivors are described in anti-MSHT systems. Following this, we explore acceptance to join the system, and identify some negative implications of survivor engagement with the system. In the last two sections, we highlight paradoxical traits of mental healthcare, education and employment services, to ultimately show how they disempower, more than support, recovery and reintegration. In the concluding section, we try to connect the difficulties in subject-remaking, encountered by survivors navigating a fallacious care system, with the elaboration of *their* sense of practical justice. This means that survivors would not subjugate to a fallacious system, but would instead contribute to the design of a fair one. Based on our conclusions, the chapter will offer some recommendations for a more survivor-centred system of care.

Subjection and the ambivalent anti-trafficking discourse

This chapter is rooted in the concept of 'subjection' (Butler, 1997) to capture the experience of survivors' subject-remaking navigating the ambivalent terrains of MSHT aftercare. As subjection draws together the simultaneous being-made and self-making process, it can be usefully applied to frame how survivors need to continually subjugate to a fallacious system, while also carving out their own spaces for rebuilding lives and identities. The system, we maintain, constructs survivors as vulnerable, but fails to provide empowering support.

Vulnerability and trauma are two key notions which often underlie how survivors are conceived and assisted, from recruitment to care. For example, in Article 3a of the Trafficking Protocol, 'abuse of a position of vulnerability' is listed among the means traffickers can employ to perpetrate the crime (United Nations, 2000). Vulnerability is also associated with life after trafficking in relation to the sociocultural exclusion and irregular status of migrants (UNODC, 2012). Additionally, vulnerability of survivors is commonly looked at as one of the consequences of the traumatic events experienced during exploitation – and to the scars these leave on survivors' wellbeing. Here, we embrace criticism of social vulnerability theories which emphasise lack of agency and subjection to structural inequalities, and which inform Western-centric and paternalistic systems of assistance (Bankoff, 2001), moulded onto the Global North subject (Fineman, 2008).

Vulnerability and trauma sit on the victimising end of the anti-trafficking discourse. On the other side, a criminalising approach over-responsibilises victims, treating them with little understanding and compassion, due to their irregular migration status or due to illegal or 'immoral' activities carried out during their exploitation (see Chapters 6 and 8, this volume). Anti-trafficking discourse builds upon stances which are, at the same time, rigidly dualistic and opportunistically ambiguous. The dualism is expressed in simplified, clear-cut oppositions, such as victims versus criminals, consent versus constraint, smuggling versus trafficking, freedom versus unfreedom. The ambiguity sees the reproduction of policies and practices which re-traumatise survivors (Dando et al, 2016), while at the same time constructing them as vulnerable.

The ambiguity in anti-trafficking discourse, we argue, is enabled by ideologies of the MSHT discourse. These ideologies favour an opportunistic oscillation between those very opposing poles on which they are built (Chuang, 2010). The oscillation is too often dictated by the interests of states and institutions (Bravo, 2019), rather than the interests of survivors. Ideologies of the MSHT discourse are linked to the anti-migration, border protectionist agenda (Aradau, 2008) and the neo-abolitionist anti-prostitution movement (Doezema, 2010) – which is in both historical and contemporary connection with women trafficking (see Chapter 5, this volume). MSHT ideologies are also blended with the postcolonial victimhood discourse of humanitarian intervention. Here, the vulnerable/traumatised survivor is framed within a broader depoliticising humanitarian apparatus of systems of intervention (Pupavac, 2001; Fassin et al, 2002). These systems, like the trafficking aftercare one, are underpinned by Western-centred biomedical knowledge of the self, wellbeing and trauma (Hinton and Good, 2016).

Against these ideological frameworks, we want to cast light onto vulnerability and trauma as political positions and not only as places of privation and desperation (de Lauretis, 1990), in need of urgent help. Trauma and vulnerability become places where 'social actors exhibit and enact new ways to re-construct and re-inhabit their own world' (Das, 2000: 223). To this end, we focus on care and support for survivors of MSHT, and survivors' own perspectives and experiences within their post-trafficking journey. We juxtapose voices of frontline practitioners from the UK and voices of survivor returnees in the Global South. We concentrate on how survivors rebuild their identity and future aspirations through therapeutic intervention, education and employment within trafficking aftercare, in the UK and the Global South. A further aim is to convey the extent to which MSHT discourse is intrinsically informed by the interplay between the Global North and the Global South, intended as two ideological constructs and as both socioeconomic and geographical realities (see Introduction, this volume). The points of view of practitioners in the UK are set in dialogue with a selection of interludes of survivor returnees extrapolated from ethnographic fieldwork conducted in Northern Vietnam, Central-West Brazil and Nepal (Lazzarino, 2015). The injection of voices from the Global South echoes grassroots perspectives in MSHT as a Global North versus South discourse.

This chapter is based on qualitative empirical investigation – fieldwork, semi-structured interviews and focus groups – with frontline practitioners and survivors in the UK and Global South contexts. The UK interviews were conducted in 2018 and 2019 by Anne-Marie Greenslade, with nine frontline practitioners, representing a cross-section of the UK's survivor support provisions, including government-funded and independent charities, and the public sector. The survivor returnees' voices from the Global South derive from a multi-country ethnography conducted by Runa Lazzarino between 2010 and 2013 using ethnographic immersion, informal conversations, in-depth interviews (122 in total) and focus groups.

Self-identification versus identification by others

The preliminary step to enter the system of assistance is to adopt the identity of MSHT victim. It also entails a decision that, in the name of that identity, becoming a 'client' is optimal. In the field of MSHT support, survivor voices are notably lacking in policy decisions and literature (Curran et al, 2017; also Introduction, this volume), despite the fact that this is slowly changing. A dearth of survivor-led input means that available information about post-intervention experiences can be unreliable (Lockyer, 2020). Furthermore, the greater focus on the sexual exploitation of women and girls eclipses the fact that men and boys can also become victims of sexual or other forms of slavery, or that labour exploitation occurs across a multitude of industries, as this volume shows. This biased focus of MSHT systems of assistance has an impact onto survivors' self-perception and decision-making processes. In fact, a significant issue for survivors is how they understand and describe what has happened to them.

MSHT survivors, particularly those who have been trafficked from abroad, but also those who return to their home, may be unacquainted with the official terminology (Doyle et al, 2019). In the UK, when authorities intervene, many victims are more inclined to focus on their asylum/immigration or reintegration needs, rather than disclosing details of their exploitation (Doyle et al, 2019). Legal terms referring to immigration or criminal justice are also unlikely to be familiar, resulting in detention at an immigration or rehabilitation centre, or even prosecution for crimes committed during exploitation (see Chapter 8, this volume). This places an emphasis on their 'otherness' as an offender in an unfamiliar country, or as an outsider treated with suspicion in their home country (see Chapter 6, this volume). Survivors' feelings of shame and self-stigma can arise from ideas that they are ultimately responsible for their unsuccessful migratory journey (Lazzarino, 2014). Moreover, this disconnect feeds into how survivors define *themselves*, as a practitioner in the UK expressed: "They would say 'My lawyer has told me that trafficking is …' so they understand what's happened to them isn't what they wanted but the language that we assign to them isn't always the language that they would assign to themselves" (Emma, Birmingham, UK, 30 October 2018). The issue of linguistic discrepancy is emblematic of the multilayered interplay between Global South and North in MSHT discourse. It shows how the spread of the current global trafficking discourse has repurposed international and local aid. The Global South–North interplay is also revealed in the language of law and policy, clashing with the experiences of irregularised migrants and marginalised citizens.

Brazil incorporated the Trafficking Protocol into national legislation after ratifying it in 2004 and implemented changes in the justice system, other statutory realms and the third sector. Examples include the creation of a National Policy to Counter Trafficking in Persons in 2006, an all-comprehensive new Law to Prevent and Combat National and International Trafficking in Person (Law 13.344 of 2016), the establishment of posts at airports and bus stations and state-level anti-trafficking offices. This progressive internalisation of the Trafficking Protocol reverberated in modifications of practices, language and ways migrants are defined and self-define:

'I think that I was trafficked yes. … I know what trafficking is because I saw a programme on TV, and yes, because I had to pay against my will and I was tricked … you know, I paid for everything to go to Europe, but it was a friend who brought me there, and she tricked me because she wanted to make money out of me, she wanted 50 per cent of each *programa* [client], but that was not the agreement, so I went to work in a brothel.' (Manuela, Anápolis, Brazil, 27 September 2012)

'There were a lot of rules, I was feeling in cage [in the brothel] because we could not go out, but I was not a victim because I knew, only I did not know about all the conditions … in women chatting here in Anápolis, in 2005, nobody was talking about trafficking, trafficking is when you go without knowing, it's the trick.' (Maia, Anápolis, Brazil, 10 September 2012)

Self-identifying as victims does not necessarily lead to entering the system, as in the case of Manuela, who had returned to Brazil years before and struggled to rebuild a life within their network of queer friends and sex workers. Conversely, Maia did not self-identify, yet received psychotherapeutic support from the local Assistance Centre for Women, where the counsellor described her as a victim of human trafficking. For many survivors, entering the system entails dealing with local authorities and other anti-MSHT actors, retelling their private life and their unsuccessful migratory endeavour, magnifying the traits of vulnerability of their journeys. It implies an act of subjugation to a public shame in relation to the discrimination they experience as queer or sex worker, failed migrant, uneducated, poor and mental health service users. Entering the system, both in the UK and elsewhere, entails facing several judgemental and demanding gazes – that of family, community and society, as well as their own. But to some, it appears as a forced choice, with no alternatives. In these cases, 'consenting' to being identified as victims/survivors is a problematic question.

Entering the system

A spectrum of reasons informs survivors' decisions as to whether to enter the system of trafficking aftercare. In 2009, the UK introduced the National Referral Mechanism (NRM), an administrative mechanism by which victims are formally identified, and individuals over the age of 18 must give informed consent to be referred. While we acknowledge the broader issue of consent, we consider consent in critical terms of compromising agency within the framework of the anti-MSHT system. Providing consent to the NRM identifies individuals as a victim and allows their details to be shared with other state authorities. Fear of repercussions, re-trafficking and further discrimination will often prevent victims from taking this option. Furthermore, most victims just want to work (Strauss, 2017) and, having left their country of origin and very often their families, the desire to create a better life is paramount. Under the NRM, however, survivors are prohibited from paid employment. This leaves many survivors with a difficult choice; although they may have previously been subjected to terrible conditions and abuse, they were at least eking out an existence: "We've got a situation where they're like 'You're offering me this NRM, I've got to sign this piece of paper, you're telling me I'll be somewhere safe for 45 days and after that you're promising me nothing, so maybe it's better to stay with the devil I know'" (Emma, Birmingham, UK, 30 October 2018). Emma felt that the goalposts had shifted from the initial aim, "which in my understanding was meant to be an administrative process and now it's become an access to support mechanism". For that reason, consent may not always be as freely given as anticipated:

> 'Survivors have said … "sure we consent but basically because people are saying that if you don't go into the NRM you are going to be homeless" or you don't have access to anything, so … it's consent with very constrained options so I fear that what people think is consent to enter the NRM is not full consent, or fully aware consent.' (Jenni, Manchester, UK, 13 August 2019)

> 'There are people who are choosing not to go into the NRM because the only reason you would choose to go into the NRM, if you're an adult, is if you're absolutely destitute and at risk. That's the only safeguarding route we have for adults at the moment.' (Caroline, Nottingham, UK, 22 November 2018)

The NRM has also been criticised for its failure to appreciate survivors' lived experience. Jenni noted that survivors are often labelled with the binary of "either pitiful traumatised or amazing resilient", neither of which acknowledges the complexities and personalities of the individual. This diminishment of identity also correlates with stereotypical perceptions of the 'ideal victim' (Christie, 1986):

> 'Victims don't always behave like victims. ... I've had quite a few victims who ... would naturally progress to drink ... to violence ... to drugs, and understanding that if you get very well-meaning people involved, that sometimes these potential victims don't always behave and so will beat people up and wreck places.' (Diana, Bristol, UK, 22 February 2019)

When no better options surface, it is more likely that survivors perpetuate their condition of dependency and precarity, and therefore accept to entrust trafficking aftercare systems with their life rebuilding. However, this does not imply exhibiting a submissive attitude. On the contrary, riding the advantages of the system does require a subtle orchestration of behaving like a victim, on the one hand, and a social actor actively pursuing different desires and plans, on the other hand (Lazzarino, 2017). Referring to Butler's concept of subjection, the moment of subjugation – the being-made within the system – is paired with expressions of agency and self-affirmation, outside of the 'ideal victim' box. These expressions can be manifestations of suffering, such as drug misuse, but also very simple ones, such as initiating an argument, or wanting to socialise with peers.

In Vietnam, sex work is illegal and stigmatised as a 'social evil' (Lazzarino, 2014). Since victims of human trafficking are associated with sex work, upon return from an international trafficking experience, they confront stigma which goes in tandem with a paternalistic approach to trafficking aftercare. Nhung, an official case of forced marriage in China, spent a year in a post-trafficking shelter for women and expressed the tension between the colliding manifestations of agency and victim:

> 'Sometimes I do not like myself, when I make a mistake, and I feel powerless ... for example with the teacher at work, I had an argument because he shouted at me and I dared shouting back, and so I quit the hairdressing school. The shelter house is not peaceful ... the social workers are nice but there are problems inside the house, there are no close friendships ... the security guards have the attitude as if we were all like prostitutes, and we do not have the right to say anything, they monitor us when we eat and they seem to say "if you went back to your hometown you wouldn't have all this food". ... I try to overcome the feeling of shame and I went back to my village only once.' (Nhung, Hanoi, Vietnam, 22 October 2011)

Several other residents manifested negative opinions in relation to their trafficking aftercare, particularly in terms of being viewed with suspicion by the managers and the guards, as well as their own families and rural communities of origins. Furthermore, self-stigma and shame are often accompanied by a sense of isolation due to the difficulty in establishing trusting relationships:

'For example, the other weekend I got permission to go out and everybody [in the shelter] thought that I went to a hotel for sex ... instead I went to the park with other people.' (Bian, Hanoi, Vietnam, 7 November 2011)

'I feel free and independent when I am here playing table pool with you [author]. I kind of liked the rules in the shelter, even if I felt angry once because my case worker did not allow me to stay out longer with my friends. Now I am grateful though, because those rules made me become more disciplined and made me avoid bad influences and temptations. The problem were not the rules ... the atmosphere there was complicated. You know, we were women having different pasts, some were trafficked, other were prostitutes by choice and escaped from the shelter to take again the route of prostitution. ... In my hometown, people's awareness is very backward. They do not care if I was a victim of human trafficking or not, they always look down upon me, even my family members. Here, in Hanoi, I do not know anybody, I do not have any friends, I do not want to tell anybody about my past.' (Xuan, Hanoi, Vietnam, 28 May 2013)

In Vietnam, which ratified the United Nations Office on Drugs and Crime Trafficking Protocol in 2011, the international MSHT discourse has been assimilated slowly at a cultural level – that is the wider level of understandings, perceptions and language. Instead, the Protocol was internalised quickly at a formal level: a series of decrees and circulars were issued, including a new Law on Prevention and Suppression against Human Trafficking in 2012 (No 66/2011/QH12). This growing corpus of documents reverberated in all domestic ministries and agencies, including new inter-agency cooperations and collaborations with international donors and non-governmental organisations (NGOs) (Tran et al, 2020). Under the law, the Department of Social Evils Prevention is tasked with assisting trafficked returnees to recovery and reintegration. Within an integral model of assistance that is found worldwide (Lazzarino et al, 2022), the section of the Vietnamese anti-trafficking law on support for victims (Chapter 5, Art 32) establishes a series of services trafficking victims are entitled to, such as medical and legal aid, and support for educational and vocational training. 'Victim supporting institutions' are to provide psychological support with the aim of having 'their psychology stabilised'.

Rebuilding through mental health support

Trafficking aftercare places survivors on an oscillating threshold between 'victim' and 'fraud'. This is evident in the model of the shelter which tends to infantilise residents (Lazzarino, 2017). This is also apparent for those survivors not deploying stereotypical victim behaviours. In broad terms, survivors are considered traumatised and in need of 'stabilisation', as specified in the Vietnamese law, however, the system is itself often re-traumatising (Contreras et al, 2017) and/or lacking adequate mental healthcare. Re-traumatisation can occur in several ways. In addition to the traumas encountered through presenting oneself as 'victim' and enter the system of assistance, suspicious attitudes, delays and insensitive support practices can further exacerbate trauma.

In 2013, the Anti-Trafficking Monitoring Group found the UK system to be lacking (Annison and ATMG, 2013). The report described delays in the identification process, the effects of which have also been highlighted by Survivor Alliance UK:

> Waiting for a decision following the interview is re-traumatising, and is a re-trafficking process. Like a trafficker, the Home Office promises you care and quality support. Like your trafficking experience, you feel that you cannot run away from the Home Office, because they know all your details and everything about you. (Browne et al, 2019: 6)

> The wait is re-traumatising. I am still waiting. … I have been for more than 900 days. This has caused serious consequences and delays to my asylum claim. I have been diagnosed with post-traumatic stress disorder, anxiety with panic attacks, and low mood by my psychotherapist, in the context of this traumatic experience and the uncertainty of whether I will reunite with my children. (Browne et al, 2019: 6)

Both quotes signify a compounding of the ordeal the survivors have already experienced. This is tragically paradoxical because trauma-informed aftercare has been gaining momentum (Wright et al, 2021), increasingly becoming the standard therapeutic approach, in the US and UK, for example (HTF, 2018). Through a trauma-informed model of support, practitioners can facilitate empowerment through collaboration with survivors, and build towards the long-term goals of self-sufficiency and self-agency (Lockyer, 2020).

Collaborative models of post-MSHT assistance are still scarce globally (see Introduction, this volume; Lazzarino et al, 2022), yet on the rise. In Nepal, co-produced assistance can coexist with non-participatory 'total institutions' (Goffman, 1990) of recovery and reintegration. In Kathmandu, an example of co-produced assistance is the first organisation founded and led by a group of women exploited in Indian red-light districts (Shakti Samuha, 2013). In the same city, another organisation follows instead a centralised, family-like model of assistance, which is radically based on religious faith and a charismatic leadership. Such was the organisation Lazzarino conducted research with in 2013 (Lazzarino, 2015). That charity was initiated by a foreign evangelical couple in 2000 and operates in MSHT prevention, as well as repatriation and reintegration, following and supporting children from their very early education up to finding them an employment. The NGO thus established its own school, vocational training programmes and activities. Meanwhile, evening gatherings around Bible reading, Friday religious celebrations and morning school prayers, all cement a strong sense of unity, to form one family close to the Christian God. This organisation is an instance of missionary aid, where the whole body-mind-soul needs of the beneficiaries are ideally catered for. One of the NGO's Nepalese leaders clarifies: "their [MSHT survivors] cognitive skills are like those of the others, it is their sentiments and soul … their emotional instability … they feel guilty, inferior, easily lose confidence … they are all traumatised by poverty and stigma" (Aditi, Kathmandu, Nepal, 1 August 2013). Surprisingly in light of this quote, psychological support was lacking. A safe sense-making space supported by a professional was not available, while a strong taboo also impeded any talk about the residents' experience. "Counselling is about finding inner strength and inner healing" (Binsa, Kathmandu, Nepal, 27 July 2013), an ex-beneficiary expressed, who was in charge of the organisation's reintegration programme at time of fieldwork. Binsa also stressed how important psychological support was, particularly for underage survivor returnees sold by their own families and ending up in Northern Indian red-light districts. This was the case of Nirmala:

'I was born in a humble rural village and when I was 16 my parents sold me to a woman who should have brought me to Kathmandu to work as a maid in a house, but instead I found myself in India. I spent there almost three years before being rescued and eventually repatriated. When I arrived in the shelter house, the first thing I looked at was the height of the enclosure around the house to evaluate if I would be able to jump and run away. I was constantly thinking about fleeing during the first days. Slowly though, I started to be persuaded by the warmth and the physical and psychological comfort that I could find in the organisation. I converted to Christianity and now I am the vice leader of my house, on the way to become a leader myself, while also studying to be a social worker.' (Nirmala, Kathmandu, Nepal, 20 July 2013)

Every survivor-leader in the organisation received brief counselling training, and a counsellor was meant to visit the shelter homes every two weeks, hosting in total over 200 minors at time of fieldwork. Apparently, the mental healthcare professional was always available to be contacted in case needed, and they could also liaise with a psychiatrist if necessary. Despite this, information, counselling and mental health support were never discussed or provided during the time of the fieldwork. It is similarly surprising that the UK legislation does not lay out clear provisions for mental health support.

On the one hand, the existence of trauma and the need for psychotherapeutic support is recognised, but this is neither officially regulated and provided, nor consistently offered and prioritised. This is not to say that Western models of formal counselling/psychotherapeutic support must be considered the best way to support survivors' recovery (Lazzarino, 2020). The spectrum of support for survivors is expanding to include alternative methods, which are less biomedical and more culturally sensitive (Lazzarino et al, 2022; Chapter 12, this volume). However, it is also questionable that radically integral, 'total' approaches – the opposite of the standard UK approach – are an ethical and culturally sensitive way to favour healing, reintegration and independence. These radical approaches are different from positive values-based support, as described by Murphy and Anstiss (Chapter 11, this volume). The Nepalese missionary case poses a further relevant issue, as the foreign NGO's denomination is a minority faith in the larger context in which it operates. It represents a case of widespread control of an organisation over the rebuilding of its, often extremely young, beneficiaries. In reference to the underlying concept of subjection, the process of becoming subordinated by power appears to exceed that of 'becoming a subject' with agency. The NGO controls several key aspects of the children's development and self-making, including their spirituality, education and often their marital and work dimensions as they grow up. This aspect is crucial as education and employment are key means to independent adulthood.

Rebuilding through education and employment

The practical aspect of becoming independent is important to the psychological transition from victim to integrated member of society, as survivors do not wish to be defined solely as someone who has experienced trauma (Lockyer, 2020). Engaging with other services and activities can be instrumental in leaving behind vulnerability and trauma, as UK providers highlight:

> 'Lots of the men and women go out and volunteer in places. … They don't turn up as an [organisation] survivor, they just turn up as "Kate" or "Sarah", and actually they can be themselves, so it's just trying to

remove that label so they can disclose it if they want to, but it's not our job to do.' (Emma, Birmingham, UK, 20 October 2018)

'It might be looking at what aspirations they've got, what educational desires they've got, what do they want to do employment-wise?' (Caroline, Nottingham, UK, 30 October 2018)

Education can provide a lifeline to survivors who are not ready for employment, but wish to develop their skills and knowledge. Survivors who were trafficked as children, or very young adults, will have had to leave school very early, if they started it at all. Manuela and Maia felt ashamed by their poor education, and they were struggling to find a decent job they could feel satisfied with. Access to education in a foreign country can be even more challenging for adults, as is the case in the UK. Very few colleges can accommodate the complex needs of survivors or deliver the type of programme that would be beneficial to them (see Introduction, this volume). Education "gives people their lives back ... it's about building their hope for the future, actually starting to make plans again, planning what you want to do next" (Nia, Newcastle, UK, 19 December 2018). As a bridge from intervention to independence, language skills and other qualifications are valuable assets in the step towards legitimate employment. In fact, one clear message from survivors is that most of them, especially men, just want to work. Unfortunately, the UK's NRM employment prohibition blocks this. Given that a central aim of any survivor-centric organisation is to empower and encourage independence, the notion of individuals identifying suitable job roles, or undertaking an interview, alone would also be an obvious natural step. However, unless an employer is also trauma-informed, they may not appreciate the additional needs of a survivor-worker:

'There is a motivation to work, it's not about not working. And they get the job and they do the job for six months and then they go and move on and then they hear a gunshot outside the house, or somebody threatens them in a way that's a trigger and they just have this sudden down spiral where their whole world falls apart.' (Ayesha, London, UK, 9 May 2019)

Acknowledging these challenges, a small number of initiatives have been founded to help develop survivors' employability skills and support them through the transition from the safe house to independence (see Chapter 11, this volume). Although employment is more likely to occur towards the latter end of survivor recovery, it can make an enormous difference in their overall wellbeing and self-esteem:

'[One survivor] said "I've worked in the UK before but never been paid. Now I even get paid holiday, I feel like a king". So not only was he being paid but actually valued enough to have paid holiday, I think you can't underestimate the impact of that on somebody who has been in exploitation. … I think a lot of survivors really value that, being in a workplace where they're valued as an individual and they can share a joke and a laugh with people and they can learn to feel safe somewhere.' (Rachel, London, UK, 9 May 2019)

The aspiration to achieve what is desired, including being 'valued as an individual', is a strong anchor that supports survivors' subject-making. Survivors' determination prevents them becoming trapped by a more powerful system to which they frequently have to subordinate in order to progress. Survivors' determination, desires and aspirations can be valued to the point that, even though the system is more powerful, the perspective is overturned: the system becomes instrumental for survivors to pursue their drive to rebuilding and redefining their identity. This is how a just system of MSHT aftercare should be.

Conclusion

We would like to conclude this chapter with a reflection around justice, intended beyond its mere legal meaning. What does justice look like for MSHT survivors? This chapter is underlined by the concept of subjection, as that universal dialectic dynamic of being-made and self-making. This angle to post–MSHT care aims to highlight how survivors navigate a paradoxical, often disempowering system, without fully subjugating or overturning it. From their attributed labels of vulnerability and trauma, survivors carve spaces to rebuild their identity and pursue their future aspirations. This happens through, and despite, the ambiguous terrains of the system of assistance.

Justice for survivors may be the possibility of re-centring their life, however this looks to the individual. We found, for example, that survivors of MSHT often express little interest in seeing their perpetrators punished. Given that most survivors originally wanted to work for a better life for themselves and their families, a lot of them desire compensation, or, when that is not an option, being able to provide for themselves and their families. In addition, while there is a reluctance to view themselves as victims, the concept of justice carries different meanings. In order to be accepted as a victim, and to receive support, trafficked individuals must subordinate to power. This necessarily feeds into their own self-image and can collide with their sense of self and agency. An internal 'victim versus subject with agency' ambivalence resonates with that of the MSHT discourse. This discourse, we have seen, is at the same time victimising and criminalising, and therefore establishes a culture of suspicion. From an even broader perspective, the negligence of governments in supporting and coordinating survivors' assistance speaks to the disparity between what we have in laws and what we have in practices. Postcolonial Global North versus South divides influence governmental policy approaches, whether this is through 'otherness' or through accepted paternalistic standpoints around people's vulnerability. It also speaks to unequal configurations within the international community. While there is unity on paper, very poor countries, for decades affected by natural disasters, political violence, wars and human-to-human exploitation of minors – such as Nepal and Vietnam – are not supported and simply lack the resources to care for their MSHT returnees.

In conclusion, we offer some recommendations for a system of care which may be more attuned with survivors' sense of justice and in full support of their 'becoming subjects'. Support that aims to empower its recipients should be designed in a way that respects the autonomy and agency of survivors. This approach realistically accepts that life for survivors does not return to a pre- or hetero-defined 'normal'. Survivors desire a normal life, and it is only they who know what that new normality should look like (Lazzarino, 2019). The trauma and experiences of subjection have been part of a survivor's life, but they do not define their subjectivity; instead, a rebalancing can take place in which the survivor can redefine themselves and make choices in line with this new identity. It is necessary to develop policies and practices of care which are survivor-centred and establish systems that show a sensitivity towards the actual support needs of survivors, and avoid re-traumatising. Consistent advocacy and support standards should be underpinned with training for all relevant practitioners in cultural and structural competence. This should be informed by survivor-led input, acknowledging the lived experiences of those who have been through these support systems and can attest to the success and limitations of various practices. Specific consideration should be given to the nature of trauma and its manifestation, by allowing survivors to decide how and when they access therapeutic intervention, and to make informed choices as to the most appropriate support for their needs.

Acknowledgements

We would like to express our deepest gratitude to all the participants of our studies, for sharing their views and experiences with us. We are also grateful to the known and unknown reviewers of the previous versions of this chapter for their constructive feedback, in particular Dr Carole Murphy and Dr Edward Wright.

References

Annison, R. and ATMG (2013) *Hidden in Plain Sight. Three Years On: Updated Analysis of UK Measures to Protect Trafficked Persons*. London: The Anti Trafficking Monitoring Group.

Aradau, C. (2008) *Rethinking Trafficking in Women: Politics Out of Security*. Basingstoke: Palgrave Macmillan.

Bankoff, G. (2001) Rendering the world unsafe: 'Vulnerability' as western discourse. *Disasters*, 25(1): 19–35.

Bravo, K.E. (2019) *Contemporary State Anti-'Slavery' Efforts: Dishonest and Ineffective*. Rochester: Social Science Research Network. Available from: https://papers.ssrn.com/abstract=3504027 (accessed 28 August 2021).

Browne, H., Esiovwa, N. and Dang, M. (2019) *The Journey of Our UK Survivor Network: Challenges & Successes*. Nottingham: Survivor Alliance UK CIC.

Butler, J. (1997) *The Psychic Life of Power: Theories in Subjection*. Stanford: Stanford University Press.

Christie, N. (1986) The ideal victim. In E.A. Fattah (ed) *From Crime Policy to Victim Policy*. London: Palgrave Macmillan, pp 17–30.

Chuang, J. (2010) Rescuing trafficking from ideological capture: Prostitution reform and anti-trafficking law and policy. *University of Pennsylvania Law Review*, 158(6): 1655–728.

Contreras, P.M., Kallivayalil, D. and Herman, J.L. (2017) Psychotherapy in the aftermath of human trafficking: Working through the consequences of psychological coercion. *Women & Therapy*, 40(1–2): 31–54.

Curran, R.L., Naidoo, J.R. and Mchunu, G. (2017) A theory for aftercare of human trafficking survivors for nursing practice in low resource settings. *Applied Nursing Research*, 35: 82–5.

Dando, C.J., Walsh, D. and Brierley, R. (2016) Perceptions of psychological coercion and human trafficking in the West Midlands of England: Beginning to know the unknown. *PLOS ONE* 11(5): e0153263.

Das, V. (2000) The act of witnessing: Violence, poisonous knowledge, and subjectivity. In V. Das, A. Kleinman, M. Ramphele, and P. Reynolds (eds) *Violence and Subjectivity*. Berkeley: University of California Press, pp 205–25.

de Lauretis, T. (1990) Eccentric subjects: Feminist theory and historical consciousness. *Feminist Studies*, 16(1): 115–50.

Doezema, J. (2010) *Sex Slaves and Discourse Masters: The Construction of Trafficking*. London and New York: Zed Books.

Doyle, D.M., Murphy, C., Murphy, M., Coppari, P.R. and Wechsler, R.J. (2019) 'I felt like she owns me': Exploitation and uncertainty in the lives of labour trafficking victims in Ireland. *The British Journal of Criminology*, 59(1): 231–51.

Fassin, D. et al (2002) *Traumatisme, victimologie et psychiatrie humanitaire: nouvelles figures et nouvelles pratiques en santé mentale: rapport final*. EHESS.

Fineman, M.A. (2008) The vulnerable subject: Anchoring equality in the human condition. *Yale Journal of Law & Feminism*, 20(1): 1–23

Goffman, E. (1990) *Asylums: Essays on the Social Situation of Mental Patients and Other Inmates.* New York: Anchor Books.

Hinton, D.E. and Good, B.J. (2016) *Culture and PTSD: Trauma in Global and Historical Perspective.* Philadelphia: University of Pennsylvania Press.

HTF (Human Trafficking Foundation) (2018) *The Slavery and Trafficking Survivor Care Standard.* London: Human Trafficking Foundation. Available from: https://www.antislaverycommissioner.co.uk/media/1235/slavery-and-trafficking-survivor-care-standards.pdf (accessed 28 August 2021).

Lazzarino, R. (2014) Between shame and lack of responsibility: The articulation of emotions among female returnees of human trafficking in northern Vietnam. *Antropologia South East Asia*, 1(1): 155–67.

Lazzarino, R. (2015) *Who Is the Subject of Human Trafficking? A Multi-sited and Polyphonic Ethnography.* Milan: University of Milano-Bicocca.

Lazzarino, R. (2017) After the shelter: The nuances of reintegrating human trafficking returnees in northern Vietnam. In S. Vignato (ed) *Dreams of Prosperity: Inequality and Integration in Southeast Asia.* Chiang Mai: Silkworm Books, pp 167–202.

Lazzarino, R. (2019) What is 'normal' in post-trafficking life? *Antislavery Early Research Association*, 22 January. Available from: https://antislavery era.com/2019/01/22/what-is-normal-in-post-trafficking-life/ (accessed 10 October 2019).

Lazzarino, R. (2020) PTSD or lack of love? *Medicine Anthropology Theory*, 7(2): 230–46.

Lazzarino, R., Wright, N. and Jordan, M. (2022) Mental healthcare for survivors of modern slavery and human trafficking: A single point-in-time, internet-based scoping study of third sector provision. *Journal of Human Trafficking*, 7(2): 1–18.

Lockyer, S. (2020) Beyond inclusion: Survivor-leader voice in anti-human trafficking organizations. *Journal of Human Trafficking*, 8(2): 135–56.

Pupavac, V. (2001) Therapeutic governance: Psycho-social intervention and trauma risk management. *Disasters*, 25(4): 358–72.

Shakti Samuha (2013) *Introduction Shakti Samuha.* Available from: http://shaktisamuha.org.np/about-us/introduction/ (accessed 29 August 2021).

Strauss, K. (2017) Sorting victims from workers: Forced labour, trafficking, and the process of jurisdiction. *Progress in Human Geography*, 41(2): 140–58.

Tran, T.H., Le, T.H. and Tran, T.P.D. (2020) Support trafficking victims through inter-agency cooperation in Vietnam: Achievements and limitations. *Asian Journal of Criminology*, 15(4): 321–44.

United Nations (2000) *Protocol to Prevent, Suppress and Punish Trafficking in Persons, Especially Women and Children, Supplementing the United Nations Convention against Transnational Organised Crime.* New York: UNODC.

UNODC (2012) *Guidance Note on 'Abuse of a Position of Vulnerability' as a Means of Trafficking in Persons in Article 3 of the Protocol to Prevent, Suppress and Punish Trafficking in Persons, Especially Women and Children, Supplementing the United Nations Convention against Transnational Organized Crime*. Vienna. Available from: https://www.unodc.org/documents/human-trafficking/2012/UNODC_2012_Guidance_Note_-_Abuse_of_a_Position_of_Vulnerability_E.pdf (accessed 5 March 2014).

Wright, N., Jordan, M. and Lazzarino, R. (2021) Interventions to support the mental health of survivors of modern slavery and human trafficking: A systematic review. *International Journal of Social Psychiatry*, 67(8): 1026–34.

10

Sexual exploitation: framing women's needs and experiences

Kathryn Hodges, Anta Brachou and Sarah Burch

Introduction

Sexual exploitation is a highly gendered crime which intersects with modern slavery and human trafficking (MSHT). Women and girls are disproportionately the victims of sexual exploitation. In addition, the ways in which exploitation is defined and addressed reflects gendered assumptions and perpetuates rigid gender roles that position women at a disadvantage with regards to the substantial exercise of their rights, such as freedom to act and to be recognised as autonomous (EIGE, 2021). There is a continuum of exploitation, and the harm women experience is represented and framed within UK legislation in multiple ways (for example, child sexual exploitation, prostitution, modern slavery and human trafficking) (Coy, 2016b). Women are vulnerable to exploitation because of their intersecting experiences of oppression. Exploitation is thus interwoven with multiple forms of complex disadvantage and cannot be understood in isolation.

This chapter brings attention to the lived experiences of sexually exploited women and the challenges they face in accessing support. Currently, women receive very different responses depending on how the exploitation they have experienced is framed. Helping services need to shift to a new understanding of how to best address women's intersecting experiences of disadvantage. How women 'are met' in services also needs to be re-evaluated, as illustrated in the Complex Experience Care Model (CECM; Hodges and Burch, 2019), which is considered in conjunction with the importance of culture competency. Culture competency and responsiveness are discussed as crucial elements that need to be embedded in support services helping women from various ethnicities and nationalities. The chapter seeks to investigate various aspects of helping services that may hinder support and that have an impact on women's help seeking experiences, and through the exploration of quotes provides recommendations on how support for women can be improved.

Throughout this chapter we draw on secondary data to include the voices of women heard in a number of previous research and service evaluations which focused on women's experience of seeking help and support (Hodges,

2018; Murphy et al, 2018; Murphy and Goldsmith, 2019). Given the limited avenues for exploited women to express their voices, service evaluations have been useful to enable these marginalised groups to speak up and shape services that are meaningful to them. To maintain confidentiality and anonymity, pseudonyms are used for the quotes provided. Additional learning is also drawn from a report bringing together learning and reflections on good practices in support provisions (Van Dyke and Brachou, 2021).

Sexual exploitation: a gendered discourse

The fact that sexual exploitation is strongly gendered is reflected in numerous ways. The term broadly refers to any sexual acts which are non-consensual or abusive, as reflected in the Modern Slavery Act 2015 (c.30). These can include pornography, trafficking and prostitution, witnessing or being coerced into sexual acts, and escorting. Yet while different types of activities can be identified, two issues are paramount. First, women and girls are the primary victims (UNODC, 2017; Home Office, 2020). Second, any differentiation between forms of exploitation obscures the fact that they are best understood as forming a continuum of risk and harm.

Studies of sexual exploitation repeatedly identify women and girls as the main target. The United Nations Office for Drugs and Crime report that 71 per cent of victims of trafficking detected globally are women and girls, a figure that rises to 96 per cent when focusing on trafficking for the purposes of sexual exploitation (UNODC, 2017). This pattern is also reflected in UK data from the National Referral Mechanism (NRM), the established framework for identifying and referring potential victims of modern slavery and ensuring they receive the appropriate support. In 2020, 90 per cent of adults referred for sexual exploitation were women. This gendered basis of exploitation can also be found in the sex industry, which Coy (2016a: 578) describes as 'a context in which sexual and physical violence, perpetrated by men against women and girls, is pervasive'. In every form of sexual exploitation, the victimising of women and girls reflects a pattern of structural violence and discrimination. According to the Convention on the Elimination of All Forms of Discrimination against Women General Recommendation No 35, violence against women is regarded as 'one of the fundamental social, political, and economic aspects by which the subordinate position of women with respect to men and their stereotyped roles are perpetuated' (CEDAW, 2017: 4).

These types of sexual exploitation are seldom discrete. Hawkins (2017: 8) argues that: 'Evidence supports the fact that child sexual abuse, prostitution, pornography, sex trafficking, sexual violence, etc., are not isolated phenomena occurring in a vacuum. Rather, these and other forms of sexual abuse and exploitation overlap and reinforce one another.' This point is also made by Farley et al (2013), who state that it is impossible to separate out different types of exploitation. Instead, they should be seen as a continuum of exploitation.

However, they are not always treated as such within policy and legislation. A failure to recognise this continuum leads to differential representation and responses to sexual exploitation. This dissonance shapes the way exploited women are met and considered by law enforcers, health and social care providers, policymakers and the wider community. Some of the implications of such interpretations of exploitation can be seen in relation to child sexual exploitation (CSE). Until the Sexual Offences Act 2003, there was no distinction in law between adults and children selling sex, therefore underage girls could be criminalised for prostitution. After 2003, this exploitation was reframed as abuse. Although this initially appears to be a more supportive response, Coy (2016b) argues that this obscures the continuum of exploitation which stems from structural inequality rather than individual vulnerability. As understanding of CSE grows, the dots need to be joined by social care professionals to understand that women involved in prostitution are frequently the same person as the exploited child (Coy, 2016b).

The tendency to distinguish between different types of victims of sexual exploitation is reflected in a range of legislative responses which can have a significant impact on the care women receive. A situation results where women and girls are seen either as victims of modern slavery and exploitation, or as having agency and making unfettered choices, with little reference to the social context, structural inequalities or lived experiences that create environments for such decisions to be made.

The demarcation between coercion and consent is often blurred. Choices are limited by circumstances, even when informed, and so the notion of an entirely free choice is illusory, and in the context of prostitution is arguably misleading (The Conservative Party Human Rights Committee, 2019). The All-Party Parliamentary Group (APPG) on Prostitution and the Global Sex Trade said 'to deny that there are no individuals for whom entry and exit into prostitution is entirely their own choice would be disingenuous … for the vast majority however, language of "choice" is deeply problematic' (APPG, 2014: 38). Many aspects can hinder women's capacity to make a free choice. Circumstances have a coercive effect and fail to provide the conditions which are necessary for genuine consent and free choice: physical safety, equal power with clients and actual alternate opportunities (Farley, 2013). Ultimately, this leaves women to make choiceless choices in a setting where power and gender inequalities prevail (Coy, 2016a).

Women who are vulnerable to exploitation are those whose lives already entail considerable precarity. This precarity stems from oppressive systems which reproduce social inequalities. These inequalities are experienced as multiple forms of overlapping disadvantage, such as poverty, lower social class, poor mental and physical health, drug and alcohol use, homelessness, lack of educational opportunities and exposure to crime. This precarity creates further vulnerability to exploitation, violence and abuse. Women's lived experiences therefore must be viewed as intersecting and interlinked.

The concept of intersecting lived experiences draws on the theoretical approach of intersectionality. Intersectionality recognises multiple identities and layers of oppression, examining the ways in which systems of discrimination such as race, gender and class interact and exploit (Crenshaw, 1991; Pittaway and Bartolomei, 2001; McCall, 2005). Women's lived experiences, the environments they inhabit and the complex multiple disadvantages they face, cannot be separated from the structure and culture in which they live (Godfrey and Callaghan, 2000; Neale, 2004).

It is undoubtedly the case that, by its very nature, much of women's exploitation remains hidden, and uncovering the extent of complex experiences of disadvantage can be difficult. Women referred to the NRM potentially represent only a fraction of cases. Nevertheless, NRM data provides an indication of some of the points of intersection for the women who are identified as referrals. The UK is both a destination country for thousands of foreign national victims, exploited in a myriad of forms, and a source country, as the majority of victims (34 per cent) identified and supported through the NRM are UK nationals (Home Office, 2020). Albanian and Vietnamese citizens are the next largest groups referred, with many women victims from Albania mostly reporting experiences of sexual exploitation (Home Office, 2020). The high number of foreign national victims identified points to the importance of better understanding cultural contexts and needs, which could enable more inclusive services and better engagement with the survivors they seek to support.

The experiences of women and girls who have been trafficked into the UK for purposes of sexual exploitation can be influenced by differing social and cultural factors. Women's exposure to the varying cultural standards and myths about sexual violence shapes how they identify themselves and comprehend their experiences (Krieger, 2020). For example, women coming from cultures where domestic and intimate partner violence is normalised might struggle to identify as victims, and consequently do not promptly seek help upon arrival in the UK. Though women from all settings may share common experiences, there will also be significant diversity. Cultural understanding and competency are therefore essential in addressing survivor needs and are further explored in this chapter.

Women commonly experience profound disadvantage both prior to and as a consequence of their sexual exploitation. The ways in which these experiences reinforce each other and interact has important implications for how helping services should be designed and how they respond to the women who need them. Some of these intersecting experiences will now briefly be considered to demonstrate the severe and multiple disadvantages which women face. This section will draw on women's testimony drawn from previous studies (Hodges, 2018; Murphy, et al, 2018; Murphy and Goldsmith, 2019) where appropriate consent for data usage had been given. The decision was taken to use secondary data in recognition of the sensitivity of talking to women about such experiences. A basic ethical principle of research with vulnerable groups is that participants should not be harmed by the experience (Moriña, 2021). Sensitive research can be an intensely emotional experience (Shaw et al, 2020), and it is vital not to re-traumatise participants by requesting them to revisit difficult events unnecessarily. Using secondary data offers a way to include women's voices in the discussion.

Intersecting experiences of disadvantage

Women's vulnerability to exploitation is often rooted in lifelong disadvantage. Women who endure severe and multiple disadvantages as adults have often experienced childhoods characterised by poverty. Poor outcomes of schooling and having experienced trauma are also common (McDonagh, 2011; Fitzpatrick et al, 2013). These experiences compromise women's ability to support themselves and their children. They may become involved in prostitution to finance basic material needs (Dalla, 2002; Hester and Westmarland, 2004), with many becoming stuck in a cycle of debt. Prostitution may also result from false promises of work in more affluent countries for MSHT victims, who find themselves trapped and isolated, with passports confiscated, in debt bondage and receiving threats of violence against family members (Lehti and Aromaa, 2006; Lee, 2011; Hales and Gelsthorpe, 2012).

Furthermore, poverty often intersects with criminal activity, violence and abuse (Rugmay, 2010). Women become drawn into the criminal justice system through a number of routes linked to their exploitation, such as prostitution, drug dealing and substance misuse, and theft (Harvey et al, 2017). When it comes to such cases where women are also labelled as offenders, in many instances the stigma associated with their actions far outweighs any acknowledgement of their experiences of exploitation.

These lived experiences are further compounded by a lack of safe and secure accommodation, compromising wellbeing and safety and heightening the risk of destitution. Rough sleeping, poor mental health and learning disabilities have been identified among trafficked British nationals (Homeless Link, 2016; Keast, 2017). Judy explains what happens when there is no safe and secure accommodation available:

> Come out of jail you've got nowhere to go, you end up here, or you end up back in jail, because you've got nowhere to go … and in the

end I got sleeping with somebody or got in somewhere which isn't good for them and putting up with things they shouldn't put up with for a place to stay, sleeping with some old man that's 70 because they've got nowhere to go. (Hodges, 2018: 102)

As recently highlighted in the *Closed Doors* report (Liisanantti and Brachou, 2020), enhanced provision of appropriate and secure accommodation is crucial for MSHT victims and essential during recovery journeys and reintegration in society. Failure to ensure safe and suitable accommodation can contribute to the continuum of risk and harm; thus, making any previous support futile and recovery progress unsustainable (Hodges and Burch, 2019; Liisanantti and Brachou, 2020).

Sexual exploitation is also frequently associated with higher levels of drug and alcohol use (Hester and Westmarland, 2004; Brown, 2013; Matthews et al, 2014). Again, however, complex interrelationships can be observed. It can be the case that prostitution becomes necessary to finance drug use, but drug use can also operate to blunt the trauma of involvement with prostitution, along with other highly damaging experiences (Young et al, 2000; Bindel et al, 2012). Debbie talked about how she had sex for drugs:

Umm well I have sex for drugs, umm I get income support at the moment, I'm only getting £24.48 every two weeks income support … umm I have friends come round, friends give me, I have sex for drugs. … Yeah I'm used to it now. … It's nice when umm my friends come and treat me and I don't have to do anything. (Hodges, 2018: 111)

Women who have past experiences of violence and abuse can carry a legacy of mental health difficulties, including post-traumatic stress disorder, anxiety and depression, psychosis, and eating disorders (Humphreys, 2003; Scott et al, 2015). Dissociation becomes a self-protective strategy which can in turn expose women to further risk if they fail to react to subsequent danger signals (Ross et al, 2003). Feelings of isolation and loneliness can be profound (Hodges, 2018).

[W]hen you're just in your own room by yourself, you end up having all these … all these thoughts you … because when you're by yourself … it's something I personally don't like when I … when I sit by myself and I sit for a very long time, I start to have all these irrational thoughts and it's something that. … I don't like so being … getting out the house, doing something, having a laugh with other people it's … it's good cause it makes you forget what … what's happening to you, what your experiences are so you don't have to think, so like it makes you less depressed. (Gloria, in Murphy et al, 2018: 54)

Women may also undergo grief and loss, often linked to separation from close networks, family or the removal of their children through safeguarding processes (Hodges, 2018). Devastating experiences such as bereavement can take place against a backdrop of past trauma and disadvantage. '[W]hen my son died, I used to be. ... I had a temper, but I just felt anger against the damn world. ... I was just thinking why me, what have I done? I must be cursed or something' (Angela, in Hodges, 2018: 104).

Severe physical health problems can also accompany sexual exploitation. Trafficked women may undergo hyper-violent multiple rapes, with consequent risk of harms such as vaginal injury, loss of blood and a range of infections (Silverman et al, 2011), along with the impact of repeated pregnancies, miscarriages and abortions (European Commission, 2016).

Attempting to seek help in dealing with these countless traumas and experiences is further compounded by complex systems and often uncertain legal status. Individuals trafficked into the UK are frequently without appropriate documentation as traffickers have taken it from them in a bid to maintain control (Home Office, 2016). Immigration status is exacerbated by convoluted legal and support systems, fear of law enforcement and additional language and cultural barriers. MSHT victims experience numerous challenges when trying to escape their situations and integrate into society. Even after many years in the UK, women can find accessing support almost impossible.

Storm (in Hodges, 2018) experienced complications with her visa leading her to have no recourse to public funds. Storm had lived and worked in the UK for around 20 years, during which time she was legitimately employed. She was sleeping on the streets and awaiting the outcome to her case; she reports her frustrations about this experience and her lack of access to services.

> I had my hearing on a Monday the judge kindly told me he was going on vacation so that's going to delay my case. Where am I now? On the street. I have to wait another month or two for a decision. Where am I? On the street. I know in my mind, I'm thinking if I get kicked and die out there so I'm saying ... you're just left to fend for yourself. (Storm, in Hodges, 2018: 109)

Sexually exploited women therefore experience a series of complex and overlapping hardships linked to their position of structural, gendered disadvantage. Addressing these needs poses challenges for traditional approaches to support. Women facing severe and multiple disadvantage face difficulties in connecting and participating with services. They may be required to access multiple agencies in relation to different needs, which is a struggle, or find that the services offer little benefit. Many may not use services at all (Cabinet Office, 2006). Single focus support services which specialise in one type of need, such as housing or help with drug and alcohol use, are unlikely to be effective as they fail to acknowledge the whole journey and the consequences of the intersecting experiences. In the next section, the focus is on the implications of these intersecting experiences for services of exploited women.

Improving support for women

The nature of service provision is critical for women. This is not only because they need to be appropriate and effective to work, but also because poorly considered services can expose victims of exploitation to the risk of further harm (Hodges and Burch, 2019). There is still a 'high prevalence of institutional misunderstanding' about the needs and experiences of women, even though there is extensive and clear research setting out approaches and methods that would improve women's position (Corston, 2007: 16; Van Dyke and Brachou, 2021). In the following section, three central aspects of women's services are explored: access and awareness; creating safe and welcoming environments; and addressing cultural barriers.

Access and awareness

The first step in help-seeking is women knowing that the experiences they have had are framed as 'needs' in policy and practice, and that there is support. While the language of need underpins policy and practice, women do not always conceptualise their experiences in this way. They talk about 'things that have happened to them' (Hodges, 2018: 52) rather than seeing their experiences as constituting needs which can or should be met. This framing of their experiences can inhibit women from becoming aware of services and how they could help. Jasmine (in Hodges, 2018: 136) said she was unsure what help was available or how she could access it: 'I didn't think that I was worthy of it.'

Awareness of the possibility of help is thus essential, followed by awareness that there are specific services that could offer support. However, knowledge alone may not be sufficient to ensure that women access services. Signposting to a service is unlikely to be sufficient, as it underestimates the impact of women's experiences and their ability to access numerous services at any one time without causing a feeling of overwhelm. As Tess comments: 'I never actually went there because I found it really hard to organise myself and I just needed someone to take me to be honest. I only ever went to things when people told me go here and they went with me' (Tess, in Hodges, 2018: 144). Women may also have language difficulties which require support:

At the beginning I had help with everything. My English wasn't good, so I needed a translator wherever I went. I needed someone to go with me as well. Now I am a lot more independent, and I am able to go to places by myself and do things independently. (Anika in Murphy and Goldsmith, 2019: 144)

In many instances, effective service delivery will entail accompanying women to appointments. This kind of emotional and practical support is essential, especially when women must negotiate numerous services with different eligibility criteria and locations. Again, this underscores the inadequacy of services which focus on a single need or problem when women need support with intersecting experiences of severe disadvantage.

Creating safe and welcoming environments

If women are to use services successfully, they must be made to feel safe and welcome. While this might seem an obvious example of good practice, it is difficult to overstate how essential it is for women who have previous experience of violence and abuse. Exposure to trauma and unsafe environments lead women to develop mechanisms such as hyper-arousal and avoidance (Elliott et al, 2005; Hopper et al, 2010) to keep themselves safe. This may prevent them from being able to trust services enough to engage. An explicit trauma-informed approach to service delivery can help create a sense of safety (Elliott et al, 2005; Covington, 2008; Witkin and Robjant, 2018), which usually needs to be in place before women can begin to address their other needs.

Safety can be found in practical terms when a space is managed well, but it also stems from how people within a service relate to the women who need support. Women say that they want to be listened to, taken seriously and understood, not just treated as a tick-box exercise (Hodges, 2018). Any sense that staff are simply going through the motions undermines the trust and acceptance that are so fundamental if women are to feel safe enough to share painful experiences and reach out for help. The following quote illustrates how central staff attitudes are to women's perception of a service: 'he looked so bored filling in the forms you know what I mean he just, didn't give a shit if I was another night on the street or not ... he couldn't be bothered he basically wanted to get me through the paperwork and go ... that's how I felt' (Jane, in Hodges, 2018: 136). In contrast, demonstrating warmth and compassion, alongside upholding commitments, conveys a sense of authentic care and support:

Megan came with me to my court case, on Monday. ... She volunteered, you know she said to me can I send a statement, a witness statement about you? And I said are you sure? No, no, I want to, so she did. Then she asked to come. ... I said you don't have to and she said, then she offered to pay ... so, that's someone who cares; she didn't have to do all of that. (Storm, in Hodges, 2018: 118)

When women do not take up services that are available to them, it is often treated as a failure of engagement on their behalf. However, women's testimonies reveal the damaging impact of being met with indifference or a lack of care. Small cues betray the sense that support staff might not be genuine or trustworthy: 'The way like they used to speak to you like it's just, like the vibe I used to get off her, do you know, and when she would speak to me she'd never look me in the eye or just wee things like that' (Anne, in Hodges, 2018: 139). Additionally, such experiences can be witnessed in discomforting non-gender-sensitive environments that also thwart women's sense of belonging, and hence their willingness or otherwise to accept the support on offer. On the other hand, women-only services can create a greater sense of security (Hodges, 2018), particularly in relation to accommodation, where gender-responsive provisions are considered more suitable for MSHT victims (Liisanantti and Brachou, 2020). 'It [single occupancy room] was very tidy ... was very ... everything was decorated ... everything was like ... it was really such nice ... it just makes me emotional. I was safe' (Faith in Murphy et al, 2018: 27).

Addressing cultural barriers

The high number of foreign national victims identified by the NRM (66 per cent of all referrals) (Home Office, 2020) means consideration must be given to cultural issues and their implications for the quality of interventions. In 2020, the NRM reported victims from roughly 90 nationalities. Therefore, cultural responsiveness, sensitivity and competency are vital when it comes to designing and delivering interventions, as well as meeting people in services. According to McFarlane (cited in Robertson, 2014: 88) cultural responsiveness 'refers to the delivery of the programme and the ability to respond to fluid, authentic situations in ways that resonate with and are therefore culturally appropriate and affirm the culture of clients'. Moreover, culturally sensitive or culture-specific services take into consideration and align with values and norms of the client group, making interventions culturally appropriate (Robertson, 2014). Such services are better equipped to unpick the subtle cultural background and context that can influence how women ask for and access help and support. For instance, where culturally specific counselling is offered, evidence suggests it enables understanding of the women's perspective in the context of their cultural upbringing, for example appreciating how challenging it may be to acknowledge and talk about intimate partners due to stigma and shame; thus benefiting the support relationship between women and such services (Brachou, 2021). It can be argued that there is added value in offering culture-specific support in women's native language to navigate many of the challenges (poor quality or availability) that are experienced when language interpretation is needed (Westwood et al, 2016). Tailored cultural provisions that respond to women's specific cultural needs and offer assistance in various languages to enable access are better placed and equipped to establish a trusting relationship with care seekers, and thus deliver appropriate and holistic support (Van Dyke and Brachou, 2021).

Additionally, given the diverse client groups in any one service, cultural competency is important to successfully interact with the women and enhance the levels of trust. The cultural competency of practitioners involves awareness, knowledge and skills to understand and discern cultural differences, with subsequent adaptation to clients' needs. As de Chesnay et al (in de Chesnay and Anderson, 2016) point out, cultural competency can be explained as the ability to use information about another's culture to provide care and support that the person can accept comfortably. By using this approach, services and practitioners are better equipped to address the needs of victims, as well as the barriers keeping them from accessing these needs.

Thus, in addition to the obvious language barriers, support services need also to be equipped first to acknowledge and address cultural barriers, and second to address them, either by implementing culturally competent and sensitive services, or through offering cultural mediation. This is a strategic approach to cultural sensitivity which creates a bridge to address the cultural gap between a migrant group, in this case women, and the host culture's support and care organisations (Davies, 2004). Cultural mediation improves the experience of seeking and providing support, to ensure effective engagement and avoid misunderstandings across both parties (Davies, 2004). In the UK, unlike elsewhere in Europe (Theodosiou and Aspioti, 2016), cultural mediators are not recognised and certified roles. Therefore, the practice is offered loosely and on an ad hoc basis by support workers and advocates, who are representatives of certain cultures. They go beyond their prescribed designated roles by being able to unpick the complex cultural dynamics that may impact how victims are perceived by decision-makers and service providers. The importance of this approach needs to be given much more attention within service design. As pointed out by a recent report (Rakovica and Ianovitz, 2021) cultural mediation can enable foreign national women who are victims of gender-based violence to make their voices heard, while navigating the various legal systems, understanding and demanding their rights and creating a safe space for integration.

The Complex Experience Care Model

The next section looks at the actions needed to improve support services for women who have experienced sexual exploitation. As has been demonstrated, a number of issues need to be taken into account when considering service design and delivery: the extreme and intersecting experiences endured by exploited women; the type of provision which is most appropriate to tackle these overlapping forms of severe and multiple disadvantage; and the actions of staff within services which can best support women to use them. The CECM (Hodges and Burch, 2019; see Figure 10.1) has been developed as a tool to help professionals comprehend the ways in which these issues operate and align. It can be used to inform the planning and commissioning of services, as well as helping professionals contextualise the experiences of women, which too often are disaggregated into a series of separate needs

Figure 10.1: The Complex Experience Care Model set within the context of cultural competency, responsiveness and sensitivity

Source: Adapted from Hodges and Burch (2019)

to meet specific single service priorities. Within this model, understanding women's experiences of trauma is key.

At the centre of the model are women themselves and their experiences of traumatic and intersecting events which have happened to them. These events influence the ways in which women make sense of their experiences and decide whether and how to seek help and from whom, as represented in the middle ring of the model. Again, these sense-making and decision-making processes are influenced by women's responses to the trauma they have suffered. The outer ring of the model reflects the implications for service delivery and commissioning when ensuring that services will be appropriate, workable and responsive to women.

The CECM can be used as a reflective tool to underpin design and decision-making in a range of service settings. However, for services which regularly seek to provide support and a place of safety for foreign national victims of sexual exploitation, it is important to acknowledge the role of culture more explicitly. In Figure 10.1, the CECM can be seen overlaid with the concepts of cultural competency, cultural responsiveness and cultural sensitivity/mediation. This overlay further informs the outer ring of service design and delivery, underscoring the necessity of culturally appropriate approaches to address cultural and gender needs. Integrating this cultural lens more overtly within the CECM fosters a focus on services which enhance recovery outcomes for victims by acknowledging the diverse cultural dynamics that impact women's lived experiences, their levels of resilience, their perceptions of help and their capacities to seek support.

Conclusion

The sexual exploitation of women must be understood as a continuum rather than a set of divergent types as expressed within the current boundaries set in policy and legislation. Vulnerabilities to exploitation are linked to things that have happened elsewhere in women's lives – they don't stand alone. This vulnerability, and the experiences which accompany it, must be seen as highly gendered. Women need to be met and supported holistically, where practitioners and services can support them in the round.

Access requirements and the ways in which services are provided can be a barrier to women who seek help, many of whom have significant histories of trauma. This reinforces precarity in women's lives and directly increases their vulnerability to further exploitation. It is therefore imperative that policymakers, practitioners and service providers understand that women's experiences influence how they seek help. This includes significant traumatic experiences which have long-term implications for mental wellbeing.

The priority must be to develop services which genuinely feel safe, supportive and respectful while being comprehensive in scope. Services should ensure cultural responsiveness and sensitivity when meeting women and providing support. Women need to place extraordinary trust in practitioners in order to be able to use services. Services must repay this trust if they are to give women the opportunity to have the time, space and support to recover.

References

APPG (All-Party Parliamentary Group on Prostitution and the Global Sex Trade) (2014) *Shifting the Burden: Inquiry to Assess the Operation of the Current Legal Settlement on Prostitution in England and Wales*. London: All-Party Parliamentary Group on Prostitution and the Global Sex Trade.

Bindel, J., Brown, L., Easton, H., Matthews, R. and Reynolds, L. (2012) *Breaking Down the Barriers: A Study of How Women Exit Prostitution*. London: Eaves.

Brachou, A. (2021) On culture sensitive support services: Data collected as part of evaluation projects. Unpublished.

Brown, L. (2013) *Cycles of Harm: Problematic Alcohol Use amongst Women Involved in Prostitution*. London: Alcohol Research UK. Available from: http://alcoholresearchuk.org/downloads/finalReports/FinalRepo rt_0108.pdf (accessed 23 June 2017).

Cabinet Office (2006) *Reaching Out: An Action Plan on Social Exclusion*. London: HMSO.

CEDAW (Convention on the Elimination of All Forms of Discrimination against Women) (2017) *General Recommendation No. 35 on Gender-Based Violence against Women, Updating General Recommendation No. 19*. Available from: https://tbinternet.ohchr.org/_layouts/15/treatybodyexternal/ Download.aspx?symbolno=CEDAW/C/GC/35&Lang=en (accessed 14 July 2022).

The Conservative Party Human Rights Commission (2019) *The Limits of Consent: Prostitution in the UK*. London: CPHRC. Available from: https:// conservativepartyhumanrightscommission.co.uk/wp-content/uploads/ 2020/03/CPHRC_Consent_Report-1.pdf (accessed 22 December 2021).

Corston, J. (2007) *The Corston Report*. London: Home Office. Available from: http://www.justice.gov.uk/publications/docs/corston-report- march-2007.pdf (accessed 23 June 2017).

Covington, S. (2008) Women and addiction: A trauma-informed approach. *Journal of Psychoactive Drugs*, SARC supplement 5: 377–85.

Coy, M. (2016a) 'I am a person too': Women's accounts and images about body and self in prostitution. In M. Coy (ed) *Prostitution, Harm and Gender Inequality: Theory, Research and Policy*. London: Routledge.

Coy, M. (2016b) Joining the dots on sexual exploitation of children and women: A way forward for UK policy responses. *Critical Social Policy*, 36(4): 572–91.

Crenshaw, K.W. (1991) Mapping the margins: Intersectionality, identity politics, and violence against women of color. *Stanford Law Review*, 43(6): 1241–99.

Dalla, R.L. (2002) Night moves: A qualitative investigation of street-level sex work. *Psychology of Women Quarterly*, 26(1): 63–73.

Davies, J. (2004) Comparing cultural mediation and cultural advocacy: As effective action research methodologies for engaging with vulnerable migrant women. *Journal of Social Work Research and Evaluation*, 5(2): 149–67.

de Chesnay, M. and Anderson, B. (eds) (2016) *Caring for the Vulnerable: Perspectives in Nursing Theory, Practice and Research*. Sudbury, MA: Jones & Bartlett Publishers.

EIGE (European Institute for Gender Equality) (2021) Gender: Glossary and thesaurus. Available from: https://eige.europa.eu/thesaurus/terms/ 1141 (accessed 14 July 2022).

Elliott, D.E., Bjelajac, P., Fallot, R.D., Markoff, L.S. and Reed, B.G. (2005) Trauma-informed or trauma-denied: Principles and implementation of trauma-informed services for women. *Journal of Community Psychology*, 33(4): 461–77.

European Commission (2016) *Study on the Gender Dimension of Trafficking in Human Beings: Final Report*. Luxembourg: Publications Office of the European Union. Available from: https://data.europa.eu/doi/10.2837/ 698222 (accessed 22 December 2021).

Farley, M. (2013) Prostitution, liberalism, and slavery. *Logos*, 13(3).

Farley, M., Franzblau, K. and Kennedy, M.A. (2013) Online prostitution and trafficking. *Albany Law Review*, 77(3): 139–57.

Fitzpatrick, S., Bramley, G. and Johnsen, S. (2013) Pathways into multiple exclusion homelessness in seven UK cities. *Urban Studies*, 50(1): 148–68.

Godfrey, M. and Callaghan, G. (2000) *Exploring Unmet Need: The Challenge of a User-centred Response*. York: York Pub. Services for the Joseph Rowntree Foundation.

Hales, L. and Gelsthorpe, L. (2012) *The Criminalisation of Migrant Women*. ESRC End of Award Report, RES-062-23-2348. Swindon: ESRC.

Harvey, H., Brown, L. and Young, L. (2017) *'I'm no criminal': Examining the Impact of Prostitution-specific Criminal Records on Women Seeking to Exit Prostitution*. London: nia.

Hawkins, D. (2017) It can't wait: Exposing the connections between forms of sexual exploitation. *Dignity: A Journal of Analysis of Exploitation and Violence*, 2(3). https://doi.org/10.23860/dignity.2017.02.03.02.

Hester, M. and Westmarland, N. (2004) Tackling street prostitution: Towards a holistic approach. Project Report. London: Home Office Research, Development and Statistics Directorate. Available from: http://dro.dur.ac.uk/2557/ (accessed 14 July 2022).

Hodges, K. (2018) *An Exploration of Decision Making by Women Experiencing Multiple and Complex Needs.* Chelmsford: Anglia Ruskin University.

Hodges, K. and Burch, S. (2019) Multiple and intersecting experiences of women in prostitution: Improving access to helping services. *Dignity: A Journal on Sexual Exploitation and Violence*, 4(2). https://doi.org/10.23860/dignity.2019.04.02.03.

Home Office (2016) *Victims of Modern Slavery: Frontline Staff Guidance.* Available from: http://www.antislaverycommissioner.co.uk/media/1057/victims-of-modern-slavery-frontline-staff-guidance-v3.pdf (accessed 29 October 2017).

Home Office (2020) *National Referral Mechanism Statistics UK: End of Year Summary 2019.* Available from: https://assets.publishing.service.gov.uk/government/uploads/system/uploads/attachment_data/file/876646/national-referral-mechanism-statistics-uk-end-of-year-summary-2019.pdf (accessed 14 July 2022).

Homeless Link (2016) *Trafficking and Forced Labour: Guidance for Frontline Homelessness Services.* London: Homeless Link. Available from: https://www.homeless.org.uk/sites/default/files/site-attachments/Trafficking%20and%20Forced%20Labour%20guidance%20-%20May%202016.pdf (accessed 26 November 2018).

Hopper, E.K., Bassuk, E.L. and Olivet, J. (2010) Shelter from the storm: Trauma-informed care in homeless settings. *The Open Health Services and Policy Journal*, 3: 80–100.

Humphreys, C. (2003) Mental health and domestic violence: 'I call it symptoms of abuse'. *British Journal of Social Work*, 33(2): 209–26.

Keast, M. (2017) *Understanding and Responding to Modern Slavery within the Homelessness Sector.* London: Homeless Link. Available from: https://www.antislaverycommissioner.co.uk/media/1115/understanding-and-responding-to-modern-slavery-within-the-homelessness-sector.pdf (accessed 26 November 2018).

Krieger, M.A. (2020) *Image-based Sexual Violence: Victim Experiences and Bystander Responses.* Windsor, Canada: University of Windsor. Available from: https://scholar.uwindsor.ca/cgi/viewcontent.cgi?article=9340&context=etd (accessed 14 July 2022).

Lee, M. (2011) *Trafficking and Global Crime Control.* London: SAGE.

Lehti, M. and Aromaa, K. (2006) Trafficking for sexual exploitation. *Crime and Justice*, 34(1): 133–227.

Liisanantti, A. and Brachou, A. (2020) *Closed Doors: Inequalities and Injustices in Appropriate and Secure Housing Provision for Female Victims of Trafficking Who Are Seeking Asylum.* London: Hibiscus Initiatives. Available from: https://www.commonwealhousing.org.uk/static/uploads/2020/12/2020_11_24-HI_Closed-Doors_Main-Report_FINAL_DIGITAL.pdf (accessed 14 July 2022).

Matthews, R., Bindel, J., Young, L. and Easton, H. (2014) *Exiting Prostitution: A Study in Female Desistance.* Basingstoke: Palgrave Macmillan.

McCall, L. (2005) The complexity of intersectionality. *Signs: Journal of Women in Culture and Society*, 30(3): 1771–800.

McDonagh, T. (2011) *Tackling Homeless Exclusions: Understanding Complex Lives.* York: Joseph Rowntree Foundation.

Moriña, A. (2021) When people matter: The ethics of qualitative research in the health and social sciences. *Health & Social Care in the Community*, 29(5): 1559–65.

Murphy, C. and Goldsmith, C. (2019) *An Independent Evaluation of the Snowdrop Project.* London: St Mary's University.

Murphy, C., Goldsmith, C., Barry, A.-M. and Hodges, K. (2018) *Independent Review of Caritas Bakhita House.* London: St Mary's University.

Neale, J. (2004) Gender and illicit drug use. *British Journal of Social Work*, 34(6): 851–70.

Pittaway, E. and Bartolomei, L. (2001) Refugees, race, and gender: The multiple discrimination against refugee women. *Refuge*, 19(6): 21–32.

Rakovica, B. and Ianovitz, S. (2021) *Cultural Mediation: An Inclusive Solution to Help Reduce the Cultural and Language Barriers Experienced by Survivors of Trafficking.* London: Hibiscus Initiatives. Available from: https://hibiscusinitiatives.org.uk/wp-content/uploads/2021/03/Hibiscus_Cultural-Mediation-Report_A4_Final_digital.pdf (accessed 14 July 2022).

Robertson, J. (2014) *Effective Parenting Programmes: A Review of the Effectiveness of Parenting Programmes for Parents of Vulnerable Children.* Wellington: Social Policy and Evaluation Research Unit. Available from: https://www.socialserviceworkforce.org/system/files/resource/files/Effective-Parenting-Programmes-Report.pdf (accessed 14 July 2022).

Ross, C.A., Farley, M. and Schwartz, H.L. (2003) Dissociation among women in prostitution. In M. Farley (ed) *Prostitution, Trafficking and Traumatic Stress.* Binghamton: Haworth Maltreatment & Trauma Press, pp 199–212.

Rugmay, J. (2010) When victims become offenders: In search of coherence in policy and practice. *Family & Intimate Partner Violence Quarterly*, 3(1): 47–64.

Scott, S., Williams, J., McNaughton Nicholls, C., McManus, S., Brown, A., Harvey, S., Kelly, L. and Lovett, J. (2015) *Violence, Abuse and Mental Health in England (REVA Briefing 1).* Available from: www.natcen.ac.uk/revabriefing1 (accessed 14 July 2022).

Shaw, R.M., Howe, J., Beazer, J. and Carr, T. (2020) Ethics and positionality in qualitative research with vulnerable and marginal groups. *Qualitative Research*, 20(3): 277–93.

Silverman, J.G., Raj, A., Cheng, D.M., Decker, M.R., Coleman, S., Bridden, C., Pardeshi, M., Saggurti, N. and Samet, J.H. (2011) Sex trafficking and initiation-related violence, alcohol use, and HIV risk among HIV-infected female sex workers in Mumbai, India. *Journal of Infectious Diseases*, 204(suppl 5): S1229–S1234.

Theodosiou, A. and Aspioti, M. (eds) (2016) *Research Report on Intercultural Mediation for Immigrants in Europe*. ERASMUS. Available from: http://www.mediation-time.eu/images/TIME_O1_Research_Report_v.2016.pdf (accessed 14 July 2022).

UNODC (United Nations Office on Drugs and Crime) (2017) *Global Report on Trafficking in Persons 2016*. Vienna: United Nations Office on Drugs and Crime Research. Available from: https://www.unodc.org/documents/data-and-analysis/glotip/2016_Global_Report_on_Trafficking_in_Persons.pdf (accessed 14 July 2022).

Van Dyke, R. and Brachou, A. (2021) *What Looks Promising for Tackling Modern Slavery: A Review of Practice-based Research*. London: St Mary's University.

Westwood, J., Howard, L., Stanley, N., Zimmerman, C., Gerada, C. and Oram, S. (2016) Access to, and experiences of, healthcare services by trafficked people: Findings from a mixed-methods study in England. *British Journal of General Practice* [online]. DOI: 10.3399/bjgp16X687073

Witkin, R. and Robjant, D.K. (2018) *The Trauma-Informed Code of Conduct*. London: Helen Bamber Foundation. Available from: http://www.helenbamber.org/wp-content/uploads/2019/01/Trauma-Informed-Code-of-Conduct.pdf (accessed 5 January 2020).

Young, A.M., Boyd, C. and Hubbell, A. (2000) Prostitution, drug use, and coping with psychological distress. *Journal of Drug Issues*, 30(4): 789–800.

11

Survivor support: how a values-based service can enhance access to psychological capital

Carole Murphy and Karen Anstiss

Introduction

Several studies have investigated the support necessities of victims/survivors of modern slavery and human trafficking (MSHT) and have highlighted the need for bespoke support and trauma informed care (Oram et al, 2016; Okech et al, 2018). Understanding the trafficking 'journey' (Zimmerman et al, 2011) can enhance knowledge of recovery trajectories and propose evidence-based solutions. Gaps in long-term support in the UK and the negative impact on outcomes for survivors identify the requirement for more tailored and well-resourced support (Murphy, 2018). To improve service delivery and remedy gaps, guidance for needs assessment, service evaluations and care standards for service providers have been developed to support specific interventions informed by practitioner experience and other research evidence (Robjant et al, 2017; Bundock and Hodges, 2020). This chapter aims to extend this knowledge base and contribute to a greater understanding of interventions in situ in a safe house and identify its relevance to policy and practice.

Between March and June 2018, 31 qualitative interviews were conducted with safe house staff (n=6), current and former guests[1] (n=11), volunteers (n=13) and partners (n=2) for the purposes of evaluating service provision and the ability to meet service aims and objectives. The interviews were transcribed and analysed using thematic analysis (Braun and Clarke, 2006: 5). Descriptive and analytical codes were developed that are representative of predetermined themes originating from concepts evident in the literature, following the approach taken by Farrell and Pfeffer (2014). In this case, themes based on concepts that were prevalent within and across all or most interviews were identified, many of which reflected the values of the service. A second level of analysis was conducted in preparation for this chapter using the framework of psychological capital (Luthans et al, 2007). Ethical approval was obtained from St Mary's University Ethics Committee.

The first author proposes that applying theoretical/conceptual frameworks could inform a deeper understanding of implicit approaches used in supporting survivors and how they operate to assist recovery. This chapter has two key interrelated aims: to offer examples of practice interventions through an examination of data collected as part of a service evaluation (Murphy et al, 2018) and to provide insights to practitioners about the application of theoretical and conceptual frameworks to practice. The application of frameworks may prove a useful tool in making implicit practices explicit, therefore opening up possibilities for measuring impacts more effectively (see also Chapter 13, this volume); and to make the case for the benefits of values-based service in enhancing survivors access to psychological capital. In proposing this framework as a useful tool for understanding recovery and rehabilitation, the lead author recognises that other frameworks for survivor recovery are in operation (see also Chapters 9 and 12, this volume), and that this is just one of many potential possibilities for furthering knowledge of best practice interventions.

The chapter is divided into four sections. First, a brief overview of recent studies that identify the journeys of survivors, before, during and after identification illustrates common themes covered in research and practice. Second, the conceptual framework of psychological capital (PsyCap) is introduced. PsyCap is a 'composite construct' that denotes an individual's positive psychological state of development (Luthans et al, 2007: 542). It has four key characteristics: self-efficacy, optimism, hope and resilience. Third, a description of a residential safe house for women, authored by the second author, the safe house manager, provides background information about the programme as seen through the eyes of the staff and volunteers. Interwoven in this overview, quotes from interviews with staff and volunteers illustrate how the safe house values of love, respect, community and spirituality underpin the day-to-day programme and are communicated to survivors in practice. Finally, analysis of interview data with survivors reveals how these values are transformed into acquisition of the four characteristics of PsyCap. The importance of these characteristics for transitioning into independence is explored. The chapter concludes with recommendations for developing opportunities for theoretically informed interventions through knowledge exchange activities between practice and academia and offers important insights to policymakers about what works.

Exemplars of common research themes and practice insights

Research on MSHT covers a range of topics as diverse as the phenomenon itself. Practitioner-informed guidance for supporting survivors is an important source of information and, set alongside academic studies, highlights the intersection of practice with academic research. Zimmerman et al's (2011) conceptual model underlines the impact of trafficking on victims along the trajectory from recruitment to reintegration or re-trafficking. The experience of trafficking has been likened to torture (OSCE, 2013) and the health, mental health and impact of trauma on support needs and survivor outcomes have been documented and argue for bespoke interventions based on an individual needs basis (Oram et al, 2016; Okech et al, 2018).

Trauma and post-traumatic stress disorder are common themes in the literature. Practitioners in varied settings have been instrumental in defining terms and developing tools for the sector (see also Chapters 9 and 12, this volume). Individual trauma is defined as 'an event, series of events, or set of circumstances that is experienced by an individual as physically or emotionally harmful or life threatening and that has lasting adverse effects on the individual's functioning and mental, physical, social, emotional, or spiritual well-being' (SAMHSA, 2014: 7). Understanding the severe and lasting impact of trauma experienced because of MSHT is therefore a key factor in supporting survivors.

Practitioner-informed guidance, based on day-to-day interactions with survivors in different settings, including safe houses, aftercare, medical, health and mental health services, is available. Some examples are care standards for support services (Human Trafficking Foundation, 2018), training standards for service providers (Bundock and Hodges, 2020) and guidelines for addressing trauma (Trauma Informed Code of Conduct; Witkin and Robjant, 2018).

However, despite this body of literature, there remain gaps in support for survivors, especially in the longer term, including lack of resources, knowledge among first responders of their role, inadequate training and barriers related to asylum-seeking status (Murphy, 2018). In response to inadequate procedures in the criminal justice system Barlow et al (2021; see also Chapter 8, this volume) proposed the Systemic Investigation, Protection and Prosecution Strategy model to assist investigators in their assessment of MSHT cases. Lundy et al (2020) evaluate whether UK practice with child victims of trafficking comply with the requirements of the Convention on the Rights of the Child. A recent report from the Centre for Social Justice (2020) outlines ongoing challenges in the fight against modern slavery in the UK. Examples such as these are generally accessible across the sector, whereas practice-based interventions in situ are less frequently reported (although see Van Dyke, 2020). Despite this growing body of literature, few reports utilise theoretical frameworks to further comprehension of the actual process of recovery. PsyCap is proposed here as a tool to contribute to filling that gap.

Psychological capital

PsyCap emerged out of the positive psychology movement first promoted by Seligman (2002) who challenged the field 'to change from a preoccupation with what is wrong and dysfunctional with people to what is right and good about them' (in Luthans et al, 2004: 46). PsyCap is a 'composite construct' that denotes an individual's positive psychological state of development and is characterised by:

> having confidence (self-efficacy) to take on and put in the necessary effort to succeed at challenging tasks; (2) making a positive attribution (optimism) about succeeding now and in the future; (3) persevering toward goals and, when necessary, redirecting paths to goals (hope) in order to succeed; and (4) when beset by problems and adversity, sustaining and bouncing back and even beyond (resilience) to attain success. (Luthans et al, 2007: 542; see also Newman et al, 2014)

Although the concept was applied and tested in workplace environments to predict work performance and satisfaction, the lead author argues that this construct could equally be applied to recovery contexts as discussed in the PsyCap and survivor voice section. Another element of PsyCap to consider in recovery for survivors is that PsyCap has an element of heritability that relates to personality traits. These traits include 'aptitudes for acquiring skills and interests; hedonic capacity and predispositions; energy level; temperament; and capacity for emotional self-regulation and effective emotional communication' (Hosen et al, 2003: 500).

PsyCap has been operationalised as a 'higher order' construct,[2] as it focuses on 'state-like' versus 'trait-like' features. These state-like features – hope, resilience, optimism, and individual efficacy, which Luthans et al (2007: 541) call 'positive psychological capital' – are regarded as more malleable and open to change (Luthans et al, 2007: 544; see also Chaplin et al, 1988). Additionally, common with all other forms of capital, negative aspects of PsyCap can contribute to lowered subjective wellbeing. These negative aspects are evident in anger, aggression, anti-social behaviour, inability to maintain relationships and can manifest in general selfishness and self-preoccupation (Hosen et al, 2003: 501).

Applying these elements of PsyCap to recovery settings is congruent with an understanding of the types of characteristics fostered in services offering psychological assistance to survivors, which aim to support the development of the 'whole person' to achieve 'higher order' states (Hosen et al, 2003). This approach redresses the negative psychological capital features that may have become embedded within experiences of exploitation and abuse. Even trait-like features (for example, personality traits; see Hosen et al, 2003), regarded as more difficult to change, may be transformed within a safe environment responsive to survivors' needs.

However, a surplus of positive states can be challenging for many survivors in recovery due to limited resources. Examined through their experiences, practitioners will recognise that access to psychological, social, economic and political capital is fundamental in determining successful recovery. For example, the impact of waiting for a (political) decision on the right to remain, living with limited independence (social and cultural) and no access to public funds (economic), impacts on opportunities to build psychological capital and can result in severe negative psychological distress (see Introduction, this volume).

In the context of this brief overview of PsyCap, the focus of this chapter will be on identifying 'higher-order' state-like features of hope, resilience, optimism and individual efficacy as aspects of positive PsyCap in recovery. Before encountering the words and phrases of the survivors, the following section, authored by the service manager, provides background information about the safe house programme as seen through the eyes of the staff and volunteers. The centrality of the core values to supporting the survivors is clearly conveyed in the quotes. The service is rooted in these values and provides an example of good practice in supporting survivors.

Love, respect, community and spirituality: the safe house values and the staff voice

The safe house Caritas Bakhita House (CBH) was established in 2015 as a residence to support women who had been trafficked into/within the UK. The values and principles of CBH are drawn from the Catholic faith:

- Love is shown in compassionate support and long-term commitment.
- We respect the dignity of every individual.
- Our community creates friendship and belonging.
- We nurture spirituality in creative activities that can bring joy and lift the spirit. (Annual Report Caritas Bakhita House, 2020)

People from all faiths and none are welcomed at CBH. The safe house is staffed 24 hours, seven days a week. Since its inception, 145 women have been supported from 44 countries. Some women are asylum seekers and many of the women enter the National Referral Mechanism.[3] When women arrive at the safe house, they have been traumatised due to exposure to both physical and mental abuse; indeed they have been dehumanised. The programme values outlined in the list are the foundations on which the women build their recovery.

'We show them love and we support them through the period of the time ... the time that they would be here ... we support them that they feel that they are worth something in their lives and we tend to that by ... what we do here in CBH we do things together.' (Staff 04)

It is especially important to immediately demonstrate the values of the programme when the women arrive, as a critical starting point for support and to counteract their negative experiences during exploitation. From the moment a woman walks through the door, the aim is to build trust through hospitality underpinned by a caring, sensitive approach. One volunteer acknowledges this and captures the sense of home in which support staff are 'present':

'I think the welcoming aspect of women in the house and the care ... and the hospitality and the delicacy and the confidentiality ... and it's a home for them above all. I think that's what they need, the presence.' (Volunteer 01)

Striving towards independence is built into all aspects of the programme. The women are actively encouraged to start making decisions early on. The first step is their individual support plan. This is based on the needs they identify and on issues which are critical in their personal development towards independence. Regular group meetings are held, where all aspects of living together are discussed and any matters arising from conversations are deliberated upon. Resolutions are determined by the women and staff with everyone having an equal voice and the right to be listened to. The women's contribution has been key to shaping the service design and delivery.

'I think looking after the wellbeing of the women I think we do well ... there are lots of ... well a lot of kindnesses and the principles of kindness are its love, its respect, its community and spirituality.' (Staff 03)

During their journey to independence, the women are encouraged to make their own decisions. They may not always choose the best path the first time, but they are taking back control, a positive step in their recovery. If a decision does not work, they have access to support in reassessing and trying again. The safe house aims to empower the women through a recognition that no one's life is perfect and that building skills to overcome obstacles and move forward with confidence is key to success, which slowly builds their personal resilience.

'I think the level of support with ... with the world outside CBH, like in terms of the Home Office and claiming asylum and job centres and all of that can seem really scary. I think to the women who don't even necessarily speak the language I think that can seem really intimidating and I think the fact that we guide them through all of that and you get accompanied to appointments ... and ... I think that's really important.' (Staff 06)

Showing respect for another person's values and opinions is the foundation upon which to build trust. As trust is built, other challenges the women may face, such as medical, asylum, family and education issues, can be addressed. Not constrained by a specific and limited duration of time as with other organisations under the Victim Care Contract – which offers a minimum of 45 days' reflection and recovery time for victims, CBH is able to 'walk alongside survivors', walking at their pace and living the programme principles:

'Just being alongside them in their journey which I don't think should ever be underestimated ... of just having someone there who is going to take each step with you when you have been through something that's ... incredibly traumatic and you might not have that familial network and so actually that support is really important.' (Staff 02)

To support recovery, responses to survivors need to be unconditional and can be shown in many ways, while also acknowledging professional boundaries. Respecting how a woman feels and recognising that this is as important as dealing with physical and material concerns is essential for empowerment towards recovery. It requires patience from staff and a commitment from every woman.

'I think you understand working with the women there's ... because there is the professional ... trying to maintain professional relationships but still there is a lot of love ... we give ... and especially this I think the many religious sisters which are involved in volunteering at CBH they maintain this gift of love I would say for what we would like to achieve love and acceptance and respect and yeah that's what we see as our CBH spirituality ... it's mainly that holding the women in it ... in that love.' (Staff 04)

Gaining insight into the internal thoughts and feelings of the women can result in difficult conversations and bring about traumatic memories. The women need to recover from their trauma and find healing. Through unconditional love demonstrated through respect and acceptance, the programme begins to help them rebuild their personal self-esteem. Trauma-informed practice underpins interventions in CBH and underlines the importance of being informed about practitioner guidelines, such as the Trauma Informed Code of Conduct (see Witkin and Robjant, 2018; see also Chapters 9 and 12, this volume).

Other activities are also important and may include events that have not been celebrated for some time in the lives of the women. Birthdays and cultural events are regularly observed and hold special meaning for the women. Small acts of kindness such as birthday cakes can mean a great deal to a person who has been exploited and abused.

> I say special thanks to (Staff) who made my first ever birthday cake when I turned 40. No words can explain how much I appreciated that. (Guest, in *Annual Report Caritas Bakhita House*, 2020)

The community spirit is also nurtured through being present 24/7, which is imperative during the first months of recovery, ensuring unconditional support is always in place. The family orientated community – epitomised especially in the shared evening meal, which is attended by staff and the women – ensures regular conversations are held. This enables the women who have already started their recovery to share what they have achieved. As they become stronger, they often want to inspire those newly arrived and more vulnerable than themselves. They will share various steps of their journeys such as learning English, volunteering and attending college, showing through lived experience what can be achieved, all things which seemed impossible when they first arrived. But the evidence of change is around the table for everyone to see.

In CBH, keeping adequate records for monitoring and evaluation purposes is important. Although the collection of usable data (see Chapter 13, this volume) is vital for understanding patterns in the sector, it needs to be integrated sensitively into a holistic model of support. The staff, in consultation with the women, have developed a model that is person-centred and embodies clear values in all interactions, moving beyond the limits of 'tick box culture'[4] as it espouses its four key values, illustrated clearly in this quote:

> 'At first it seemed imperative to have the right forms full of boxes and sections to tick, but a person is more than a form, a life is more than a tick box. The women are strong as proved by the fact they have survived the most horrendous conditions and stayed alive. We now need to support their onward journey by stimulating their desire to move forward, taking back control and feeling valued. A person's recovery cannot be determined by age, gender or length or type of exploitation. Quite simply everyone is an individual. For us recovery is about being person centred not time centred.' (Staff 01)

While ticking the right boxes can be crucial in ensuring victims receive the correct support, addressing the limits of 'tick box culture' is also imperative. Throughout their stay in the house, the women are part of the creation of a home which gives them a sense of safety; safety being something they may recognise over and above terms such as MSHT (see Witkin and Robjant, 2018). The women feel safe enough to express their own opinions while growing towards independence. The core values underpin what the service strives to do, enabling every woman to live an exploitation-free life. One of the staff captures the essence of these themes:

> 'There is a sense of social ... cohesion and fun ... which is really important because it's a home at the end of the day. It is a home and it's not ... it needs to have that feel ... that it's a safe, homely, comfortable place where they want to be and where they feel safe and looked after.' (Staff 02)

This overview, as presented by the service manager, reveals how the values of the safe house are embedded in the service narratives and implicitly communicated to the women. The safe house also provides a firm foundation in which to develop the four core features of PsyCap. The following section will apply an alternative analysis, using the lens of PsyCap, to reveal how the women articulate elements of higher order features of PsyCap that extend beyond the programme's core values and how the safe house values are transformed into development of positive PsyCap.

Positive psychological capital and transitions into independence: survivors' voice

A critical element of recovery journeys for the women in this study was in the creation of a home, a safe place. Embedded in all interactions, the values of CBH are communicated to the women through the words and actions of the staff. The quotes in the previous section represent the implicit understanding of the benefits of love, respect, community and spirituality. To supplement this knowledge and understand how PsyCap intersects with these values, responses from interviews conducted with survivors in this safe house, as part of an evaluation of the service, were examined. Examination of this type of data, supported by theoretical and conceptual frameworks, provides an additional layer of analysis in which to understand the complexity of the deeper transformations taking place. It is within this context that the overview of PsyCap provided in this chapter aims to contribute to greater comprehension of the dynamics at play, illustrated in the following analysis. Responses have been grouped under the themes of hope, resilience, optimism and individual efficacy, which are, as aforementioned, PsyCap key features.

Hope

In the following extracts, a critical element of the development of hope includes experiencing respectful support that inculcates learning opportunities for change. Survivors speak about the change that occurred within them/ their lives, contextualised within a discourse of support from staff:

> 'Yes everything, everything … because here really, I change my life, because being here, everything for me … and then my life maybe it was like this, but now it's like this … all … all from here because I learn here that it takes … what is life, what … what can I do with it, something … with everything … my life … everything.' (Guest 03)

Changing a life, learning 'what it takes' and 'what I can do with it' epitomise hope for this guest. Likewise in the following quote, the guest acknowledges how the support helped her to change herself and move from feeling lost, scared and stressed to engaging with new people and new activities:

> 'They give me too much support, not just the support but they change me like a person because I was completely different when I came at first here in this house and it's not just the support they gave me but they change me … because at the beginning I was … feeling too lost and I didn't have hope at all. I was so scared even from the people here at the beginning because I didn't know anyone and it was my first time that I have contact … like talking and chatting with people that I don't know and very different cultures and traditions and stuff like this and at the beginning I was so, so lost and so stressed.' (Guest 04)

Moving from a position of hopelessness about the future, this quote also embodies hope:

> 'I was so sad, I was so down, and I thought I can't … can't think it about it for the future and I can't move forward for my life but thanks to them because they help me a lot to move forward. I don't have enough words to be honest to say how much and how helpful it was this house was for me … it was amazing. … It was really, really great job.' (Guest 05)

This sense of being 'completely different' in the beginning, being sad and lost, unable to think about the future, to moving forward and experiencing change, encapsulates the hope engendered within the environment of the safe house.

Resilience

The extracts in this section capture the way in which survivors have built skills in managing their lives and overcoming adversity and developing resilience, from first 'walking like a baby':

> 'I walk like a baby you know just doing my first steps at the beginning I couldn't. ... I didn't know anything, I didn't know even to go ... where is the nearest shop here. ... I didn't know anything at all and even English, you know my English, I couldn't speak even English.' (Guest 04)

Dealing with everyday situations, such as shopping, also poses challenges for survivors often negotiating a new culture and language. Facing these challenges, with a helping hand, builds internal resilience to grow:

> 'Yeah, they supported me, and they didn't push me to do it ... they said that if you feel ... unsure to talk or you feel bad to talk don't do it ... they just are supporting me ... but in a very, very good way but they never push me to do something. Everything I done, I've done ... because I wanted to do that but not because they pushed me to do that.' (Guest 05)

This guest encapsulates the struggle to deal with previous traumatic experiences. The safe house provides a safe space from which to try new things and develop strength and resilience:

> 'I think it's [activities] good cause it doesn't ... you don't stay at home because when you're just in your own room by yourself, you end up having all these ... all these thoughts you ... because when you're by yourself ... it's something I personally don't like ... when I sit by myself and I sit for a very long time, I start to have all these irrational thoughts and it's something that. ... I don't like. So being ... getting out the house, doing something, having a laugh with other people ... it's good cause it makes you forget what ... what's happening to you, what your experiences are so you don't have to think, so like it makes you less depressed.' (Guest 06)

This final quote particularly addresses how resilience is developed through engagement in activities and having fun with others. Support of staff and volunteers and the structured activities available are important factors in developing resilience that supports independence.

Optimism

The experience of 'being pushed' into independence by staff features strongly in many of the interviews. At first, there appears to be resistance, but eventually, respondents realise that they have grown through taking risks, developing resilience and optimism along the way.

> 'But after you know, they keep talking to me and stuff like this, telling me and I started doing courses and different stuff and just keeping myself busy … they push me to change for good and they did it. At the first time you don't realise how good is here. It looks like you know people here just push you know like to do stuff and sometimes people here usually they think that, oh why they are pushing me to do this because they don't realise it's for our better, you know it's good for us, it's knowledge for us and everything.' (Guest 04)

Building educational and work experience are critical to reintegration. The safe house supports the women to engage in external activities and develop supportive networks:

> 'I work in volunteering and I'm studying at school and I'm thinking for the future to get the job and it's a good step and I have such a good network around of me and I meet such different people and which I didn't have that opportunity and so that is good for me to say "oh yes, I'm moving forward" so that is something I get it in here.' (Guest 05)

The extracts show how challenges made by staff to engage more with the 'outside world', although initially resisted, eventually offer a payoff to the women. Taking safe risks in a supportive environment is then internalised into a realisation that this is a push for change for the better, to move forward, build networks and take advantage of opportunities.

Self-efficacy

Building individual efficacy incorporates creating personal resources that can be relied on and utilised to support independence. At first, this could be in the form, as in the following quote, of a compliment or recognition for personal achievements:

> 'They say "you're great", because whenever I do English the teacher give like five star … I say "only five star?" I make it like

you know joke ... "alright ten star" ... because every time you say you're doing it very good ... even though I don't understand everything, I have to search in the Google, what is this meaning and then I have to look my book as well because before I had it in my book, what is this meaning ... so whenever I had homework and everything I had to organise it ... my support worker, I said this is my homework result and then they say I'm proud of you, you're doing it very good and so they're proud of me and I'm proud of myself too.' (Guest 01)

Likewise, having trusted staff support to 'hold your hand' during stressful encounters enables survivors to overcome challenges and recognise personal self-efficacy, illustrated in this quote:

'To be honest when I arrive in this country which I say I didn't speak any English, I didn't know any place, I didn't know how to start my life, I didn't know what to do and to be honest I never sleep in the hospitals and I had phobia for the doctors and I can't go there and all the ways they was with me taking from my hands and say, you are going to do, you do it, and I say, no ... you'll do it because you're strong and you are going to do it ... and thanks to them so I did ... so I know how to ... get the things what I need and I know how to go to ask for help if I need something, somewhere and because of them, because they ... first they came with me and told me you are going to need to go there and there and then they say try it by yourself. In the beginning I was saying why you do this, why not just don't come with me but after I started to say, oh that is for me because I'm going to leave this house and I need to do things by self, so I need to learn, that is good to learn because where you come sometimes with someone always you never do learn and I have to say really ... that is really helpful.' (Guest 01)

As a person reflects on their personal experiences, they can begin to recognise their growth and achievement for themselves, and to understand that they have enough knowledge and experience to be independent and individually efficacious.

'Because to be honest to be in one country alone and without language and you don't know nothing there, you don't know about the place, you don't know about the route, you don't know about nothing and it's hard, but I get the support from them and so now I know things how they go. ... I don't know perfectly but I have idea ... how to go, where I need to go and what I need to do.' (Guest 05)

'When I leave here, I have everything, I know how to treat my life, I know how to go somewhere, I know how to connect to people, everything for my life I start in this house.' (Guest 02)

In this final short extract, the respondent says that "everything for my life I start in this house". Recognition of the possibilities and opportunities to develop skills and confidence within a safe house environment that offers structured support and opportunities for growth is not surprising to those involved in the sector. Viewing survivors' experiences through the lens of PsyCap clearly demonstrates the great strides that can be made in a supportive environment, dedicated to preparing individuals for independence.

Conclusion

Drawing on interview data, this chapter examined the practice of support in situ in a safe house for women in the UK and explored the experiences of survivors through the lens of the safe house values (love, respect, community and spirituality) as expressed by staff and volunteers. It highlighted how each of these values and principles of action underpin the day-to-day support offered. We also showed how, in turn, survivors experiencing these values within the support received can develop PsyCap, both within the safe house and during reintegration into the community.

Theoretical and conceptual frameworks, such as PsyCap, can be used to understand experiences of recovery, and the impact of interventions on the psychological wellbeing of survivors. The integration of these resources into survivors 'toolkits' for independence are evident and have the potential to improve outcomes. The application of theory to practice aims to promote a deeper engagement by practitioners with theoretical frameworks that will support richer understanding of the usefulness of concepts, such as PsyCap, to their practice. The positive outcomes demonstrated through the internalisation of PsyCap features – hope, resilience, self-efficacy and optimism – are illustrated in the words and actions of the women in this analysis. PsycCap features have the potential to be useful as a tool for measuring impact in services.

Survivors thrive in supportive environments that embody a set of values based on safety and mutual respect. This chapter has shown how practitioners, working within a specific set of values, embody these values and communicate them to the individuals they are supporting. However, the specific values and ethos of this service are unique to that service, especially as these values are based within a framework of Christianity within a female-only safe house. There are large gaps in knowledge about other types of support available to survivors, including non-faith-based and services for men, which would aid understanding of what works to promote recovery more broadly.

Working alongside practitioners, academics have a role to play in identifying research gaps, communicating findings from research and offering additional opportunities for knowledge exchange. Recently, there has been a welcome shift in the sector, with more research being funded (for example, by the Modern Slavery and Human Rights Policy and Evidence Centre in the UK) which is relevant, impactful and will result in findings disseminated more widely to practitioners, policymakers and academics. This chapter has attempted to contribute to this knowledge base. It has done so through an examination of the support offered in one safe house, and how that is experienced by survivors, staff and volunteers. Our chapter has demonstrated how the values of the programme – including love, respect, community and spirituality – intersect with and contribute to building PsyCap, in terms of its key features of hope, resilience, self-efficacy and optimism.

It is through focused studies such as this one that deeper appreciation can be gained about survivors' experiences and interactions with support programmes. There is an urgent need to identify outcomes for the sector that clearly outline indicators for recovery. Once achieved, larger, longitudinal studies could more effectively establish what interventions work to develop resilience for long-term success. A clearly defined conceptual model that aids in gaining insights into survivors' recovery journeys in safe houses, both within and outside the National Referral Mechanism, would prove invaluable in informing policymakers about what works in the longer term. This would ensure that recovery is not a roulette wheel (Bourdieu, 1986), with outcomes left to chance.

Acknowledgements

The authors would like to thank the survivors, staff and volunteers who participated in service evaluation interviews. Thanks also to the external reviewers, Rachel Witkin, Julie Christie-Webb and Maria Mellins.

Notes

[1] The service uses the term 'guest' to refer to women who access their service, which fits with the ethos of the service overall.

[2] A higher order construct is any large, coherent construct that is used to organise information and to integrate it into one's general knowledge (American Psychological Association Dictionary of Psychology).

[3] The National Referral Mechanism is a framework for identifying and referring potential victims of modern slavery and ensuring they receive the appropriate support (Home Office, nd).

[4] See Lee's (2021) research based in medical settings on how a 'tick box culture' interferes with compassionate nursing, equally applicable to MSHT statutory and third sector services.

References

Barlow, C., Kidd, A., Green, S.T. and Darby, B. (2021) Circles of analysis: A systemic model of child criminal exploitation. *Journal of Children's Services*. Available from: https://www.emerald.com/insight/content/doi/10.1108/JCS-04-2021-0016/full/html

Bourdieu, P. (1986) The forms of capital. In J. Richardson (ed) *Handbook of Theory and Research for the Sociology of Education*. New York: Greenwood, pp 241–58.

Braun, V. and Clarke, V. (2006) Using thematic analysis in psychology. *Qualitative Research in Psychology*, 3(2): 77–101.

Bundock, L. and Hodges, K. (2020) *Modern Slavery Training Standards, Identification, Support and Care of Victims of Modern Day Slavery*. Skills for Care. Available from: https://www.skillsforcare.org.uk/Learning-developm ent/ongoing-learning-and-development/Modern-slavery/Modern-Slav ery.aspx

Caritas Westminster (2020) *Annual Report Caritas Bakhita House*. Available from: https://issuu.com/rcwestminster/docs/gads1505_-_caritas_bh_-_year_end_2020_web_single-p

Chaplin, W.F., John, O.P. and Goldberg, L.R. (1988) Conceptions of states and traits: Dimensional attributes with ideals as prototypes. *Journal of Personality and Social Psychology*, 54(4): 541–57.

Farrell, A. and Pfeffer, R. (2014) Policing human trafficking: Cultural blinders and organizational barriers. *The Annals of the American Academy of Political and Social Science*, 653(1): 46–64.

Home Office National Referral Mechanism (NRM) (nd) Available from: https://www.gov.uk/government/publications/human-traffick ing-victims-referral-and-assessment forms/guidance-on-the-national-referral-mechanism-for-potential-adult-victims-of-modern-slavery england-and-wales

Hosen, R., Solovey-Hosen, D. and Stern, L. (2003) Education and capital development: Capital as durable personal, social, economic and political influences on the happiness of individuals. *Education*, 123(3): 496–514.

Human Trafficking Foundation (2018) *Trafficking Survivor Care Standards*. Human Trafficking Foundation. Available from: https://static1.squaresp ace.com/static/599abfb4e6f2e19ff048494f/t/5bcf492f104c7ba53609aeb0/150311355442/HTF+Care+Standards+%5BSpreads%5D+2.pdf

Lundy, L., Kirk, T., Gordon, F., Dunhill, A. and Kidd, A. (2020) Responses to child victims of modern slavery in the United Kingdom: A children's rights perspective. *Child and Family Law Quarterly*, 32: 2.

Luthans, F., Luthans, K.W. and Luthans, B.C. (2004) Positive psychological capital: Beyond human and social capital. *Management Department Faculty Publications*, 145. Available from: http://digitalcommons.unl.edu/manag ementfacpub/145 (accessed 15 July 2022).

Luthans, F., Avolio, B.J., Avey, J.B. and Norman, S. M. (2007) Positive psychological capital: Measurement and relationship with performance and satisfaction. *Personnel Psychology*, 60(3): 541–72.

Modern Slavery Policy and Evidence Centre Funded Projects (2021) Available from: https://modernslaverypec.org/research-projects/core-outcome-set

Murphy, C. (2018) *A Game of Chance? Long Term Support for Survivors of Modern Slavery*. London: St Mary's University. Available from: https://www.stmarys.ac.uk/research/centres/bakhita/docs/2018-jun-a-game-of-chance.pdf

Murphy, C., Goldsmith, C., Barry, A. and Hodges, K. (2018) *Independent Review of Caritas Bakhita House*. London: St Mary's University.

Newman, A., Ucbasaran, D., Zhu, F.E.I. and Hirst, G. (2014) Psychological capital: A review and synthesis. *Journal of Organizational Behavior*, 35(S1): S120–S138.

Okech, D., Hansen, N., Howard, W., Anarfi, J.K. and Burns, A.C. (2018) Social support, dysfunctional coping, and community reintegration as predictors of PTSD among human trafficking survivors. *Behavioral Medicine*, 44(3): 209–18.

Oram, S., Abas, M., Bick, D., Boyle, A., French, R., Jakobowitz, S., Khondoker, M., Stanley, N., Trevillion, K., Howard, L. and Zimmerman, C. (2016) Human trafficking and health: A survey of male and female survivors in England. *American Journal of Public Health*, 106(6): 1073–8.

OSCE (2013) Office of the Special Representative and Co-ordinator for Combating Trafficking in Human Beings in partnership with the Ludwig Boltzmann Institute of Human Rights and the Helen Bamber Foundation, *Trafficking in Human Beings Amounting to Torture and other Forms of Ill-treatment*, Occasional Paper Series no. 5 (June 2013). Available from: http://www.helenbamber.org/publications/

Robjant, K., Roberts, J. and Katona, C. (2017) Treating posttraumatic stress disorder in female victims of trafficking using narrative exposure therapy: A retrospective audit. *Frontiers in Psychiatry*, 8: Article 63. https://doi.org/10.3389/fpsyt.2017.00063

SAMHSA (Substance Abuse and Mental Health Services Administration) (2014) *SAMHSA's Concept of Trauma and Guidance for a Trauma-Informed Approach*. HHS Publication No. (SMA) 14-4884. Rockville: Substance Abuse and Mental Health Services Administration.

Seligman, M.E. (2002) Positive psychology, positive prevention, and positive therapy. *Handbook of Positive Psychology*, 2: 3–12.

Van Dyke, R. (2020) *What Looks Promising for Tackling Modern Slavery: A Review of Practice-based Research*. Bakhita Centre, St Mary's University. Available from: https://www.stmarys.ac.uk/research/centres/bakhita/docs/modern-slavery-report-what-looks-promising-a4-brochure-21-031-feb21-proof-2.pdf

Witkin, R. and Robjant, K. (2018) *Trauma Informed Code of Conduct*. Helen Bamber Foundation. Available from: https://www.helenbamber.org/sites/default/files/2021-05/Trauma%20Informed%20Code%20of%20Conduct_April%202021.pdf

Zimmerman, C., Hossain, Z. and Watts, C. (2011) Human trafficking and health: A conceptual model to inform policy, intervention and research. *Social Science and Medicine*, 73: 327–35.

12

Imagining otherwise: art and movement as tools for recovery

Anna Westin

Introduction

The world, like our physical body, is always present to us. It is regaining 'this naïve contact with the world' that is the fundamental task of phenomenology (Merleau-Ponty, 2002: i, vi). In a similar way, phenomenology also allows us to regain contact with the medium through which we experience the world: the body. This 'naïve' contact with the world around us, experienced through the body, blurs the dichotomies with which we organise experience. Phenomenology invites us to merge the subject with the object and presents us with a world of experience in which the separate elements of consciousness, material objects and ethical relationships are fully 'intertwined' (Sallis, 2019: 12).

As a Pilates and Somatic practitioner working with survivors of modern slavery and human trafficking (MSHT), this phenomenological approach has been a particularly helpful methodology for me to employ in my work. Often the women that we work with have undergone experiences that cause significant psychological and physical trauma. The interrelational traumas experienced in sex trafficking, in particular, can cause complex experiences of woundedness that extend far after individuals are removed from the experience. Allowing a phenomenological reading of trauma enables me to engage in the interconnectivity of the world that situates the individual in a 'whole', where the body and the world around it are not separated. Whereas often trauma discourse can focus on siloed methods for healing trauma, situated in the symptoms of the body, I would argue that a phenomenological engagement with bodily movement, through Pilates and dance in particular, enables the survivor to heal through seeing her story unfold as a living creature. The survivor experiences herself as a conscious being, moving as a particular body. This connection to her own body, expressed through the movement of musculature and skeletal structure, through an awareness of breath and heartbeat, enables a bodied connection to others who, likewise, move their own bodies, respond to sensation, and are capable of experiencing pleasure and pain.

In this chapter, I will use phenomenology to assess how the arts can be used as a phenomenological instance of healing the wounds experienced from MSHT. First, I will explore how philosophy can give us language to reconceptualise healing as an interconnected experience of embodiment in relationships. Here, the work of Merleau-Ponty and Ricœur shows us that in order to heal, we have to understand how we relate. Merleau-Ponty develops this through a phenomenology of the body, and Ricœur shows us the significance of the imagination in restoring broken connection. The imagination is often defined with some ambiguity. Wielded as a phenomenon through which the unseen is expressed in reality, it has the paradoxical power of bringing about new revelation, or further ambiguity. In the process of trauma healing, the imagination is often either criticised or held as a tool of impressive healing capacity, through the embodied medium of the arts.

In the second part, the chapter starts getting into the particular experiences of suffering that require healing. Here, I explore the traumatic experiences that survivors of sex trafficking face, the impact that these traumas can have on relationships, and what forms of healing might be particularly helpful. In this instance, I suggest that individuals require practices of embodied imagination that can help them to both be present to the trauma that they continue to suffer in the present, and reimagine a life beyond the trauma. This is explored through Kearney's phenomenology of hospitality that recognises both the connection that can be made to others, and the appropriate limits to this openness to others. Movement and limit is then expanded on in the third section, where I suggest that body-based practices, such as Pilates, have the potential to contain elements of both imagination and reconnection that are important to the healing process. We are in the early stages of applying this work through classes offered by the JAM Network UK, a small collective that supports survivors through movement and arts practices. The concept of this embodied imagination and its practices are further developed in the fourth section on the role of music in recovering from trauma. The chapter concludes by offering a short reflection on the power of enabling situations of reconnection between the body and the imagination, in safe environments, as ways of practising healing, hospitality and a reclaiming of embodied agency.

Merleau-Ponty and body in trauma

Maurice Merleau-Ponty (1908–61) was a French phenomenologist. He developed a theory of bodied consciousness that brings experiences of the body into the complex web of interconnected life experiences. For him, the body is both that which touches the world, and is touched by it. For Merleau-Ponty, the world that we live in is a 'field of possibility'. It is not an abstract place, but a place that we inhabit, a space that we perceive.

Merleau-Ponty shows that 'I am conscious of the world through the medium of my body' (2002: 221). However, he goes further by also exploring how the body connects us with the world around us. The body is joined to the wider world in its lived expression. It is in relation to this wider world that 'the subject and object are seen to be moments of a whole, a totality, rather than two distinct things' (Sallis, 2019: 12). What Sallis shows here is that both the experience of consciousness and the body constitute one experience, rather than being separated into distinct moments of experience. This interconnected phenomenology of the subject-object is particularly important for making sense of the problematic dualisms between the body and the mental life that occur in trauma theory, as I will discuss in this chapter.

Though trauma itself has been around since the beginning of human history, trauma theory is a relatively new phenomenon. Sigmund Freud (1856–1939) provided important theoretical insight into the phenomenon when he noticed that shell-shocked veterans who returned from the First World War seemed to prefer returning to their experiences of pain rather than the usual preference for pleasure. The trauma that Freud saw in his patients suggested that the life drive (*Eros*) was being overwhelmed by the death drive (*Thanatos*) (Kearney, 2020). Kearney shows us that Freud's initial insight on the role of the body was curtailed by the emphasis on mind cures. Breaching the pleasure-pain principle, trauma, which had been previously interpreted through external events only, became internalised in the psychic narrative of the individual. The narrative association and telling of the individual's story then became central to healing the inner psychic rupture caused by trauma that was not linked to an external event.

However, the emphasis on mind cures, further developed through Jung, Lacan and colleagues in the psychoanalytic tradition, could not fully account for the 'somatic question of affect' that was left in the bodies after trauma (Kearney, 2020: 2). While the narratives of the mind were being reconstructed, it seemed that the body still cried out for healing. In his work with survivors of trauma, psychiatrist Bessel van der Kolk noticed that the affect in the body lingered even after the trauma narrative had been reconstituted. He recognised the urgency in treating the body as itself a part of the trauma memory. In examining the underlying symptom of dissociation characteristic of many traumatic experiences, van der Kolk explains it by invoking the body: 'The overwhelming experience is split off and fragmented, so that the emotions, sounds, images, thoughts and physical sensations related to trauma take on a life of their own' (2015: 66). It is 'the sensory fragments of memory' that then cause the post-traumatic intrusion in the present, 'where they are literally relived' (2015: 67).

A bodied reading of trauma is sympathetic with Merleau-Ponty's exploration of bodied perception. But Merleau-Ponty also maintains the connection to consciousness that body-based psychotherapeutic theory requires in order for the human experience to be located uniquely. In *The Structure of Behaviour* (1984), Merleau-Ponty highlights this incarnate consciousness when he examines the nervous system. Rather than emphasising the effects of trauma on the body over consciousness, or vice versa, a Merleau-Pontian reading requires that we analyse the bodily exchange between dimensions of perception. The 'effect of cerebral influences', he suggests, 'is to reorganise behaviour as a whole: the central nervous system is the place in which a total image of the organism is elaborated, and this image governs the distribution of responses' (Sallis, 2019: 19). This means that the body and consciousness are constantly adapting; it is this adaptation that then connects the subject and object, and the self to the wider world. This is important for trauma theory, because Merleau-Ponty is showing how theories of the mental aspects of trauma required a bodied account as well (and vice versa) in order to encapsulate the totality of the traumatic experience.

But it is not just theoretically important. Merleau-Ponty's phenomenology of embodied consciousness permits us to understand extreme human experiences with more clarity. Trauma, for instance, can benefit from this reading. In trauma, the relational structures of experience are broken. Philosopher and psychologist Yochai Ataria suggests that Merleau-Ponty's phenomenology can address the experience of body dis-ownership that can occur through intense and long-term traumatic experience. In this experience, he suggests, an individual dissociates her relation to the body, seeing it as 'a pure object' that is 'an integral part of the hostile environment' through which she was traumatised (Ataria, 2016: 217). This dissociated state breaks what Merleau-Ponty refers to as the 'subject-object' phenomenon of being one's body. For Merleau-Ponty, the observed body cannot be separate from the observing body: 'as a perceiver it is subject, yet at the same time it is an object which does not leave me' (2002: 103). Ataria notes how trauma can place the body at odds with itself. He names this 'disownership', in which the lived body (*lieb*), or the 'body-as-subject', is torn apart from the corporeal body (*körper*), or the 'body-as-object' (2016: 226). This is particularly true in experiences of trauma where the body has been the site of suffering, inflicted at the hands of other humans.

Ricœur's relational imagination

I would suggest that, just as Freud's theories of trauma require somatic engagement, so can Merleau-Ponty's carnal phenomenology also benefit from being read alongside Paul Ricœur's narrative phenomenology. Here the body is understood through language. Ricœur also situates the subject in a bodied state, as a being alongside others. This subjectivity, however, has a narrative structure.

For Ricœur, the self requires a 'subjective sense of self-continuity' (Ezzy, 1998: 239). The challenge of trauma, which Freudian theory accounts for, is that traumatic experience can often break an individual's sense of narrative continuity. The duality of life forces, between death and life, are ruptured through the silent dominance of death. Ricœur's phenomenological exposition opens up a preliminary grappling with the subject as embodied. He shows how the body is central to the experience of selfhood. For Ricœur, the subject exists hermeneutically, that is, through an interpreted and relationally contextualised self. The subject has a place of origin, a body and a language for communicating with the others around her. She cannot be reduced to the narrative self. This enables Ricœur to pose the question: 'What mode of being, then, belongs to the self, what sort of being or entity is it?' (1992: 297). This phenomenological question posits the problem of narrative self-continuity in an extended relation: relationship to oneself as a body, and to oneself alongside others. 'One's own body', Ricœur says, 'is the very place – in the strong sense of the term – of … belonging, thanks to which the self can place its mark on those events that are its actions' (1992: 319). Ricœur further expands on the relationship between suffering and the self through his insight on language and suffering. He not only looks at suffering as an experience of physical pain and facelessness. He also wants to connect this to meaning making and the possibility of hope, by re-engaging the conceptualisation of suffering with the imagination.

The role of the imagination, then, enters in Ricœur as a transitory movement that brings the enigmatic experience into a language of sense-making and order. The imagination, Ricœur explains, connects our experiences to one another through the use of language and symbol, as, for instance, seen in myth and metaphor (1995: 166). Using myth and metaphor to mediate experience becomes a way of reconnecting the self-continuity, while the body ushers us into a reality beyond mythic reductions. Mircea Eliade, as Ricœur recalls, proposes that mythic imagination can incorporate 'our fragmented experience of evil into a greater narrative of origin' (cited in Ricœur, 1995: 251). The role of the mythic imagination is not to bring a definite moral explanation. Rather, it serves as a situation for ordering and re-finding relation. In drawing on the imagination, the experience of the subject is connected to multiple modes of experience. The subject can both be victim of trauma, and subject to a life beyond trauma, with a full capacity for consciousness and relationship. How can this work? Ricœur writes that in engaging the imagination in relation to the other, tools such as myth act as 'not a false explanation by means of images and fables, but a traditional narration which relates to events that happened at the beginning of time … and, in a general manner, establishing all the forms of action and thought by which man understands himself in this world' (1967: 5). Because we cannot connect myth to a concrete history or geographical place per se, myth evades the confines of theodicy and explanation. But what it does do is that it opens space for meaning making. In its use of symbols and metaphors (its 'symbolic function'), it reveals 'the bond between man and what he considers sacred' (1967: 5). This is particularly interesting because it implicates our understanding of suffering. However, what I want to see is whether this discourse can connect with a more practical situation, namely, connecting this phenomenology of imagination to artistic practice. This connection, I will suggest, can, if rightly understood, develop an embodied method of hopeful resistance.

I am particularly interested in how this hopeful resistance can enable the transformation (with 'formation' being a key word in referencing the embodiment of human being) of the traumatised experience of a survivor of trafficking. Ricœur writes that, even in the undergoing of suffering, there is hope.[1] But experience shows us there is still a broken relation present. For instance, in relation to the body, Levine shows us that the traumatic incident can compromise the central nervous system activity long after the event has happened (1997). Thus, the self is taken up in the 'impatience of hope', which marks an expectation of an experience that is, as yet, not fully present. This is what Ricœur refers to as a belief '*in spite of* evil' (1995: 260). It also references the 'plenitude' in the experience of lacking. While still undergoing the suffering, there is a possibility that the future will not be the same as the suffering past. But this needs tools for us to consider: the cause and effect relation has to be reasserted in a new direction, despite the presence of traumatic effect still being lived in the body. Here, the role of the imagination becomes a powerful vessel for transformation. The imagination, reaching beyond the isolated situation, through such practices as lament and myth, can connect to others beyond the experience of stigmatised and isolated suffering. This brings the phenomenon out of 'defilement', or self-blame, or isolation (Ricœur, 1967: 31), which the ambiguity of suffering can slip into. This suffering is not one of fault (Ricœur, 1967), and therefore beyond rationalisation, but it is still a phenomenon of relation, and thereby of justice and hope.

Ricœur uses the imagination as a tool for understanding human experience, as bodied consciousness. But he does not want to keep it at a merely theoretical level. This hopeful imagination can contain the key for the reorientation of experience, and thus stretches into conversations of healing and ethics. For Ricœur, it is the imagination that can help us to hopefully resituate ourselves to the world, even after the narrative of our identity, the relationships and way in which we saw the world, is ruptured. This permits a phenomenological laboratory of exploration that can enable us to 'think' experience beyond the limits of the immediate present. This means both attending to the trauma of the present that is found in the body, while reorienting oneself towards an open future, beyond that trauma. In referencing this phenomenology of hope, Espen Dahl suggests that it can be embodied in something as small as just getting up and continuing on with the task of living. Through this phenomenological interpretation of the imagination, we are given new resources, however subtle, to engage with trauma, by reworking the fragments of life into a full-bodied experience that extends the past through to an experience of the future.

Traumatic experiences and art therapy in sex trafficking

The trauma comes with the individual through the body that remembers and was a part of the traumatic experience. For this, I would argue that experiences of sex trafficking have the preconditions in which the individual can experience herself as object. The body is experienced by the other as a source of pleasure, which is not problematic per se. Rather, it is when the conscious and free experience of the bodied subject is continuously usurped for the experience of pleasure that the relation becomes problematic, because it contravenes the autonomy and the will of the subject. When coercion is present as a criterion in the relation, then the sexual relation moves from one of pleasure as mutual goal, facilitated through free response, to one of more problematic experiences of domination and vulnerability.

Sex trafficking can imply several forms of trauma through its complex nature. Often the relationships that wound the individual are already intertwined in one's identity: a woman is sold by a family member; a boy is sold by a boyfriend. The conditions of experience can have their own alternate traumas: poverty, political systems, mental illness, intergenerational abuse (Sethi, 2007), coercion and rape. Sex traffickers control through fear tactics, abandonment, manipulation, domination, the building and abuse of trust, rape and forced addiction (Contreras and Farley, 2011; Hom and Woods, 2013). Trauma from sex trafficking therefore differs from other experience of sexual trauma, and it is important to always consider the heterogeneity of experiences in this field. Unique factors are attributed to sex trafficking often extending long-term, the role of the abuser as an intimate acquaintance, and the multiple perpetrators engaged in the abuse (Gerassi and Nichols, 2018).

Evidence reveals increased rates of complex post-traumatic stress disorder (PTSD) in survivors of sex trafficking, attributive to the complex interconnection of abuse individuals suffer. Their trauma incorporates symptoms related to the physical, emotional and sexual abuse and violence that individuals experience. This does not mean that all survivors of sex trafficking are presented with PTSD. Figures on this vary significantly (see, for instance, Ottisova et al, 2016). Rates of PTSD range from 33 to 84 per cent (Clawson et al, 2009: 16). Furthermore, though some experiences may be attributed as traumatic, other individuals have interpreted their experiences through other descriptors such as shame, isolation and depression (Gerassi and Nichols, 2018). All this evidence suggests that the trauma that individuals might experience can be complex, if they do (see Briere and Spinazzola, 2005). Nevertheless, sexual abuse is a particularly destructive experience that can cause survivors to feel extreme forms of shame, physical pain (including sexually transmitted infections and pregnancy without medical care), and excessive physical and emotional disconnection from other people (Levine, 1997). Given the statistically significant figures of traumatic symptoms in survivors of sex trafficking, survivor-centred and culturally sensitive trauma-informed care is essential in order for individuals to heal from their experiences and lead healthy and whole lives that are future-focused (see Chapters 7, 9 and 11, this volume).

In the previous sections of this chapter, I explored how trauma benefits from a phenomenological engagement that situates the individual in relation to the whole world. Through exploring the embodied and 'holistic character' (Sallis, 2019: 12) of our experience, and the role of the imagination in resituating a fractured narrative experience, I am interested in how bodied imaginative healing practices can enable a traumatised sex-trafficked survivor to regain a sense of agency. This sense of agency would situate herself in holistic relation to the world.

An example of an approach that aims to address trauma through connecting the lived experience to the imagination is art therapy. Studies have suggested that art therapy offers 'emotional catharsis and strengthens concepts of the inner self to enhance resilience' to future adversity (Kometiani and Farmer, 2020: 101582). Art therapy encompasses a wide range of expressions, ranging from writing to music, from art to movement. Research suggests that using this 'multi-media approach' allows individual participants to explore and ease the process of self-expression, whereas the group container enables a supporting presence and space in which gentle reconnection with others is made possible in a safe space. While much of art therapy focuses on the catharsis and meaning-making of trauma experiences (Kometiani and Farmer, 2020), the work that we have been engaging with, as I show in the next section, is less therapeutically concerned. Reading experience phenomenologically, through the subject-object in the world, the imagination is invoked as an experience in which participants can explore themselves in relation, not just to their trauma, but to the integration of the whole life.

Healing through movement: JAM Network UK

I direct a collective of survivors, artists, movement specialists and activists in London and Kent. The name of our organisation is the JAM Network UK, which references the communal practices that we facilitate for survivors.

We work with a group of survivors, and the activities that we engage with are largely developed through conversations with women about their felt needs at particular stages of their journey. Some participants have just come out of situations of trafficking. In these instances, the retreat format of our work is to create safe spaces to explore imagination-based practices such as art and movement, in a gentle and natural context. For women who are living independently and who might have other roles in the community, the work of JAM is to facilitate spaces for them to connect to their bodies and imagination in more autonomous formats. This can, for instance, look like facilitating group trauma-informed Pilates classes or developing particular artistic skill sets such as writing, dance or dramatic production. The aim is not to focus on the trauma itself; there are plenty of organisations offering this important work. Rather, we hope to provide tools to facilitate an existential and phenomenological exploration of what imaginative and embodied agency might look like after trauma.

In developing this work further, with an awareness of the role of the body in mediating experience, we have sought to develop trauma-informed movement practices for individuals. This has taken place through, as mentioned, Classical Pilates mat classes, in which individuals are gently invited to re-engage in the agency of their own bodies.[2] While being trauma-informed, and situated in Somatic body psychotherapy, the movement practice is decidedly non-therapeutic. That is, it is primarily about getting the body integrated and moving, so as to facilitate the aims of the method, namely, improving concentration, muscular integration and body wellbeing, breath, coordination and stamina (Murray, 2018). The goal of the JAM Network's activities is therefore to assist survivors of trafficking in bridging from their experience of trauma to a wider experience of the world in connection to other people. The trauma-informed practices mediate the arts-based disciplines that the Network provides for its participants. The aim is for the healing to occur in the outworking of the whole life story, where survivors can become 'more than' survivors, and where they are experienced as artists, writers, movement specialists and musicians. The creative and movement-based arts are used as the primary expression of the recovery of a life. The individual practice of participants is the manifest reintegration of the pieces broken in their unique experience of trauma.

In my role as director of the JAM Network UK, I have tried to employ this phenomenological model of healing to our network practice. As a community of experts and amateurs in the field of MSHT activism, each person comes with the primary concern for the other. More specifically, the relation between the self and the other is perceived as one of hospitality. Kearney defines hospitality as an openness to the stranger: 'The other inscribed within me as an uncontainable call from beyond ... breaks the closed circle of the ego–cogito and reminds us of our debts to others. Here, the very ipseity of the self exposes itself, paradoxically and marvellously, as openness to otherness. Real hospitality' (Kearney, 2011: 81).

The primary tool for engagement with the other for us, however, is through the arts. It is in the engagement with the other, through 'a carefully open listening', or 'an attentiveness' (MacKendrick, 2011: 98), that the life of survivor becomes present to us, and we to her. But this requires careful engagement; the survivor of trafficking is used to having boundaries broken, and the process of opening up to the other, developing a relationship of trust and listening, facilitated through the boundaries of movement and art, requires what Ricœur calls a 'courage to discern' (Kearney and Fitzpatrick, 2021: 8). This means that the activities we provide will have a very specific orientation. While other organisations might focus on punishment of the traffickers, or directing individual moralisation through 'vigilante activism', our role is to re-engage the isolated narrative of the victim/survivor back into the community narrative.

Because of the complex challenges surrounding MSHT, there is often a blurring of this ambiguous experience of suffering: the stigmatisation of irregular migration, racism, unseen-ness, language barriers and complex social and psychological trauma can develop a phenomenon where the ambiguity of suffering is confused between fault and victim, between blame and lament. Situating the role of hospitality here, then, is important because it clarifies the phenomenon, bringing the sufferer an exit through relation, without reducing it to an isolated and self-imposed self-rupture. Ricœur stresses the relational resituation developed through language via the hopeful imagination, as said. It is through reimagining identity, with the help of narrative structures such as myth, that we might be able to re-posit our experience beyond the rupture of meaning that suffering has created, as also argued in this chapter. However, Merleau-Ponty reminds us that this imagination requires a perceiving body, who engages with the world as subject-object. Contemporary trauma theory teaches us that both the body and the mind require integration, and that the sensing body needs to integrate the traumatic memory in order to heal (Kearney, 2020: 6).

The role of Pilates movement in recovery

The language of recovery has become central to the way in which we have engaged with experiences of MSHT with survivors in the UK. There was an experience of a life before trafficking, and now, this present, however dominated it is by the past, is an experience which extends into a future beyond trafficking. But recovery requires understanding that it will take some effort to restore the sense of self that trafficking has taken. As briefly mentioned in this chapter, I am interested in situating this recovery as a phenomenological moment of hospitality. Ataria's phenomenology of body disownership is a helpful way of understanding how a survivor's body may be experienced after trafficking. In sex trafficking, where the body is the site of rape, coercion, pleasure and violence, the phenomenology of the body is of central concern to the recovery of an individual's sense of future. I would argue that the body of a survivor of sex trauma requires particular consideration in any context of care that is provided.

If this body has become instrumentalised through sexual traumatisation, then it is critical that the subjectivity of the self, the 'lived body' (Ataria, 2016: 226), is transformed. Levine and van der Kolk suggest that trauma localises itself in the unspoken tales of the body through the dysregulation of the central nervous system, and that healing is restored through practices of touch. However, in order to restore the experience of the touching-touched subject–object that Merleau-Ponty describes, the body that is 'made of the same flesh as the world' (1968), the individual needs to be able to re-occupy her own body state, as subject. Often for an individual who has survived sex trafficking, the body can be experienced as 'a place of violence' (Ataria, 2016: 225). The aim of recovery is to restore connection to the body-mind states through the healing of the body, but this is a healing that takes place through integrating the individual in relation to their future. Here, the imagination can be used as a tool to introduce healing as an instance of play. The imagination is thereby mediated through the movement of the body itself, a sensing, autonomous body capable of responding to the world around her.

I would suggest that Pilates offers a particular practice in which individuals can regain the experience of integration, through playful movement. This offers a titrated experience of imaginative movement, in a supported context. While work has been done to show the important connection between yoga and trauma healing (see, for instance, Emerson and Hopper, 2011), the unique concentration facilitated by playfulness that is offered in a Classical Pilates mat class can enable survivors to explore movement in their own bodies, integrated to their breath, dynamic and full of vitality. In order to reduce barriers to accessibility, it is important for the practices to be easily accessible to participants, which is one of the great benefits of mat-based exercise (Namy et al, 2022). Offering trauma-informed Pilates classes to participants gives them a supported opportunity to explore the interconnection of their body's movement, its health and sense of agency, in a way that is safe and playful.

Pilates' unique engagement with the imagination, through visualisation and movement cues (Montuori et al, 2018), as well as his conscious attempt to keep individuals grounded and concentrated on the present, offers a context of integration that can help the individual to feel through an experience of the body as a site of playful imagination. As a circus performer himself, and working predominantly with ballet dancers in New York City, Pilates designed a method that would integrate the body structures to optimise the playful yet intentional movements of the body (Fiasca, 2009). The instruction scaffolds the learning; participants are not left alone, and the instructor's training in appropriate methods of touch therapy offers an alternate non-sexual exploration of human contact (Emerson and Hopper, 2011; Gomes Silva, 2014). This is particularly important for sex trafficking survivors, though it is not appropriate in all circumstances, and the practitioner needs to have training in this modality. The classes that we have offered have been primarily non-contact, as I wanted participants to develop personal internalisation of the exercise prior to feedback from outside. How I integrate touch in future lessons has been discussed with my mentors, in both Somatic Experiencing and Pilates, in order that it continues to facilitate healing processes and reintegration, rather than causing any re-traumatisation to participants. The emphasis has been on restoring the playground of the body for participants to explore for themselves, through safe professional guidance.

The role of music in recovery

Another layer of relationality that we use to engage with survivors of sex trafficking is through the careful use of music, facilitated by professional musicians. In Martin Daughtry's book *Listening to War*, he analyses how traumatic brain injury found in the Iraq War was caused 'not by shrapnel or bullets, but by the sounds of war' (Dietsche, 2017: 67). Engaging with sound, then, as with movement and touch, presents a two-fold phenomenological moment: it has the potential to mirror the moment of rupture, and the possibility of reconnection. Latent with meaning, music richly intertwines the somatic experience with the experience of narrative consciousness.

The positive effects of music in helping to alleviate trauma symptoms have long been documented (see, for instance, Garrido et al, 2015; Landis-Shack et al, 2017). Drumming has been seen to alleviate PTSD symptoms, through increasing openness, 'togetherness, belonging, sharing, closeness, and intimacy, as well as achieving a non-intimidating access to traumatic memories, facilitating an outlet for rage and regaining a sense of self-control' (Bensimon et al, 2008: 34). Developing the embodied practices of Pilates, music extends the bodied 'being-in-the-world', through connecting the body to narrative and sound exploration. Emerson and Hopper write that 'people who are traumatised need physical and sensory experiences to unlock their bodies, activate effective fight/flight responses, tolerate their sensations, befriend their inner experiences and cultivate new connection patterns' (2011: 5). Through using music to express emotional states, connect with the wider group, and relay narrative, the individual is given a safe context for interrelational and intersensory mediation. This is another phenomenological moment to practice individual interconnection through an accessible and universal modality.

As with Pilates, music is not used therapeutically with the focus on expressing and processing the trauma. This is a secondary outcome of the experience. In JAM Network, we are not working with music therapists, but rather with professional musicians who seek to develop the survivors' capacities as musicians. As such, music becomes a mode of engaging with the interconnected states of being, between language, body, object and other, in a way of restoring vitality to the lived experience and reconnecting the individual to the relational and sensory life.

Conclusion

Echoing the exchange between analytic and somatic accounts of trauma, Merleau-Ponty and Ricœur phenomenologically illustrate the need to integrate bodied consciousness. For them, this is a work of the flesh and the imagination. In my work with survivors of sex trafficking, I have tried to use the embodied imagination to engage with the ruptured relation between the survivor, the trafficked individual and the community, thereby restoring this relation as one of hospitality. But this requires reimagining the relation.

The relation of hospitality, both to oneself as a body and to others, through the embodied imagination, is thereby re-posited through embodied acts of music-making and movement in community. The use of arts, through music, movement, drama and painting, can bring the 'more' into the 'less' of the present. It presents an opportunity for reimagining a future that is not a repetition of the past, while also acknowledging the rupture of suffering, and resituating the relation towards the other in responsibility. These are, at the heart, simple practices of human ritual; ones that our participants have themselves asked for, ones that connect us as a community through our bodies and imaginations, and ones that survivors repeatedly say they simply 'enjoy'. This enjoyment, in the end, feels the most important of all.

Acknowledgements
With thanks to colleagues at SOSI and Pi Studios London, Holly Murray, Deborah Feldman, Jo, Elspeth Messenger, Carolyn Westin, Trevor Stammers, Cheryl Mvula and Richard Kearney.

Notes
[1] Ricœur situates this phenomenology of hope in Christian eschatological myth. He writes that if we believe that in Christ God has conquered evil, we must also believe that evil can no longer annihilate us; it is no longer permissible to speak of evil as if it still had power, as if the victory were only in the future (1967: 61).

[2] As we are still piloting many of the programmes due to the disruption of COVID-19 and my visa, there are limited cases and opportunities for reporting, but a full new programmme will start rolling out in January 2022.

References

Ataria, Y. (2016) I am not my body, this is not my body. *Human Studies*, 39(2): 217–29.

Bensimon, M., Amir, D. and Wolf, Y. (2008) Drumming through trauma: Music therapy with post-traumatic soldiers. *The Arts in Psychotherapy*, 35(1): 34–48.

Briere, J. and Spinazzola, J. (2005) Phenomenology and psychological assessment of complex posttraumatic states. *Journal of Traumatic Stress*, 18: 401–12.

Clawson, H.J., Dutch, N., Solomon, A. and Grace, L.G. (2009) *Human Trafficking into and within the United States: A Review of the Literature*. US Department of Health and Human Services, Office of the Assistant Secretary for Planning and Evaluation. Available from: http://aspe.hhs.gov/hsp/07/humantrafficking/litrev/#barriers

Dietsche, S.J. (2017) Listening to war: Sound, music, and survival in wartime Iraq by J. Martin Daughtry (review). *Notes*, 74(1): 67–9.

Emerson, D. and Hopper, E. (2011) *Overcoming Trauma Through Yoga: Reclaiming Your Body*. Berkeley: North Atlantic Books.

Fiasca, P. (2009) *Discovering Pure Classical Pilates: Theory and Practice as Joseph Pilates Intended*. Pure Pilates Net.

Garrido, S., Baker, F.A., Davidson, J.W., Moore, G. and Wasserman, S. (2015) Music and trauma: The relationship between music, personality, and coping style. Frontiers in Psychology, 6: 977.

Gerassi, L. and Nichols, A. (2018) *Sex Trafficking and Commercial Exploitation: Prevention, Advocacy, and Trauma-Informed Practice*. New York: Springer.

Gomes Silva, S.M. (2014) *Engaging Touch and Movement in Somatic Experiencing Trauma Resolution Approach*. New York: IUGS.

Hom, K.A. and Woods, S.J. (2013) Trauma and its aftermath for commercially sexually exploited women as told by front-line service providers. *Issues in Mental Health Nursing*, 34(2): 75–81.

Kearney, R. (2020) Healing touch: Hermeneutics of trauma and recovery. *Journal of Applied Hermeneutics*, 10: 1–13.

Kearney, R. (2021) *Phenomenologies of the Stranger: Between Hostility and Hospitality*. New York: Fordham University Press.

Kearney, R. and Fitzpatrick, M. (2021) *Radical Hospitality: From Thought to Action*. New York: Fordham University Press.

Kometiani, M.K. and Farmer, K.W. (2020) Exploring resilience through case studies of art therapy with sex trafficking survivors and their advocates. *The Arts in Psychotherapy*, 67: 101582.

Landis-Shack, N., Heinz., A.J. and Bonn-Miller, M.O. (2017) Music therapy for posttraumatic stress in adults: A theoretical review. *Psychomusicology*, 27(4): 334–42.

Levine, P. (1997) *Waking the Tiger*. Berkeley, CA: North Atlantic Books.

MacKendrick, K. (2011) The hospitality of listening: A note on sacramental strangeness. In R. Kearney (ed) *Phenomenologies of The Stranger: Between Hostility and Hospitality*. London: SAGE, pp 98–108.

Merleau-Ponty, M. (1984) *The Structures of Behaviour*, translated by A. Fisher. Pittsburgh, PA: Duquesne University Press.

Merleau-Ponty, M. (2002) *Phenomenology of Perception*. London: Routledge.

Montuori, S., Cucio, G., Sorrentino, P., Belloni, L., Sorrentino, G., Foti, F. and Mandolesi, L. (2018) Functional role of internal and external visual imagery: Preliminary evidences from Pilates. *Neural Plasticity*. Doi: 10.1155/2018/7235872

Murray, H. (2018) 'Classical Pilates Comprehensive Training Manual'. London: Pi Studios.

Namy, S., Carlson, C., Morgan, K., Nkwanzi, V. and Neese, J. (2022) Healing and resilience after trauma (HaRT) yoga: Programming with survivors of human trafficking in Uganda. *Journal of Social Work Practice*, 36(1): 87–100.

Ottisova, L., Hemmings, S., Howard, L.M., Zimmerman, C. and Oram, S. (2016) Prevalence and risk of violence and the mental, physical, and sexual health problems associated with human trafficking: An updated systematic review. *Epidemiology and Psychiatric Sciences*, 25(4): 317–341.

Ricœur, P. (1967) *Philosophie de la volonté, Finitude et Culpabilité II. La symbolique du mal*, edited and translated as *The Symbolism of Evil*, by E. Buchanan. New York: Harper and Row.

Ricœur, P. (1992) *Oneself as Another*, translated by K. Blamey. Chicago, IL: University of Chicago Press.

Ricœur, P. (1995) *Figuring the Sacred: Religion, Narrative, and Imagination*, edited by M.I. Wallace, translated by D. Pellauer. Minneapolis, MN: Fortress Press.

Sallis, J. (2019) *The Logos of the Sensible World: Merleau-Ponty's Phenomenological Philosophy*. Bloomington, IN: Indiana University Press.

Sethi, A. (2007) Domestic sex trafficking of Aboriginal girls in Canada: Issues and implications. First Peoples Child & Family Review, 3(3): 57–71.

Van der Kolk, B. (2015) *The Body Keeps the Score*. New York: Penguin.

13

Monitoring and evaluating anti-trafficking measures

Ruth Van Dyke and Mike Dottridge

Why is it vital to measure the impact of anti-trafficking responses?

Since the UN Trafficking Protocol was adopted in 2000, a great deal has been published about cases of human trafficking. In some countries, information about trafficking cases is collected by a statutory 'monitoring' agency, such as Portugal's Observatory on Trafficking in Human Beings.[1] However, monitoring involves more than collecting figures: it includes making a quality judgement on whether measures implemented to stop human trafficking meet standards set by international or national law. Since 2000, there have been numerous initiatives to develop methods for monitoring the implementation of anti-trafficking laws, policies and related measures, to see if they are having their intended effect and to find out if they are having other, unintended effects.

The most advanced international monitoring procedure comes from the Group of Experts on Action against Trafficking in Human Beings (GRETA), the treaty-monitoring body created by the Council of Europe's Convention on Action against Trafficking in Human Beings (2005). However, at national level, both governmental and non-governmental organisations (NGOs) routinely want to assess whether progress is being made with respect to a wider range of anti-trafficking laws, policies and other measures, so there continues to be interest in alternative methods. For example, in 2007 a Global Alliance against Traffic in Women[2] report criticised anti-trafficking measures that cause harm to people other than traffickers (GAATW, 2007). The title, *Collateral Damage*, brought into the mainstream the idea that well-intentioned anti-trafficking measures could have unintended and adverse impacts on trafficking victims. It emphasised the importance of monitoring these impacts, so that remedial action could be taken.

Suitable questions to assess the results of anti-trafficking measures might seem straightforward (suggestions usually focus on, 'Have there been more arrests?' and 'Are more trafficking victims being identified and assisted?'), but in practice it is useful to distinguish between the short-, medium- and long-term effects of measures taken. The terms used in English to distinguish between these timeframes are 'output', 'outcome' and 'impact'. These distinctions can be difficult to understand. In effect, 'output' refers to the immediate result of an activity, for example, at the end of a training activity, '20 judges have been trained' while 'outcome' refers to the medium-term effect of the activity, for example, 'Judges take notice of statements by experts about the effects on a victim of being trafficked'. While finding out whether outputs have been delivered is a management responsibility, discovering the results (the outcomes) usually requires proactive investigation. Impact evaluation has to be done some time after the intervention and the strict timeframes of project financing routinely mean that no long-term impact assessment occurs. The 2002 lexicon on evaluation is the Organisation for Economic Co-operation and Development (OECD) Development Assistance Committee (DAC) *Glossary of Key Terms in Evaluation and Results Based Management*. It describes measures to bring about change as 'development interventions'. It defines monitoring as 'a continuing function that uses systematic collection of data on specified indicators to provide management and the main stakeholders of an ongoing development intervention with indications of the extent of progress and achievement of objectives and progress in the use of allocated funds' (OECD DAC, 2002: 27). The Glossary defines evaluation as:

> The systematic and objective assessment of an on-going or completed project, programme or policy, its design, implementation and results. The aim is to determine the relevance and fulfilment of objectives, development efficiency, effectiveness, impact and sustainability. An evaluation should provide information that is credible and useful, enabling the incorporation of lessons learned into the decision-making process of both recipients and donors. Evaluation also refers to the process of determining the worth or significance of an activity, policy or program. (OECD DAC, 2002: 21–2)

Table 13.1 offers other helpful definitions.

When the DAC Glossary was developed, the term for the chain of activities deemed necessary to achieve a particular result (the 'logic' of an initiative) was 'Logical Framework'. In the past decade this has been largely replaced by the term 'Theory of Change'. The term 'indicator' in this context should not be confused with the 'indicators' that are tell-tale signs that a crime has been committed or that a particular individual has been trafficked. In the context of monitoring and evaluation it refers to an 'indicator of success' where success is an observable qualitative or quantitative change.

Table 13.1: Definitions of other relevant terms

Logical framework	Management tool used to improve the design of interventions, most often at the project level. It involves identifying strategic elements (inputs, outputs, outcomes, impact) and their causal relationships, indicators, and the assumptions or risks that may influence success and failure. It thus facilitates planning, execution and evaluation of a development intervention.
Indicator	Quantitative or qualitative factor or variable that provides a simple and reliable means to measure achievement, to reflect the changes connected to an intervention, or to help assess the performance of a development actor.

Source: OECD DAC (2002)

Importance of baseline information

Unless organisations know what the situation is at the outset before activities to bring about change begin, they are unlikely to find out whether their subsequent endeavours had the desired effect. This applies whether the goal is ambitious (for example, planning 'to end all cases of human trafficking') or more focused (for example, 'to increase the capacity of specialist police to organise proactive investigations of possible trafficking cases'). Documenting the situation before constitutes 'baseline' information. To those in a hurry to bring about change, it seems a waste of resources to try and quantify the situation *before* changes occur. However, without baseline information, it is more difficult to conclude whether interventions genuinely contributed to change. In Europe, this was a general weakness of anti-trafficking responses during the first decade after the adoption of the UN Trafficking Protocol.

Three categories of monitoring in the context of human trafficking and slavery

Type 1 concerns 'projects' and 'programmes', that is, time-bound interventions with specific budgets and specific objectives or 'expected outcomes'. Projects financed by overseas development assistance are expected to use 'results-based programming', often measured as 'relevance' ('Was the proposed intervention likely to achieve the project's objective?'), 'effectiveness' ('Did the project achieve its objectives?') and 'efficiency' (measuring the use of resources and value for money).

Although premature, evaluators are routinely asked to find out about a project's impact. They routinely conclude that whatever outcomes have been achieved will not be sustained without further project 'inputs'. Occasionally, they are asked to comment on 'participation' by talking to beneficiaries about the specific effects for them. However, until recently, it was apparent that there was a marked tendency *not* to consult trafficking victims either before or after they were affected by an anti-trafficking measure.

Many initiatives to *prevent* human trafficking fall into this Type 1 category, as does some government support to victims. For example, in 2019 and 2020 the UK financed a project in Nigeria entitled 'Stamp Out Slavery in Nigeria'[3] and another in Vietnam entitled 'Tackling Modern Slavery in Vietnam'.[4] These were one-off projects with a results-based approach but (so far) little evaluation of impact.

A variant on this type of evaluation involves assessing the results of a set of projects with similar objectives, in order to draw general conclusions about what methods are most effective. For example, one of the authors visited four places in Southeast Europe in 2004 (Albania, Kosovo, Moldova and Romania) to assess initiatives to prevent children from being trafficked either within the borders of the countries or transnationally (Dottridge, 2006).

Type 2 involves an evaluation of a country's national response to trafficking or modern slavery. In some countries it is a national statutory body, such as the Netherlands' National Rapporteur on Trafficking in Human Beings, which is tasked with preparing such an analysis and publishing regular annual reports (BNRM, 2002). The UK's Independent Anti-Slavery Commissioner (IASC) has played a somewhat similar role. Rapporteurs, like ombudspersons, are expected to be independent of government interference, though the extent of this independence varies.

In other cases, an international body, such as the treaty-monitoring body, the Council of Europe's GRETA,[5] evaluates the national situation. Other relevant bodies include regional groupings of countries, such as the Coordinated Mekong Ministerial Initiative against Human Trafficking, involving six countries in the Greater Mekong sub-region working together (China, Cambodia, Laos, Myanmar, Thailand and Vietnam).

Another Type 2 evaluation is prepared by an NGO, sometimes to influence their governments directly or to submit information to international bodies such as GRETA or the UN Special Rapporteur on Trafficking in Persons. The Anti-Trafficking Monitoring Group (ATMG) performs this role in the UK.

Type 3 involves evaluations carried out by organisations of their own work, to improve it. This might involve a law enforcement agency scrutinising its own methods or an NGO evaluating its assistance to victims. Some evaluations of this type are carried out in the framework of project-based funding, but both statutory bodies and NGOs aim to evaluate the organisation's work overall as well as for individual beneficiaries. An example of this type is the 2013 review of Nigeria's National Agency for the Prohibition of Trafficking in Persons. Reportedly financed by the United States and several European countries, it was not made public.

Finding out from trafficking victims ('survivors') what the effects of anti-trafficking practice were for them

Although it is more than two decades since the UN Trafficking Protocol was adopted, there is still no standard 'off-the-shelf' method for consulting trafficking victims about the effects they have felt from efforts to protect or assist them. Further, the methods for evaluating prevention measures are often so simplistic as to generate meaningless data. This is partly because many prevention measures are not well designed, for example assuming simplistically that a person who is told about the existence of traffickers and the dangers of falling under their control will behave differently, if they migrate.

Understanding how trafficked women, men and children are affected by anti-trafficking measures should be key for almost any monitoring system, whether it involves prevention, protection or prosecution. Nevertheless, national authorities and specific projects have routinely been reluctant to collect information directly from people who have been trafficked, sometimes arguing that this might re-traumatise them or that trafficked persons change their 'stories' and are therefore unreliable.

Feedback from trafficking victims that is useful for monitoring purposes can be obtained in a range of ways. For example, the UK's ATMG quotes comments by anonymous trafficked persons, made in public or to an organisation providing a service to them (such as a lawyer). A recent review of practice-based research in the UK noted the importance of survivors' voice in programme evaluation in order to build more effective responses (Van Dyke and Brachou, 2021).

Some research projects have set out directly to collect feedback from trafficked persons to identify shortcomings in responses. For example, in 2005 one of the authors designed a structured interview for adolescents who had been trafficked in Southeast Europe (Dottridge, 2006). A supplementary report issued by UNICEF in 2008 summarised comments made by adolescent respondents in greater detail (Dottridge, 2008).

Examples of 'Type 2' (monitoring a country's anti-trafficking responses)

Monitoring a country's treaty obligations to respond to human trafficking: the Group of Experts on Action Against Trafficking in Human Beings

Since 2010, the work of the treaty-monitoring body created by the Council of Europe's Anti-Trafficking Convention, GRETA, has developed substantially, making it a world leader. However, monitoring has been principally at national level, finding out how national systems perform against the standards set in the Convention; it has not yet proved possible for

GRETA to assess the effectiveness of the cooperation and coordination that is supposed to occur bilaterally between countries, but which is often flawed.

Alongside reports that follow a country visit (first shared with the government concerned and published with the government's comments), GRETA also publishes annual reports about its activities and has used these to comment on specific issues as a result of its in-country findings. For example, its 6th General Report on 2017 focused on child trafficking, while its 8th Report on 2018 presented general findings about the provision of assistance.

Monitoring the quality of responses by criminal justice systems to human trafficking

A project funded by the Australian government focused over almost two decades on developing the capacity of criminal justice systems (police, prosecutors and courts) in countries in Southeast Asia belonging to the Association of Southeast Asian Nations (ASEAN) to detect cases of trafficking and bring traffickers to justice. In both 2006 and 2011, after a space of five years, the project conducted a general survey of these countries' responses to human trafficking and published the results as formal ASEAN reports.

An important starting point for establishing this monitoring system was the observation that statistics on the performance of a criminal justice system (numbers of traffickers arrested, numbers of cases referred for prosecution, numbers of trials and convictions, lengths of sentences, and so on) did not tell the whole story. Indeed, if put under pressure to provide more arrests or convictions of traffickers, it was recognised that the authorities might manipulate cases (and statistics) in order to impress outsiders, but without actually improving their performance. The project consequently developed a series of minimum standards, based on human rights consideration, against which the performance of a national criminal justice system could be monitored and assessed objectively.

The seven (minimum) quality standards were on the following issues:

1. a comprehensive legal framework in compliance with international standards;
2. a specialist law enforcement capacity to investigate human trafficking;
3. a frontline law enforcement capacity to respond effectively to trafficking;
4. a strong and well informed prosecutorial and judicial response to trafficking;
5. victims are quickly and accurately identified and provided with immediate support and protection;
6. victims of trafficking are fully supported as witnesses; and
7. systems are in place to enable effective international investigative and judicial cooperation on human trafficking cases.

The details required to meet each standard were published (ARTIP, 2011). For example, meeting standard '3' required that 'Front line law enforcement officials know how to respond effectively to trafficking cases'. This was assessed by four separate sets of standards, with a total of 28 specific issues on which the performance of frontline police was monitored. The monitoring system was not simple to use, but it revealed the salient details that police force managers, ministers of justice or elected politicians needed to assess how their systems were performing and whether adjustments were required. Although devised for use in Southeast Asia, almost every aspect would be applicable in countries in other regions. Over the past five years, a similar system has been tested in parts of Southeast Europe, in the expectation that national rapporteurs will eventually be appointed to take on responsibility for independent monitoring (see BAN, 2016).

Monitoring standards set for other governments: the US Trafficking in Persons report

The most controversial monitoring publication is issued on an annual basis by the US Department of State, which monitors developments in more than one hundred countries and ranks the performance of each in one of four categories, according to criteria agreed by the US Congress, rather than by the UN (US Department of State, 2021). A US diplomat based in each US embassy is responsible for collecting data from both governmental sources and NGOs and forwarding it to specialists in the Department of State to draw up the annual report.

Monitoring of national responses by civil society organisations

In the absence of a functioning national rapporteur, civil society organisations have monitored their country's anti-trafficking responses and made recommendations to their government. The findings of a monitoring or evaluation exercise usually has less impact if prepared and published by a single organisation than if published by a coalition of different organisations. In the UK, the ATMG was formed in 2009 to coincide with the entry into force in the UK of the Council of Europe Anti-Trafficking Convention.[6] Its first publication (ATMG, 2010) reviewed the protection and assistance available to trafficking victims in the UK and highlighted shortcomings. Subsequent publications focused on other aspects of the country's anti-trafficking system, including prevention and the National Referral Mechanism (ATMG, 2021). The methods that have been used for collecting data have usually been qualitative rather than quantitative. The reports are intended mainly for advocacy purposes, to influence the UK government and its officials responsible for anti-trafficking policy.

Examples of 'Type 3' (monitoring the performance of individual organisations)

Service providers may commission an evaluation to improve their service or determine if it is effective, achieving their objectives, and for whom. They may also seek to determine if there are gaps in the services they provide. Survivors' voice has been recognised as important in research design and in identifying what and how services should be delivered (Van Dyke and Brachou, 2021).

Organisations have developed a series of methods for assessing their own performance. For example, in 2012 International Justice Mission (IJM) developed a tool to measure 'survivor outcomes and progress toward restoration' (IJM, 2018: 4). IJM calls the 'rehabilitation process "restoration", defined as survivors' ability to function in society with low vulnerability to revictimization' (IJM, 2018: 6). The Assessment of Survivor Outcomes (ASO) tool has been through a process of validation which has indicated that measures of survivors' progress towards restoration are accurate and reliable. This tool is based on six domains and sets out what restoration would look like for survivors in each of the domains: safety, legal protection, mental wellbeing, economic empowerment and education, social support and physical wellbeing. For the IJM, the ASO tool is important to the individual in terms of improvements in wellbeing as well as vulnerabilities. This data can be used to assess how effective programmes are in enabling survivor restoration, and to inform future programming.

IJM suggests three data collection points using the ASO tool: at intake, to assess strengths and vulnerabilities and to develop a care plan; at exit, to assess if the survivor is restored or needs further services; and after a year, to assess how far the survivor's restoration has been sustained (IJM, 2018). Professional judgement is used to score the survivor in relation to the many sub-domains.

In a more recent development, some English NGOs are using external evaluations to assess their effectiveness. These have also acted as formative evaluations that drive service improvements. The methodology employed consists of interviews with stakeholders, including staff and survivors, and analysis of records kept by the NGO (Van Dyke and Brachou, 2021).

One of the barriers to effective evaluation is NGO methods of data collection. While the NGOs reviewed engaged in holistic and people-centred support, they did not use standardised methods to measure recovery and did not measure regularly or consistently. This hampered the ability of NGOs to assess their impact or to better understand variations in recovery (Van Dyke and Brachou, 2021). Other examples of Type 3 practice are set out in the following sections.

Victim Navigator programme

Developed by the British NGO, Justice & Care, an independent support worker is placed in a police force. They support victims of modern slavery from an early stage, enhance a victim-centred response by police officers, and encourage victims to engage with a criminal investigation. Justice & Care developed its Case Management System to record data for evaluation purposes from the beginning and the scope expanded over time (Justice & Care, 2020) reflecting the Victim Navigator Theory of Change model (see Figure 13.1). Indicators were developed to capture victims' forms of engagement with police, criminal justice outcomes associated with victims' contacts with police, and victims' recovery outcomes. These outcomes are seen as arising from the activities of Victim Navigators, based on their Theory of Change about how this is likely to influence police and victims' behaviours.

To track and assess survivors' recovery journey over time, Justice & Care developed a 'victim assessment tool' that uses Likert scale questions[7] to explore a survivor's wellbeing across six key domains: mental and emotional health; physical health; financial stability; social connection; safety; and legal status. This assessment was developed in two symmetrical parts: survivors' self-reported feelings and Navigators' professional observations. These can be compared as well as combined to form an overall picture of recovery. The purpose was threefold: that victim's voice and perspective play a central role in assessment of recovery; that data be triangulated; that effects of trauma on survivor's self-assessment be studied, for example, how trauma affects survivor ability to identify risk to themselves. The Justice & Care approach contrasts with the IJM tool which is based solely on professional judgement of recovery.

The Victim Navigator programme promoted victim engagement with police. A typology of engagement was developed and translated into a scale of six levels assessed by Victim Navigators:

1. no engagement;
2. willing to take phone calls with police but not give information on record;
3. providing intelligence or information on record;
4. making a witness statement;
5. providing an 'Achieving Best Evidence' interview; and
6. willing to support a prosecution.

In addition, indicators were devised to collect data on the outcomes of victim engagement. These included: further victims identified; suspects identified; locations of interest identified; new lines of enquiry or case kept open; arrests; and suspects charged. Through the evaluation process Justice & Care sought to measure criminal justice outcomes that could be linked to the Victim Navigators through its Theory of Change but, in addition,

Figure 13.1: Theory of Change (Justice & Care)

Victim Navigator Programme ToC:

Mission: Sustainable reduction in the prevalence of human trafficking in counties served by VN programmey

E Survivors are not re-trafficked thanks to their decreased vulnerability (IOM 2010) Increased convictions deter or disrupt trafficking business model

B No external factors (e.g. natural disasters or political crisis) drive a new increase in trafficking prevalence due to increased supply of vulnerable people or demand for slave labour

Assumptions:

B Belief

W Weak evidence

E Evidence-based

EXTERNAL FACTORS:
Regulation of supply chains
Demand for cheap labour, sexual services
Logistics for trafficking businesses eg borders
Public attitudes and reporting Govt focus
Safeguarding, welfare, care systems

IMPACT

INCREASED MODERN SLAVERY PROSECUTIONS AND CONVICTIONS

REDUCED RE-TRAFFICKING OF SURVIVORS

SYSTEMIC IMPROVEMENTS IN QUALITY AND COORDINATION OF SERVICES FOR VICTIMS

E Survivor voice used to hape future training and service models

B Survivors do not experience additional financial crises such as ill health, new debts or addiction in the family/household

Survivors have improved outcomes across the rehabilitation/reintegration domains of physical health, menta health, safety, economic stability, legal support or social integration according to their needs

LONG TERM OUTCOMES

W CPS maintain and increase willingness and capacity to charge, prosecutors understand and present cases capably, cross-border collaboration where needed

Survivors provide increased intelligence and evidence to police and prosecutors

Force-wide increase in capacity to investigate modern slavery cases
Increasein potential victims identified by police
Increase in potential exploiters identified by police
Increase in quality admissible evidence obtained by police
Increasein potential exploiters arrested

Figure 13.1: Theory of Change (Justice & Care) (continued)

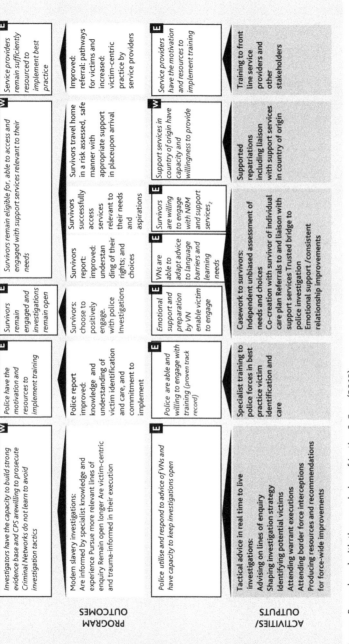

Source: Reproduced with the permission of Justice & Care (2019)

could be used to assess any significant relationship between outcomes and level of engagement.

Helen Bamber Foundation

The Helen Bamber Foundation is an NGO based in London that provides psychological therapies to survivors of human trafficking and torture, as well as advocacy for policy change. It has a specialist Counter Trafficking Team working alongside therapy, legal, housing and welfare, medical advisory and integration teams. They work with survivors to help them thrive and live independently. An integrated package of care is based on listening and responding to what recovery signifies to survivors, and staff also use recognised psychological assessment tools. For example, the therapy team offers National Institute of Clinical Excellence recommended interventions for more common problems of post-traumatic stress disorder (PTSD) and depression.

In monitoring individuals, they use tools such as the Clinical Administered PTSD Scale (CAPS-5) and the PCL-5 for PTSD, and the PHQ-9 depression scale before and after treatment. This allows evaluation of the person's progress and the efficacy of the intervention. They also measure the survivor's quality of life and wider difficulties and needs by using the Work and Social Adjustment Scale and a clinical interview to explore strengths and needs in areas such as management of everyday tasks, relationships and friendships, study and career planning. They assess for risk and safeguarding concerns and use clinical reviews to enquire about any difficulties the survivor may have in keeping safe, making choices, asserting themselves and getting help when they need it. Assessments conducted during and post therapy help understand the individual journey. Such assessment tools have also been used for research purposes as a means to examine whether specific therapies aid the recovery of trafficking survivors (for example, Robjant et al, 2017; Brady et al, 2021). These findings could help promote the use of effective interventions for survivors who have symptoms of PTSD, and/or in particular settings.

Chab Dai

Chab Dai is an NGO based in Cambodia. It is one of the few organisations supporting trafficking survivors to monitor and evaluate impact of recovery and reintegration support over the long term. Their Butterfly Longitudinal Research began in 2010 with data collection completed in 2019. This prospective longitudinal study was intended to better understand the process of recovery by following the same cohort of survivors over time. It aimed 'to understand the perspectives and experiences of survivors as they journey through rebuilding their lives' (Cordisco Tsai et al, 2018: 9). It provides evidence that could inform programme and policy development and enhance wider debates. Chab Dai was able to overcome many of the common barriers to longitudinal studies and assessment of impact by obtaining funding from donors, reducing the participant attrition by earning their trust, relationship building, and developing a strong research team despite staff changes (Miles, 2020).

Chab Dai identified shelters as one of the key forms of support available to survivors in Cambodia. The Butterfly Longitudinal Research interviewed its participants multiple times and recorded their perspectives about their stay in shelter care and their transition into the community. The 2018 report sets out these findings as well as recommendations derived from participants' experiences (Cordisco Tsai et al, 2018). The Chab Dai study is critical for those seeking insight into long-term monitoring of anti-slavery initiatives.

Monitoring against standards of care and assistance

The Human Trafficking Foundation is a British civil society organisation set up to support, and add value to, the work of organisations addressing human trafficking and modern slavery in the UK. It established an Expert Working Group to discuss ways to improve support to victims of human trafficking. This Working Group published the *Trafficking Survivors Care Standards* in 2014 which can be used as a framework for monitoring and evaluation in the form of external inspections. Their standards (updated in 2018 as *The Slavery and Trafficking Care Standards*) aimed to ensure 'that adult survivors of trafficking would consistently receive high quality care wherever they are in the UK' (Roberts, 2018: 12). Standards were to be used as the driver for improved service provision to ensure better survivor outcomes. While the British government indicated in October 2017 that it would include the Trafficking Survivors Care Standards in future National Referral Mechanism (NRM) victim care contracts, it was not until 2021 that they started formally influencing service provision. They have been embedded in the 2021 victim care contracts and form part of the inspection framework as set out by the Care Quality Commission (CQC, 2021). For the first time support to survivors will be the subject of monitoring and inspection and rated against five key questions: are services safe, effective, caring, responsive and well-led? Key lines of enquiry and prompts have been influenced by the Modern Slavery Victim Care Contract and *The Slavery and Trafficking Care Standards*. The instigation of an inspection regime is geared towards improving service delivery to survivors, but the CQC has no power of enforcement in relation to the contracted modern slavery care providers. Nevertheless, for the first time there is policy and practice that is intended to improve survivor support, to ensure it meets standards established by practitioners working in the modern slavery sector, and which is likely to impact on survivors' outcomes in England and Wales. An important element of the inspection is to give survivors an opportunity to share their experiences and views about the service (CQC, 2021). In addition, they will describe good practice as well as areas for improvement and associated recommendations. The CQC (nd) began its inspections of safe houses and outreach services in 2021 and expects to complete in 2022. Reports will be made available to each care provider, the Home Office and to the Salvation Army, but they are not scheduled to be published; instead, those interested in monitoring and evaluating service provision, and survivors' perspectives on services, will have to rely on an annual report concerning all its inspections, which 'will focus on the themes we identify in relation to survivors' experiences and will include examples of good practice and details of any areas where improvements are needed' (CQC, 2021: 12).

Monitoring to understand the victim profile, to aid service delivery and for equality purposes

It is evident at international and national level that governments are collecting some data on those entering an official process of victim identification (in some countries a NRM). The United Nations Office on Drugs and Crime (UNODC) includes human trafficking data on the characteristics of identified victims of human trafficking (in terms of gender, age and nationality) in the global reports it publishes every two years, for example the 2020 *Global Report on Trafficking in Persons*. These reports may comment on reasons for differences in vulnerability to human trafficking and can aid understanding at an international level as well as at a national level about the populations that are at risk. It can be used to devise appropriate preventive and protective measures.

The data collected by national bodies can be used for a variety of purposes, for example to seek to understand the drivers and experiences of victims from leading source countries. In the UK research was commissioned which focused on Vietnam (Silverstone and Brickell, 2017); Albania, Nigeria and Vietnam (Hynes et al, 2019); and on developing prevention programmes upstream, as in Nigeria (Department for International Development, 2018). It can also inform victim care by ensuring there are adequate spaces in safe houses to reflect needs based on the gender characteristics of adult victims or the scale of support that might be required for child victims in particular locations. Nationality and ethnic origin too might play a role in helping professionals understand the need to provide interpreters, have resources in different languages and consider the cultural needs of victims in terms of food, ability to engage in religious practices and possible stigma. The recent UK Skills for Care Training Framework (Skills for Care, 2020) states that professionals working in the modern slavery space need to be aware of the role cultural factors play in human trafficking, in identifying victims and in providing appropriate support. The sharing of cultural context material with police officers by Victim Navigators raises awareness of the nationality and diverse needs of victims so that Victim Navigators' and police officers' engagement with victims is more effective.

The UK Black and Minority Ethnic Anti-Slavery Network (BASNET), established by the charity AFRUCA –Safeguarding Children, launched its Action Plan in July 2021. It is a call for action to promote equality, diversity and inclusion within the modern slavery sector, based on its observations in relation to race and discrimination (see also discussion of implicit forms of racism in both the statutory and non statutory sectors and the consequences for criminalisation, Chapter 7, this volume). A key priority is the collection and publication of data on the race, nationality and ethnicity of victims by the Home Office as part of the NRM process. The BASNET Plan (2021) recommends this action for two race equality purposes. Firstly, this data can be used to monitor the impact on victims/survivors across the full NRM process from initial referral by first responders to when victims/survivors exit the NRM. Secondly it can be used to evaluate if there is equitable treatment and decision-making for all victims at all stages of the NRM, and thereby provide evidence that can be used for advocacy purposes where decision-making may not reflect the government's public sector equality duty.

BASNET's aim to promote equality, diversity and inclusion within the modern slavery sector also has implications for service providers. Data is needed to ensure provision reflects the needs of its users, but it is also required to assess if access to services or outcomes for survivors is equitable and fair. Without examining whether services are effective for different groups of survivors, providers, whether in the statutory or civil society sector, are not well prepared to identify what if any changes are required to achieve more equitable and inclusive outcomes. Monitoring staff profiles also provides an opportunity to develop new recruitment practices in order to encourage a more diverse workforce. In light of Black Lives Matter, many institutions have recognised that institutional racism needs to be addressed.

Independent evaluators who are able to develop trust with survivors will be in a position to listen and learn from them about how responsive providers are to their diverse needs (for example do staff have the necessary cultural intelligence[8]), and if they feel they have been subject to discrimination based on their race, nationality, ethnicity, religion or gender. Equality can become part of the evaluative landscape.

Lessons learned from different types of monitoring and evaluation

Since organisations involved in anti-trafficking responses realised that some forms of monitoring and evaluation were needed, a wide range of techniques have been tried. Often these have been flawed by the lack of involvement of monitoring and evaluation specialists, with plans containing objectives that are too general (not 'SMART') and the intended end results are therefore not clear enough to assess whether they have been achieved or not. Others have been undermined by the lack of independence of those doing the monitoring, for example some have been part of a government machine and feel obliged to follow an 'official line' that everything is going well.

Considering the vast number of national plans against trafficking that have been designed and implemented in Europe it would be reasonable to expect national anti-trafficking coordination structures (such as national commissions, inter-ministerial coordination groups or NRMs) to have developed considerable monitoring expertise. It might be expected that regional organisations (the Organization for Security and Co-operation in Europe, the Office for Democratic Institutions and Human Rights, the European Commission and the Council of Europe) and donors (notably the US) would have played a role in ensuring that the best aspects of plans and monitoring systems were shared, and the least effective aspects abandoned. However, the turnover of staff, fluctuations in funding and national action plans, often shopping lists rather than meaningful anti-trafficking intentions, have all undermined progress. Lack of adequate funding for monitoring and evaluation purposes from inception, and of sufficient duration to capture outcomes and impact also undermines robust collection of what works for whom and under what conditions, as well as any unintended consequences. On the positive side, GRETA continues to emphasise the importance of effective monitoring to the governments of all the countries that have ratified the Council of Europe Anti-Trafficking Convention.

In the UK there has been increased impetus to monitor and evaluate UK government spending on modern slavery, to improve data collection, to better understand the scale and nature of modern slavery, and to evaluate the effectiveness of programmes to support survivors. The Independent Anti-Slavery Commissioner is helping to drive some of this work by prioritising the value from research and innovation and improving the evidence base (IASC, 2021). In addition, the £10 million investment of public money in the Modern Slavery and Human Rights Policy and Evidence Centre (MS PEC) is funding new collaborative research partnerships that may influence change in law, policy and practice.

At the programme level, some NGOs have sought funding to evaluate their work, although Chab Dai stands out for its effort to resource long-term impact studies. However, service providers have tended to create their own outcome measures in relation to victim recovery or engagement with criminal justice actors. To better understand 'what works', a project funded by MS PEC aims to develop and implement a Modern Slavery Core Outcome Set (MS-COS) that will promote a more robust set of indicators.

The MS-COS will set out a minimum standard set of outcomes that should be measured and reported when assessing the effectiveness of programmes that support survivors and will include items identified as important to the recovery of survivor. This is a promising development that can only help improve the outcomes for future survivors.[9]

Acknowledgements

Thanks to Sara Cottingham, Eileen Walsh from the Helen Bamber Foundation, Naomi James-Davis from Justice & Care and Dr Alicia Kidd from the Wilberforce Institute.

Notes

[1] See www.otsh.mai.gov.pt/
[2] The Global Alliance against Traffic in Women is an alliance of NGOs coordinated from Thailand.
[3] Funded by the UK's Department for International Development and implemented by a company, Palladium. The initial budget was for £2,249,999, but the project ended prematurely in 2020 as a result of UK government cuts. See https://devtracker.fcdo.gov.uk/search?query=Cleen%20Foundation&includeClosed=0
[4] Funded by the UK Home Office and implemented by a consortium composed of the International Organization for Migration, British Council and World Vision. See https://vietnam.iom.int/en/tackling-modern-slavery-viet-nam-tmsv-project. One of the project's three objectives was to prevent 'vulnerable populations' in Vietnam from being trafficked (see www.britishcouncil.vn/en/programmes/society/tackling-modern-slavery-vietnam).
[5] Details of GRETA's monitoring procedures can be found at http://www.coe.int/t/dghl/monitoring/trafficking/Docs/Monitoring/default_en.asp
[6] Information about the ATMG was accessed at www.antislavery.org/what-we-do/uk/anti-trafficking-monitoring-group/
[7] Allows respondents to indicate their level of agreement or disagreement to a statement.
[8] Cultural intelligence means being able to navigate different cultures and work successfully across cultural boundaries.
[9] See www.mscos.co.uk

References

ARTIP (Asia Regional Trafficking in Persons) (2011) *Progress Report on Criminal Justice Responses to Trafficking in Persons in the ASEAN Region.* Available from: documentation.lastradainternational.org/doc-center/2829/progress-report-on-criminal-justice-responses-to-trafficking-in-persons-in-the-asean-region (accessed 26 July 2021).

ATMG (Anti-Trafficking Monitoring Group) (2010) *Wrong Kind of Victim? One Year on: An Analysis of UK Measures to Protect Trafficked Persons.* London: Anti-Slavery International.

ATMG (2021) *A Review of the National Referral Mechanism Multi-Agency Assurance Panels.* London: Anti-Slavery International. Available from: https://www.antislavery.org/wp-content/uploads/2021/02/MAAPs_report_final.pdf (accessed 1 September 2021).

BAN (Balkans ACT Now!) (2016) *Monitoring and Evaluation of Anti-Trafficking Policies: A Handbook for Victims' Advocates*. Belgrade: Balkans ACT and ASTRA. Available from: www.astra.rs/en/monitoring-evaluat ion-anti-trafficking-policies-handbook-victims-advocates/ (accessed 1 September 2021).

BASNET (2021) *Promoting Racial Equality, Diversity and Inclusion: An Action Plan For The UK Modern Slavery And Human Trafficking Sector*. Available from: www.bmeantislavery.org (accessed 26 July 2021).

BNRM (Bureau Nationaal Rapporteur Mensenhandel [Bureau of the Dutch National Rapporteur on Trafficking in Human Beings]) (2002) *Trafficking in Human Beings: First Report of the Dutch National Rapporteur*. The Hague: Bureau NRM.

Brady, F., Chisholm, A., Walsh, E., Ottisova, L., Bevilacqua, L., Mason, C., von Werthern, M., Cannon, T., Curry, C., Komolafe, K., Robert, R.E., Robjant, K. and Katona, C. (2021) Narrative exposure therapy for survivors of human trafficking: A feasibility randomised controlled trial. *BJPsych Open*, 7(6).

Cordisco Tsai, L., Vanntheary, L. and Channtha, N. (2018) *Experiences in Shelter Care: Perspectives from Participants in the Butterfly Longitudinal Study*. Available from: https://static1.squarespace.com/static/55a81f9be4b01a300 79bb9d3/t/5b7cc46e03ce64d96fe0f15c/1534904019664/Shelter+Exec Summary+ENG.pdf (accessed 22 July 2021).

CQC (2021) *How CQC Inspects Safehouses and Outreach Services*. Available from: https://www.cqc.org.uk/sites/default/files/How_CQC_inspects_ safehouses_and_outreach_services1.pdf (accessed 14 July 2021).

CQC (Care Quality Commission) (nd) *Inspection Framework: Safehouse and Outreach Service Provision*. Available from: www.cqc.org.uk/guidance-provid ers/healthcare/how-cqc-inspects-safehouses-outreach-services (accessed 14 July 2021).

Department for International Development (2018) *UK Aid to Stop Modern Slavery in Nigeria*. Available from: https://www.gov.uk/government/news/ uk-aid-to-stop-modern-slavery-in-nigeria (accessed 22 July 2021).

Dottridge, M. (2006) *Action to Prevent Child Trafficking in Southeastern Europe: A Preliminary Assessment*. Geneva and Lausanne: UNICEF and Terre des hommes.

Dottridge, M. (2008) *Young People's Voices on Child Trafficking: Experiences from South Eastern Europe*. UNICEF Innocenti Working Paper 2008-05, Florence. Available from: www.unicef-irc.org/publications/pdf/iwp_2008 _05.pdf (accessed 1 September 2021).

GAATW (Global Alliance against Traffic in Women) (2007) *Collateral Damage: The Impact of Anti-Trafficking Measures on Human Rights around the World*. Bangkok: GAATW.

Hynes, P., Burland, P., Thurnham, A., Dew, J., Gani-Yusuf, L., Lenja, V. and Hong Thi Tran, H.T. (2019) *'Between Two Fires': Understanding Vulnerabilities and the Support Needs of People from Albania, Viet Nam and Nigeria Who Have Experienced Human Trafficking into the UK.* London: University of Bedfordshire and International Organization for Migration. Available from: www.beds.ac.uk/trafficking (accessed 14 July 2021).

IASC (Independent Anti-Slavery Commissioner) (2021) *Independent Anti-Slavery Commissioner Annual Report 2020–2021.* Available from: www.anti slaverycommissioner.co.uk/media/1642/independent-anti-slavery-commi ssioner-annual-report-2020–2021.pdf (accessed 29 August 2021).

IJM (International Justice Mission) (2018) *Assessment of Survivor Outcomes: Guidance Manual.* Available from: ijmstoragelive.blob.core. windows.net/ijmna/documents/studies/ASO-Guidance-Manual.pdf (accessed 12 July 2021).

Justice & Care (2020) Victim Navigator Interim Evaluation, September. London: Justice & Care

Miles, G. (2020) *The Butterfly Longitudinal Research Project: A Chab Dai Study on Re/integration Researching the Lifecycle of Sexual Exploitation & Trafficking in Cambodia.* Available from: static1.squarespace.com/ static/55a81f9be4b01a30079bb9d3/t/601232693125e10067e5db78/ 1611805294060/Research+Evaluation+of+Chab+Dai+Longitudinal+ Butterfly+Research+Project.pdf (accessed 22 July 2021).

OECD DAC (Organisation for Economic Co-operation and Development, Development Assistance Committee) (2002) *Glossary of Key Terms in Evaluation and Results Based Management.* Paris: OECD. Available from: www.oecd.org/dac/evaluation/2754804.pdf (accessed 27 July 2021).

Roberts, K. (ed) (2018) *The Slavery and Trafficking Survivor Care Standards.* London: Human Trafficking Foundation. Available from: static1.squarespace. com/static/599abfb4e6f2e19ff048494f/t/5bcf492f104c7ba53609aeb0/ 1540311355442/HTF+Care+Standards+%5BSpreads%5D+2.pdf (accessed 12 July 2021).

Robjant, K., Roberts, J. and Katona, C. (2017) Treating posttraumatic stress disorder in female victims of trafficking using narrative exposure therapy: A retrospective audit. *Front Psychiatry*, 8: 63. Available from: www.ncbi.nlm. nih.gov/pmc/articles/PMC5451503/ (accessed 22 July 2021).

Silverstone, D. and Brickell, B. (2017) *Combating Modern Slavery Experienced by Vietnamese Nationals En Route to, and Within, the UK.* London: Independent Anti-Slavery Commissioner. Available from: www.antislaverycommissio ner.co.uk/media/1159/iasc-report-combating-modern-slavery-experie nce-by-vietname-nationals-en-route-to-and-within-the-uk.pdf (accessed 22 July 2021).

Skills for Care (2020) *Training Framework: Identification, Support and Care for Victims and Survivors of Modern Slavery and Human Trafficking*. Available from: www.skillsforcare.org.uk/Learning-development/ongoing-learning-and-development/Modern-slavery/Modern-Slavery.aspx (accessed 14 July 2021).

United States Department of State (2021) *Trafficking in Persons Report June 2021*. Washington. DC.

Van Dyke, R. and Brachou, A. (2021) *What Looks Promising for Tackling Modern Slavery: A Review of Practice-based Research*. Bakhita Centre for Research on Slavery, Exploitation and Abuse, St Mary's University.

Conclusion: Interrupting the journey

Carole Murphy and Runa Lazzarino

This volume has been a multifaceted and four-dimensional exploration of the journey of the victim/survivor of modern slavery and human trafficking (MSHT). The reader, we hope, should now be able to 'connect the dots' making up this tragic journey, from recruitment through to representation and (re)integration, from the macro perspective of organised crime and large business, to the micro-physics of the processes of self- and sense-making of assisted survivors; from how legal cases are conducted in the UK, to how the demand from the UK impacts the online sexual exploitation of children on the other side of the world; and including the intersection of MSHT with other discourses, in media, films, and services. This volume has had the ambition of drawing a comprehensive picture of the MSHT victim/survivor trajectory. The main aim has been to offer a critical, yet 'down-to-earth', overview of the victim/survivor journey, intended both in actual and metaphorical terms. To try to achieve this, we have put together contributors from different fields and views, from practitioners to consultants (who may have an 'activist' vision, or an approach which is removed from any positivist or constructivist model of knowledge production). Different approaches are also present across the chapters coming from academics, or mixed authorship (academic-and-practitioner or academic-with-practitioners). While some draw from critical theories (in power, race, migration, gender, epistemology), others are more descriptive of a specific phenomenon of investigation.

Taken together, the effort of all contributions is directed at bridging a few apparent disconnections, in order to start laying the foundations for a more integrated terrain in critical modern slavery studies, where survivors/victims will ultimately have more *power*. One key disconnection is the one between ideologies/representations and practices: several authors show how MSHT sit at the intersections of discourses (race, the nation, gender, biomedicine) which impact practices in all four Ps of prevention, protection, prosecution and partnership. Another key disconnection this volume tends to glue together is the one between the structural injustice allowing 'cultures of exploitation' to flourish, and the after-trafficking apparatus of assistance, in other words the recruitment and the recovery moment. It is time to examine these two phases as part of the same tragic trajectory of the survivor/victim, and to argue for survivor-led structural interventions to bring about effective change. Another separation the volume criticises is the one between Global North and South. If the former is setting the agenda and claiming to lead the fight against MSHT, with new legislation and supporting the expression of 'survivors' voices', it also bears strong, historical and current responsibilities towards the establishment and the perpetuation of human-to-human exploitation. Manichean views of bad versus good, victim versus perpetrators, freedom versus unfreedom, as argued in several chapters of this volume, do not reflect the complexity of the political and economic forces informing MSHT nor of the experiences of victims/survivors. Overcoming rigid dualisms in this field is something other scholars have attempted to achieve (O'Connell Davidson, 2010, 2015). Beyond the philosophical implication of this fascinating effort, it is important to see how this is useful in practice. And in fact, along with an improved ideological awareness and a critical approach to MSHT studies, this book has aimed to bridge the academic–practitioner gap. This is directed to inform improved policies and practices which can together be more considerate of the structural forces (economic, political and social) determining MSHT, and of survivors' experience, needs and culture. One of the ways to achieve this is to look at practices, as we have argued in the volume introduction and done throughout the chapters of this book.

Furthermore, this volume has had no intention to support any conjecture/ ideology around freedom/unfreedom in the context of survivor experience. It points to the need for de-centring, and de-Westernising, our focus on MSHT and the value systems underpinning its operation. If a family member sells another family member for profit; if people's bodies are trafficked and making money dominates all; if exploitation, and even 'slavery', can mean different things in different contexts and in different times, but often bear colonialist and postcolonialist marks; if people keep searching for better lives and opportunities, and their desires and needs are such as to render them vulnerable to injustice; and if services and justice later encountered make little sense to survivors, probably it is time to pause and listen. In this sense, this volume suggests that it is time to build the road for a new journey, one which starts with embarking in non-tokenistic, fully integrated academic– practitioner–survivor bottom-up knowledge production to inform fresh actions to combat MSHT.

Certainly, this volume could not be all-comprehensive, and there are several areas of MSHT that could not be covered, as well as some other viewpoints and perspectives. Additionally, as MSHT studies is a growing field, new directions for investigation and practice are also emerging and looking promising. An area of interest only briefly mentioned in this collection (see Chapter 4) is that of rehabilitation of survivors into employment opportunities. There is currently very little academic literature available on this. Scholars have primarily focused on acute support and, as one of the longer-term aspects of rehabilitation, fewer survivors are able to give their narrative on this subject. Research indicates, though, that a major obstacle for survivors in the UK is finding and sustaining employment. Under the National Referral Mechanism, those survivors claiming asylum are not allowed to work. Even after a positive Conclusive Grounds decision, their immigration status may still be a barrier to securing a job. Furthermore, time in captivity, plus an extended period of prevention from legally working, will also mean long gaps in the CV (Hodkinson et al, 2020). This is something which survivors may not wish to discuss in applications or interviews; unless an employer is trauma aware, they may not appreciate the additional needs of a survivor-worker. Although permanent, paid employment is more likely to occur towards the latter end of survivor recovery, it can make an enormous difference in their overall wellbeing and self-esteem. This has been particularly noted in male survivors, for whom a strong part of identity is traditionally based in their livelihood (Aldridge-Morris, 2017). In fact, the security and esteem that paid employment engenders can ultimately result in greater results for the wider system. There is strong potential for further research in this area, including longitudinal studies of survivor rehabilitation and multidisciplinary work around wellbeing and identity.

Attention to policing practices and attitudes and how they contribute to vulnerability of victims/survivors of MSHT and undocumented migrants (Plambech, 2014; Boon-Kuo, 2017; Leser and Pates, 2019) is a further area which has not been elaborated in our collection. In the UK, two of the key barriers to accessing support, and particularly engaging with the criminal justice process, has been victims' fear, or distrust, of the police. This goes along with the lack of awareness of MSHT among frontline professionals and their responsibilities to victims. Ross et al's (2015) research highlighted National Health Service staff's lack of knowledge of how to identify victims and how to respond if they had concerns. Haughey's review (2016) of the Modern Slavery Act one year on pointed to the lack of awareness among law enforcement which was corroborated by Her Majesty's Inspectorate of Constabulary Fire & Rescue Services 2017 report. However, promising initiatives are taking place. The Human Trafficking Foundation's London Project sought to promote referral pathways for victims of modern slavery within London local authorities (HTF, nd) as well as ensure that they were aware of their responsibilities to support and care for victims (Anti-Slavery London Working Group, nd). Finding ways to help victims engage with police was identified as crucial to improving criminal justice. A report documented how three London NGOs shared their experience of working with Chinese national women who are vulnerable, and some who are trafficked, to improve the response to this group by service providers and the police (Van Dyke and Brachou, 2021). This report shares examples of practice which recognises the fears and concerns of this group who is at risk of exploitation and MSHT. However, more work needs to be done to change attitudes and policies which are engrained in ideologies around migration, gender, race and victimhood – all issues explored in this collection.

Finally, we recognise that, as noted in the Introduction, there is a dearth of survivor-informed research due to various barriers, including cost and time, especially in terms of building relationships with practitioners as gatekeepers. Arguably though, this gap is narrowing as academics, such as many of those writing for this text, have built strong relationships with practitioners over several years, and have co-authored chapters with practitioners or are themselves practitioner/academics. From these relationships, access to survivors has become easier to attain. But to frame it in terms of 'access to survivors' is problematic to the overarching intention of this book. Survivors are respected as autonomous individuals who are invited to participate in this text as equals, in terms of providing insights and analysis into their own personal experiences, as opposed to being subject to, or object of, analysis by others. Policymakers and practitioners are then invited to engage with these narratives to understand the lived experiences of survivors, so to inform policy that works well in practice. Each chapter has provided tangible recommendations for practitioners that can lead to action in practice.

Overall, survivors of MSHT are increasingly attributed an active role in their recovery and reintegration and their voice as activists and advocates is also growing. Their involvement in shaping the services that are provided to support their recovery is recognised as crucial, yet still lacking, as we have covered in the Introduction to the book. Firstly, more nuanced and substantive investigations are necessary in order to place at the centre the racialised, cultural and gendered experiences of those marginalised by historic and contemporary configurations of inequality. Only experience-near, participatory studies can contribute to the establishment of an evidence base for the development of appropriate categories, policies, interventions, terminologies and healthcare responses. The voices of marginalised individuals in some form of unfreedom, as well as governmental and non-governmental bodies from the Global South, must be allowed to decide to speak or not (Spivak, 1988), if a de-monopolisation of the discourse of MSHT is to be achieved. This book is advocating for those voices and experiences to be placed at the centre of studies, interventions and policies.

Having said this, this book is also somewhat lacking the presence of first-person survivors' voice, aside from the survivors co-authoring the introduction. We are aware that the lack of survivors' voice can be linked to, but can also be a totally different thing from, lack or presence of postcolonial theory. However, on the one hand, we have made a tangible act of inclusion of two survivors as co-authors. This is per se a reflexive political act aiming at decentring our perspective and knowledge production in this book. On the other hand, we have tried to frame both the issue of survivors' voice, and the discourse of MSHT more broadly, drawing on key postcolonial scholars and theories – in particular postcolonial feminism, which wraps the whole collection (and underpins in particular Chapters 7, 9 and 10). The Foucauldian language employed, especially the use of 'discourse', embeds in itself a constructivist, critical approach to MSHT, sensitive to power dynamics and knowledge/practice production. As hopefully clarified here, the presence of practitioners, being themselves academics/writers, or co-authoring with academics, is one of the ways whereby grassroots and participatory knowledge production is integrated. Many of the authors contributing to this edited collection have extensive experience of consulting survivors to understand their recovery journeys in the UK context, and beyond. We believe that participatory (action) research and co-production – what has been called the 'participatory Zeitgeist' of our times (Palmer et al, 2019) – is one of the evolutions/substantiations of postcolonial theory/postmodernism. The Babylon of voices in participatory research, something more secularly called multi-stakeholder research, can imply that some of these voices are more positivistic, and less concerned with theory altogether. This is because their perspective comes from practice, and from inside the systems/apparatuses of the discourse of MSHT in this case. Therefore, it is ultimately important to attempt to foster collaborations between scholars, service providers and service users: to critically join knowledge and practice production. This is what this book has tried to do.

The volume is also missing a deeper contextualisation of Global South settings, intended in a geographical sense. It is not ethnographic depth that contributors aimed to provide on this occasion. The aim has been instead to offer comparative scenarios/voices/insights around similar issues from non-Western contexts (for example, MSHT recruitment and source settings in the chapters of Part I of the volume). Ethnographic (Chapter 9) or qualitative empirical research (Chapters 3, 10 and 11) is informed by drawing from those contexts. Furthermore, the Western-focused perspective we are challenging is not achieved, in this collection, via a deep contextualisation of non-Western contexts in some chapters, or via the foregrounding in each chapter of such perspective. The West/self is an ideological construct (Said, 2003) – in addition to being a political and economic dominant reality. Symmetrically, the Global South is a geographical, but mostly a political and ideological construct that we can use to refer to the transversal community of vulnerabilised subjects. In light of this, the way this book has tried to decolonise the discourse of MSHT is via: assembling contributions from different positions and roles to fragment a monolithic view on the phenomenon, that is the bad guys, the victims, and the saviours; assembling contributions casting light on different moments of MSHT – what we have called the victim journey – to show the complexity of the phenomenon, its local and international character where several actors share responsibility; and promoting a more integral approach to tackle MSHT. Such an approach should entail a joining of forces from several actors and put in place in- and cross-country, collaborative interventions. These interventions should tackle both structural factors (economic and sociocultural) and enhance micro-practices whereby individual survivors' voices and needs are listened to. MSHT decolonisation occurs also via a grassroots critical view formulated by those at the frontline – the political Global South – of current anti-MSHT systems. This formulation can be particularly poignant in the UK, which is a prolific Global North country in the production of new knowledge, practices and pieces of legislations. Supposedly a positive model in anti-MSHT, UK anti-MSHT is instead exposed in several ways, in the pages of this collection, for example in its economic and political embeddedness with some of the dark sides of the MSHT 'demand', anti-migration ideologies, victims' representations, fallacies in the justice and assistance system, and so on. This collection intends to promote an approach and an awareness of contexts favouring survivors' self-inclusion, which is anti-tokenistic, respectful, reflexive and conscious of ethical and power dynamics. This approach ultimately tends to interrupt all the horrendous journeys of current and future victims and survivors and to build effective pathways of prevention and care.

Acknowledgements
This text has benefited from inputs kindly provided by Dr Ruth Van Dyke and Dr Anne-Marie Greenslade, for which we are very grateful.

References

Aldridge-Morris, K. (2017) The importance of ESOL for the victims of modern slavery. *Language Issues*, 28(2): 63–5.

Boon-Kuo, L. (2017) *Policing Undocumented Migrants: Law, Violence and Responsibility*. Abingdon: Routledge.

Haughey, C. (2016) *The Modern Slavery Act Review*. London: UK Government.

Her Majesty's Inspectorate of Constabulary Fire & Rescue Services (2017) *Stolen Freedom: The Policing Response to Modern Slavery and Human Trafficking*. Available from: www.justiceinspectorates.gov.uk/hmicfrs (accessed 27 July 2022).

Hodkinson S., Lewis, H., Waite, L. and Dwyer, P. (2020) Fighting or fuelling forced labour? The Modern Slavery Act 2015, irregular migrants and the vulnerabilising role of the UK's hostile environment. *Critical Social Policy*, 41(1): 68–90.

HTF (nd) *Local Authorities' Referral Pathway for Adult Victims of Modern Slavery*. Available from: https://static1.squarespace.com/static/599abfb4e6f2e19ff 048494f/t/5b164e6b562fa7121fa39da3/1528188528869/LWG+Local+ Authorities+Modern+Slavery+Protocol+%28adults%29+-+Adult+ NRM+Pathw....pdf (accessed 27 July 2022).

Leser, J. and Pates, R. (2019) On the affective governmentality of anti-trafficking efforts: An ethnographic exploration. *Journal of Political Power*, 12(3): 339–57.

O'Connell Davidson, J. (2010) New slavery, old binaries: Human trafficking and the borders of 'freedom'. *Global Networks*, 10(2): 244–61.

O'Connell Davidson, J. (2015) *Modern Slavery: The Margins of Freedom*. London: Palgrave Macmillan.

Palmer, V.J., Weavell, W., Callander, R., Piper, D., Richard, L., Maher, L., Boyd, H., Herrman, H., Furler, J., Gunn, G., Iedema, R. and Robert, G. (2019) The participatory zeitgeist: An explanatory theoretical model of change in an era of coproduction and codesign in healthcare improvement. *Medical Humanities*, 45(3): 247–57.

Plambech, S. (2014) Between "victims" and "criminals": Rescue, deportation, and everyday violence among Nigerian migrants. *Social Politics: International Studies in Gender, State & Society*, 21(3): 382–402.

Ross, C., Dimitrova, S., Howard, L.M., Dewey, M., Zimmerman, C. and Oram, S. (2015) Human trafficking and health: A cross-sectional survey of NHS professionals' contact with victims of human trafficking. *BMJ Open*, 5: e008682. doi:10.1136/bmjopen-2015-008682

Said, E.W. (2003) *Orientalism*. London: Penguin Books.

Spivak, G.C. (1988) Can the subaltern speak? In C. Nelson and L. Grossberg (eds) *Marxism and the Interpretation of Culture*. London: Macmillan, pp 271–313.

Van Dyke, R. (2020) *Improving our Response to Modern Slavery and Exploitation: Supporting Chinese Women*. London: Centre for the Study of Modern Slavery, St Mary's University.

Van Dyke, R. and Brachou, A. (2021) *What Looks Promising for Tackling Modern Slavery: A Review of Practice-Based Research*. London: Bakhita Centre for Research on Slavery, Exploitation and Abuse, St Mary's University.

Index